White Space Revisited

White Space Revisited

Creating Value
Through Process

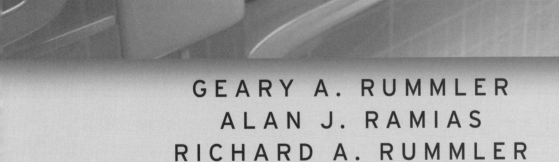

GEARY A. RUMMLER
ALAN J. RAMIAS
RICHARD A. RUMMLER

FOREWORD BY PAUL HARMON

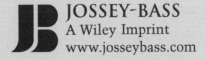

JOSSEY-BASS
A Wiley Imprint
www.josseybass.com

Published by Jossey-Bass
A Wiley Imprint
989 Market Street, San Francisco, CA 94103-1741—www.josseybass.com

Readers should be aware that Internet Web sites offered as citations and/or sources for further information may have changed or disappeared between the time this was written and when it is read.

Jossey-Bass books and products are available through most bookstores. To contact Jossey-Bass directly call our Customer Care Department within the U.S. at 800-956-7739, outside the U.S. at 317-572-3986, or fax 317-572-4002.

Jossey-Bass also publishes its books in a variety of electronic formats. Some content that appears in print may not be available in electronic books.

Library of Congress Cataloging-in-Publication Data
Rummler, Geary A.
    White space revisited: creating value through process / Geary A. Rummler, Alan J. Ramias, Richard Rummler;
  foreword by Paul Harmon.
        p. cm.
    Includes bibliographical references and index.
    ISBN 978-0-470-19234-4 (cloth)
1. Industrial productivity.   2. Value added.   3. Performance.   4. Organizational effectiveness. I. Ramias, Alan J., 1947- II. Rummler, Richard, 1961- III. Title.
    HD56.R864 2010
    658.5'15—dc22

                                                                                          2009035519

Printed in the United States of America
FIRST EDITION
HB Printing   10 9 8 7 6 5 4 3 2 1

CONTENTS

FIGURES

TABLES

Businesses have likely been trying to improve processes for as long as there have been businesses. One imagines that ancient Egyptian pottery shop owners worried about how to make production of pots faster, better, and cheaper. Systematic efforts at business process improvement are usually thought to have begun when Fredrick Winslow Taylor published his best-selling book, *The Principles of Scientific Management*, in 1911, just about the same time that Henry Ford was revolutionizing manufacturing with his ideas about a continuous production line.

Throughout the early half of the twentieth century, industrial engineers carried the torch for process improvement and often met at annual Work Simplification conferences. In the years following the Second World War, process work came into its own. Factories in Asia and Europe had been destroyed in the war and needed to be rebuilt from scratch, and everyone wanted to be sure that their new factories were as efficient as possible. Quality control engineers like W. Edwards Deming and Joseph Juran played a major role in helping companies design efficient processes. In the late 1980s a group of people at Motorola combined process work with quality control techniques to create Six Sigma, a popular approach to improving the quality and consistency of processes. In 1990, James Womack, Daniel Jones, and Daniel Roos wrote *The Machine That Changed the World*, which reported on the huge strides that Toyota had made and coined the term *lean*.

In a similar way, the rapidly evolving field of computing led to massive and widespread changes in the way business processes were organized. Companies had begun to use computers to automate their processes in the 1960s. In the 1980s, with the introduction of the personal computer, automation became available to managers and office workers. In the 1990s, gurus like Michael Hammer, James Champy, and Tom Davenport urged companies to reengineer their processes to take better advantages of the improvements that process-oriented computer systems could offer.

In addition to the gurus in the quality control and automation traditions, there have always been process advocates among business management theorists. Michael Porter, for example, is known for his work on strategy and value chains, and James Heskett has led a reevaluation of how organizations relate to employees and customers. The leading guru in the management tradition, however, was Geary Rummler.

Dr. Rummler began his career in Michigan in the 1960s. He earned his MBA and his doctorate at the University of Michigan and proceeded, over the course of the remaining decades of the twentieth century, to elaborate an integrated methodology for improving processes in organizations.

In reality, Geary Rummler never focused on processes as such. Instead, he focused on corporate performance and on how companies could be organized and managed to produce superior performance. When I think of Rummler's impact, I usually think first of his performance matrix, which is pictured in Table F.1. More than anything else, the matrix suggests the scope of Geary Rummler's vision. He imagined an organization comprised of three levels: one concerned with the organization as a whole, one concerned with the specific processes the organization used to accomplish work, and one focused on the concrete activities that people and systems performed. He assumed that at each level organizations would define goals and measures, create designs for achieving their goals and measures, and establish management practices that would assure that the designs achieved the desired goals and measures. Thus, although process was extremely important to Rummler, it was always just one part of a comprehensive approach to performance improvement, and it was important only because it supported the goals of the organization.

When I first started working with Geary, in the late 1960s, he was already using flowcharts to describe business processes, although he had not yet arrived at the "swimlane" diagrams that he made ubiquitous when he joined with Alan Brache to publish *Improving Performance* in 1990. Similarly, in the 1960s, the Activity Level of the Organization Performance Matrix was entirely focused on the employees who performed activities. Thus the Activity Level focused on how goals were defined for employees and how they were trained, managed, and motivated to perform their jobs. In the course of the 1980s and 1990s, like the rest of us, Rummler struggled to understand the role of computers in modern organizations and to incorporate software systems into the Activity Level of the Performance Matrix.

Table F.1 Rummler's Performance Matrix

	Goals and Measures	*Design and Implementation*	*Management*
Organizational Level	Organizational goals and measures of organizational success	Organizational design and implementation	Organizational management
Process Level	Process goals and measures of process success	Process design and implementation	Process management
Activity or Performance Level	Activity goals and measures of activity success	Activity design and implementation	Activity management

In the 1980s, Geary Rummler joined with Alan Brache to form Rummler-Brache and undertook a number of consulting engagements that widely influenced how people today think of process change. To provide two examples: it was during the 1980s that Rummler worked at Motorola, revising processes and teaching the process analysis techniques that laid the groundwork for Motorola's subsequent development of Six Sigma, which marries process and quality control techniques. In a similar way, IBM practitioners took courses from Rummler-Brache and then went on to create LOVEM, an IBM business process reengineering methodology that relied on Rummler's diagramming concepts. Today we find those same concepts in the latest flowcharting notation: BPMN. Many would emphasize the swimlanes that provide business people with insights into who is responsible for managing specific activities. In fact, the idea of always placing the customer of the process in the top swimlane and then diagramming every interaction between the customer and the business process is probably the more valuable insight. The latest approaches for improving service industry processes rely on an ability to model a customer's activities and then change the service business's activities to create a better customer experience.

Geary Rummler achieved widespread recognition in the 1990s. Hammer, Champy, and Davenport convinced companies they needed to reengineer but didn't provide much specific guidance about exactly how processes were to be analyzed and redesigned. Many companies, once they decided to commit to reengineering, looked around for a systematic methodology and discovered *Improving Performance* and the Rummler-Brache training courses. There was an irony here, since Geary Rummler was never a fan of reengineering. He had always advocated a more comprehensive, systematic approach and thought that reengineering's emphasis on radical change would be too hard to implement. In hindsight, Rummler was right, but in the meantime a whole generation of process practitioners learned to approach process change projects using the Rummler-Brache methodology.

Rummler sold his interest in Rummler-Brache and retired at the end of the 1990s. Within a couple of years, however, he realized, as he once told me, that he had "failed retirement." There were still too many problems he wanted to investigate, too many new insights he wanted to incorporate into his performance improvement methodology. Thus, in the early years of this decade, Geary joined with a group of colleagues to create Performance Design Lab (PDL), a new consulting and training company that provided Geary an organizational base from which he could continue to explore ways to improve organizational performance and elaborate his comprehensive approach to performance analysis and organizational design.

Geary Rummler died unexpectedly on October 29, 2008. In the year before his death, Geary, his son, Rick Rummler, and his longtime colleague, Alan Ramias, had begun work on a new book that would pull together all the insights they had garnered during the previous two decades. The book was nearly done when Geary died. Rick and Alan have done the entire business process community an important service by completing the book and seeing it through publication.

To my way of thinking, Geary Rummler was always the performance analyst's performance analyst. He didn't promote himself in the way that others did and was never as well known to the general public as process gurus like W. Edwards Deming or Michael Hammer. On the other hand, over the course of his career, he did more to influence the way process improvement work is done today than anyone else I know. The quality control community owes the emphasis on defining processes at the core of Six Sigma to Geary's work at Motorola. Similarly, the IT community owes its current swimlane-based, customer-focused BPMN diagrams to Geary's efforts to create flow diagrams that business people could easily understand. We all owe Geary thanks for his relentless emphasis on process change that improved corporate and human performance.

Over the years *Improving Performance* has been a bible to many process practitioners. Reviewers have consistently said that it was the best book to give to business managers who were looking for an introduction to process. Predictably, this new book, summarizing Geary Rummler's latest thinking about process analysis, process management, and organizational performance, will be widely read by new managers who are trying to make their organizations more process centric, and by today's process practitioners who are trying to figure out how to fit all the various technologies together into a whole.

Isaiah Berlin famously divided great thinkers into two types: Foxes and Hedgehogs. Foxes, he explained, knew many different things, but Hedgehogs knew one big thing. Geary Rummler was a hedgehog. He knew that organizations were systems that transformed customer needs and raw materials into valuable products or services. He knew that everything was connected to everything else and that effective change required a comprehensive knowledge of how the whole system worked to achieve its goals. His vision of the performance system that used processes to create value is one of the key managerial insights of our time. Other process gurus had a similar vision, but Geary Rummler's vision was uniquely powerful because he continually stressed the importance of a systematic, integrated approach.

So many things are changing. So many new techniques become available each day. It's very easy to get lost in the details. We are lucky to have this new book to provide us, once again, with Geary Rummler's comprehensive vision of how we can systematically improve the performance of our organizations.

This Preface was found in Geary's notes. It is rough and probably incomplete, but it contains his own words on the purpose for writing this book.

What we wish to present is a view with an edge. We need to elbow our way into a crowded, noisy field. It's sort of a "Hello! Remember, it's still about work!" The only way a business creates value for its customers and an organization for its stakeholders is through its value-adding work processes.

Unlike in the first book in 1990, which laid the foundation for the field, it is now an established, mature, and increasingly confusing field. There are endless lectures, articles, journals, conferences, and workshops devoted to process modeling tools, BPMS products, maturity models, governance models, design and improvement methodologies, process culture, business process leadership, process management, process-centered organizations. . . .

But despite all this activity, the undercurrent of a recent Gartner conference [in February 2008, where Geary was a keynote speaker] was, "Where are the results?" "Is BPM a fad?"—the whole thing powered by technology and training vendors who themselves are busily maneuvering and consolidating. I guess we would say that BPM is, at best, stalled. It certainly has not realized the potential we saw in 1984 when doing our early work at Motorola.

From our perspective, the BPM/process movement has gotten off track. In fact, it is even hard to find a reference to what we think are the basics: identifying and improving the work required to deliver organizational results. "Process" was not some invention to improve productivity; "process" was itself a process that started not with the work but with the results desired and worked backward from there to identify and redesign the work that must produce those results. That is the essence of industrial and process engineering.

Yet the "field" of BPM seems to be all about the "means," with no connection to the end. It's about how to model a process, how to automate a process, how to automate the management system. It's about the technology to run a process, the tools and techniques for projects, the organization culture to support a process orientation, and about BPM leadership. Which leaves us far off track from the core concept—which is about work.

We think it is way past time to get back to some basics: like understanding the organization results we are trying to deliver, realizing that there are no shortcuts to value creation in any business, and identifying, designing, and managing the work required to achieve those results—and treating process as the best-known way to engineer those results.

Thus this book . . .

ACKNOWLEDGMENTS

SPECIAL ACKNOWLEDGMENT

To our partner and friend, Cherie Wilkins, who contributed greatly to this book, not only writing parts of it but also giving an endless amount of inspiration, ideas, energy, and material. In particular, she wrote the Sara story, which provides the reader with a detailed walk-through of the Rummler Process Methodology. Bravo, and deepest gratitude.

ACKNOWLEDGMENTS

For contributing to the concepts and methodology

Mark Munley

Jaime Hermann

Klaus Wittkuhn

For providing opportunities to develop the ideas in their organizations

Steve Hassenfelt, for whole enterprise PPMS design

Richard King and Bert Kerstetter, for management system design and application of RPM to custom application development

José Luis Luna, Homero Reséndez, and the many talented members of the Processes and IT department, for business process framework design and integration of process and technology change

Steven Teal, Stacey Rachilla, Susan Erwin, Trevor Sparrow, and Ruth Henderson, for value creation portfolio management

T. J. Elliott and Willa Thomas, for process management and contributing sub-processes

Yvette Montagne and Rick Wills, for management system design

Mark Munley, for management system design in a service-based industry

Catherine Plowman and Oren Hester, for application to a shared service environment

Kerry Sharp, for business process architecture design and technology/process integration

Joyce Wells, for whole business redesign

For helping in the writing of this book

Dale Brethower

T. J. Elliott

Kregg Hale

Paul Harmon

Lorena Lanese

Pat Murphy

Fred Nickols

Chris Ramias

Klaus Wittkuhn

SPECIAL THANKS

To Paul Harmon, for writing the Foreword

To Leslie Stephen, for expert editing

To Matt Davis and Lindsay Morton, for leading us through publication

GEARY A. RUMMLER

Dr. Geary A. Rummler was the founding partner of the Performance Design Lab (PDL), where he was continuing his lifelong work on organizational performance improvement in complex systems. He died on October 29, 2008. At the time of his death, Geary was working with his partners on two books. One was this book; the other addresses management and focuses on the design and operations of an effective management system from a process perspective.

Prior to founding the Performance Design Lab, Geary was the founding partner of the Rummler-Brache Group, an organization that became a leader in the business process improvement and management business in the 1980s and 1990s. Prior to that, Geary was president of the Kepner-Tregoe Strategy Group, specialists in strategic decision making; cofounder (with Thomas F. Gilbert) and president of Praxis Corporation, an innovator in the analysis and improvement of human performance; cofounder (with George S. Odiorne) and director of the University of Michigan's Center for Programmed Learning for Business.

Geary was a pioneer in the application of instructional and performance technologies to organizations and brought this experience to the issue of organization effectiveness. His clients in the private sector included the sales, service, and manufacturing functions of the aircraft, automobile, steel, food, rubber, office equipment, pharmaceutical, telecommunications, chemical, and petroleum industries as well as the retail banking and airline industries. He also worked with such federal agencies as IRS, SSA, HUD, GAO, and DOT. Geary's research and consulting took him to Europe, Japan, Korea, Malaysia, China, and Mexico.

In addition to consulting, teaching, and presenting at conferences, Geary published a steady stream of articles and a variety of books ranging from labor relations to the development of instructional systems and his articles appeared in numerous professional and management journals and handbooks. In 1988, he coauthored *Training and Development: A Guide for Professionals*, with George S. Odiorne. In 1990, he coauthored *Improving Performance: How to Manage the White Space on the Organization Chart*, with Alan P. Brache.

Geary received his MBA and PhD from the University of Michigan and served as:

- The national president of the International Society for Performance Improvement (ISPI)
- A member of the board of directors of the American Society of Training and Development (ASTD)
- A member of the editorial board of *Training* magazine

Geary's professional accomplishments include:

- Induction into the Human Resource Development Hall of Fame in 1986
- The Distinguished Professional Achievement Award from ISPI in 1992
- The Enterprise Reengineering Excellence Award from *Enterprise Reengineering* magazine in 1996
- The Distinguished Contribution Award for Workplace Learning and Performance from ASTD in 1999
- The Lifetime Achievement Award from the Organization Behavior Management Network in 1999

ALAN J. RAMIAS

Alan J. Ramias is a partner of the Performance Design Lab (PDL). He was employed by Motorola for ten years as an internal consultant on organizational performance. As a member of the team that founded Motorola University, he was the first person to introduce Geary Rummler's pioneering concepts in process improvement and management to business units within Motorola. Alan advocated and led several of the first groundbreaking projects in process improvement that evolved to the invention of Six Sigma and Motorola's winning of the first Malcolm Baldrige Award in 1988.

After joining the Rummler-Brache Group (RBG) in 1991, Alan led major successful performance improvement engagements within Fortune 500 companies. His experience spanned several industries and the full spectrum of corporate functions and processes, such as strategic planning, manufacturing, product development, financial management, and supply chain. Major clients included Shell, Hewlett-Packard, 3M, Citibank, Motorola, Steelcase, Citgo, Hermann Miller, Louisiana-Pacific, and Bank One. After leading many high-profile projects, he became a partner and managing director of consulting services at RBG. He led development of much of RBG's products and services, and was responsible for selecting, training, and mentoring RBG's consultant teams. He joined PDL in 2005.

Alan can be reached at aramias@ThePDLab.com.

RICHARD A. RUMMLER

Richard A. Rummler is a partner of the Performance Design Lab (PDL). He brings more than fifteen years of consulting experience in the analysis, design, and implementation of organization performance systems. He has worked with organizations in Asia, Europe, and North America to achieve improvements in organization performance.

Rick's consulting experience includes a wide range of interventions, including process improvement and reengineering, organization redesign, and measurement and management system design. These projects have addressed various business sub-systems, such as customer acquisition, manufacturing, product development, and customer service. Organizations that have benefited from Rick's consultation and project leadership include ABB, Applied Materials, GE Plastics, and Sun Microsystems.

An experienced presenter of the concepts and tools espoused by PDL, Rick has delivered training programs to manufacturing and service organizations as well as government agencies and the military. Organizations that have specifically requested his training delivery services include Citibank, DuPont, and Hewlett-Packard.

Rick can be reached at rrummler@ThePDLab.com.

White Space Revisited

Introduction

This is the book that Geary Rummler had long been planning to publish. His 1990 book, *Improving Performance: How to Manage the White Space on the Organization Chart*, coauthored with Alan Brache, became a bible to thousands of process improvement/management believers scattered throughout the business world, academia, and government. Ever since then, at conferences, client meetings, and public gatherings, admirers would sidle up to him and ask, "When are you going to write the sequel to the 'white space' book?" That became the working title of the manuscript that went through years of slow development, the final result the book you hold in your hands.

This book is considerably more than an updating of *Improving Performance*, however. For example, that book said relatively little about information technology. By contrast, this book says a lot about that subject, because the world has changed remarkably in the past quarter-century due in great part to the impact of information technology on organizations. And so as technology became more and more entwined with organizational performance and processes, Geary and his partners at the Performance Design Lab (PDL) went back to school, so to speak, to learn and understand the implications of this convergence of work processes and information systems and to ask how well this merger has been happening.

Sadly, Geary did not live to see the publication of this book. He passed away suddenly on October 29, 2008, just as the final chapters were in development. But he was heavily involved in creating this book, in structuring it, and drafting large sections of it—and even more important, in crafting the ideas that propelled him from his earliest discoveries in process thinking back in the 1960s, '70s and '80s to his latest work with the clients of his most current company, the Performance Design Lab. What drew him onward was learning something and then sharing what he found out. Because, among the many characteristics of his uncommon personality, Geary was uncommonly generous with his intellectual output.

And so you will see as you read these pages. This book amounts to a tribute to Geary, yes, but even more so, it's an outpouring of what Geary and his colleagues continued to learn about process for the past twenty-five years. You can hear Geary in many of the passages, you can read some lines and you'll recognize that he said exactly those words in some setting, to someone's face, with that particular mix of wry insight and passionate conviction that he was known for. For example, a classic Geary observation about the rather troubled management of IT, "They [senior executives] need to pay at least the same amount of inattention to IT as they do to all the other functional areas."

OUTLINE AND PURPOSE OF THIS BOOK

This book is composed of three parts, which together provide a conceptual foundation, a thorough methodology, and a set of working tools for doing process work in a vastly significant way, and a series of observations about the practice of what is commonly called Business Process Management (BPM) that are meant to aid the process practitioner in being more effective.

Part One: White Space Revisited

Our purpose in this part of the book is to review the past, assess the current state, and pose a model for the future of what we can call the "process revolution" that today is BPM.

First, we attempt a retrospective of the movement from our own vantage point as instigators of many of the concepts and tools in common use today. We identify and comment on the achievements of the "process revolution," on its major milestones since the first work done at Motorola in the 1980s that triggered the revolution, and try to characterize what we think the "state of the state" is regarding this all-important concept in business thinking.

We then move to an updating of the key concept of "white space" in organizations. We pose this new definition of the white-space problem as the pivotal one that continues to bedevil organizational performance because of a long-established fixation on resource management to the detriment of value creation. At the same time, we argue that this problem is, for process practitioners, still the richest opportunity for improvement, and one that has barely been touched.

From there we pose our solution to the resource versus value dilemma by introducing and describing a concept and model called the Value Creation Hierarchy. We walk through each level of this model in detail, describing how it helps to define a business and its processes and why an understanding of the hierarchy is critical to organizational performance.

Part Two: Designing or Improving the Value Machine

In Part Two, we use the Value Creation Hierarchy as a foundation for retooling the process practitioner. We provide tools and methodology for doing work that we firmly believe will yield results far beyond standard current practice.

We provide a rich toolkit for defining processes in organizations, on the scale that, in our view, the work should be taking place but often isn't. We walk through this architecture of tools, giving examples of how and when to use them.

We then address the challenging subject of process management, giving our definition of what it should be and how it can be effective while describing the many pitfalls and errant practices we see in companies.

Then we walk through, in a highly detailed case study, the Rummler Process Methodology for doing process definition, improvement, and management work—the culmination of our collective experiences in the years since *Improving Performance* launched us and so many others on the path of process improvement.

Part Three: Implications

In Part Three we directly address the important relationship of information technology to process. Having worked in numerous IT shops, we share our observations on the nature of doing process work with this set of practitioners. Then we outline a set of changes in its role, principles, and work methods that we believe would greatly improve IT's success and impact on organizational effectiveness, including the introduction of a model, roles, and process for identifying, funding, executing, and managing improvement efforts for better results.

Finally, we address other audiences relevant to process work and identify important implications of the ideas in this book for those constituencies. We close by summarizing the intent and major points of this book.

WHO THIS BOOK WAS WRITTEN FOR

When *Improving Performance* was first published in 1990, there were no people running around inside corporations calling themselves the "Process Excellence" Department, or "Chief Process Officer," or "Process & Technology Specialist." Now we can't keep up with all the variations in titles of both jobs and functional areas that purport to do process work.

Improving Performance was written for managers, and the book found its way into the hands of people who became what we call in these pages "process practitioners." This book is primarily for you, the practitioner. Our intention is to share all that we have learned about process that we believe will help you be more effective and have a bigger impact in your organization.

The other audience for whom this book is intended is, once again, managers and leaders of organizations that want to achieve greater, and lasting, results. For you, who are likely to play the role of sponsor or senior participants in some of the process work described herein, the details in this book may be alarmingly dense. But our purpose is to arm those people who help you do this kind of work inside your organization with all the tools and methods we can. Rely on them to explain. In addition, in 2010 we will publish a companion book especially for managers on the same topics covered in this book, but with a distinct slant toward your role as leaders.

PART ONE

White Space Revisited

CHAPTER ONE

The Silver Anniversary of Process

CIRCA 1985

In April 1985, we (Geary and Alan) were invited to make a presentation at the annual conference of the National Society of Performance & Instruction (NSPI)[1] because somebody had told the society that we were doing some "experimental stuff" at Motorola.

At the time Geary was founding partner of the consulting company, the Rummler Group, and Alan was a training manager and internal consultant for the Semiconductor Products business groups in the Phoenix area. Over the course of about two years, we had developed a new improvement methodology, and in late 1984 we got a chance to apply it to a business unit that was suffering from some significant delivery, product quality, and coordination problems. They were losing business to competitors. We got the senior management team to sit down and assess their way of managing the work flow. Most important, this team was composed of heads of several different business groups who had been asked to create and support this line of business but who had never acted as a coherent management team. It was during one of those work sessions that Rummler first posited the notion that the job of the team was "managing the white spaces on the organization chart."

At the time we had no name for this new methodology. During the NSPI presentation we laughingly referred to it as "our thing," like *La Cosa Nostra*, but we weren't quite sure what we had—it had started as a training program, morphed into a kind of problem-solving approach, and ended as a management "team-building" intervention, for want of a better label. But while we had the methodology and tools worked out in a primitive way, we didn't yet have any results to show.

Two months later, that changed. In June 1985, we reconvened the original team, now headed by a new senior executive, to see if any good had come out of the effort. It turned out that cycle time had been cut from fourteen weeks to seven weeks in nine months. The business—addressing a vital new segment for the sector—had turned completely around, and now the competition was chasing them.

That was the beginning. We had invented and then evolved the first systematic process design, improvement, and management methodology. Yes, we recognize that many other pioneers made great contributions to the field of what is now "business process management" (BPM)—among them, Frederick Taylor and W. Edwards Deming—long before us. But their ideas were adopted mostly by manufacturing companies, and *process* meant the production process. It was not until the 1980s that the business process movement—meaning design, improvement, and management of all important processes inside organizations—took hold, and that, in our view, was the beginning of BPM.

Our methodology was eventually employed in most of the major business units at Motorola, then was married to Motorola's version of TQM and rolled out in the late 1980s as Six Sigma. By 1990, "our thing" had had a major impact on the transformation of Motorola from a company with quality problems to a world-class leader in innovation and continuous improvement. In 1990, A. William Wiggenhorn, founder of Motorola University and the man who had brought Rummler into Motorola, estimated that the impact of these improvement efforts came to $950 million in savings for what was a $10 billion company at the time. During our years there, revenues tripled.[2]

Along the way, we had both invented and proved the benefits of an improvement methodology that yielded tangible business results with often startling speed. By the late 1980s, the methodology was being endorsed by the CEO on down, and Geary, as a member of the Motorola Management Institute from 1984 to 1995, taught the key concepts and approach to a generation of senior to midlevel managers.

Not that the path to success was always swift and smooth. At first we did not know how to describe this new approach to improvement nor how to educate clients on the importance of processes. The most receptive areas at first were in manufacturing, where TQM was practiced and the concept of process was familiar (although everyone meant the manufacturing process only, not the larger business processes); outside of manufacturing, the notion of process was entirely foreign. Gradually, though, we learned to articulate the benefits of a process view, and we gained adherents one by one.

During that period, Motorola was the most fertile ground for this pioneering work, but there were other takers. Geary built out the methodology as he also did work with other large corporations, including Ford, GTE, Douglas Aircraft, GM, GE Plastics, Sherwin-Williams, Ryder Truck, Capital Holding Corporation, Hillenbrand Industries, Sematec, and VLSI.

Characteristics of the Approach

What made the methodology work so well? There were several characteristics of these early projects that we think made all the difference:

1. Our process improvement projects at Motorola were conducted directly with the senior executives of the business units where we operated. Instead of having intermediary teams of specialists and lower-level managers on "design teams," the executives functioned as

both "process owners" and designers in what we called an Executive Process Improvement Project. That is one reason why results were often achieved so quickly. Instead of months of analysis, process modeling, and commitment building with midlevel executives and other stakeholders, the people with the power to make things happen were the ones who had designed the improvements and wanted them implemented post haste. There was little time needed to create consensus and seldom much resistance. These people had competitive pressures and were serious. (We note that when we went to other companies, we ended up creating design and steering teams because the Executive Process Improvement Project was a hard sell.)

2. The focus of the improvement projects was on critical business issues such as total customer satisfaction, value creation, and growth of the business. These were issues that executives cared most about and would put their energies into addressing. We didn't do "process work" merely because it seemed like a good thing to do; we did it only in service of a burning business issue.

3. Because of the focus on critical business issues, the processes that we helped to redesign tended to be the core, value-adding processes that create and deliver products and services right to customers. We were not buried in "enabling processes," although we often dealt with them in order to make them more effective in serving the core processes.

Assumptions on Which We Built the Approach

The process improvement methodology that started at Motorola went through innumerable upgrades throughout the 1980s and 1990s as we, with our clients, learned more and more about process design, discovered additional tools and techniques, and covered greater ground in the quest to make it a comprehensive approach for change. In the early years, for example, there was no material on implementation. We relied on our clients to install their redesigned processes, and many did so, but some stumbled hardest at the point when the design work was complete but the organization at large had not accepted it. We added an additional phase to deal with implementation and change management.

There were, however, some basic assumptions about processes and organizations that were used in developing and applying the methodology, and they have proved to be true over the decades.

1. Organizations as Systems

We believe that every organization, public or private, is a system of interdependent parts and is subject to systems logic. The concept of systems applies at any level of a given organization, whether it's an entire enterprise existing within a larger, super-system of market, environmental, and competitive forces, or a business unit or even a single department, existing inside as a system within systems. Figure 1.1 is a diagram of any business organization sitting inside its super-system.

Figure 1.1 The Organization as a System

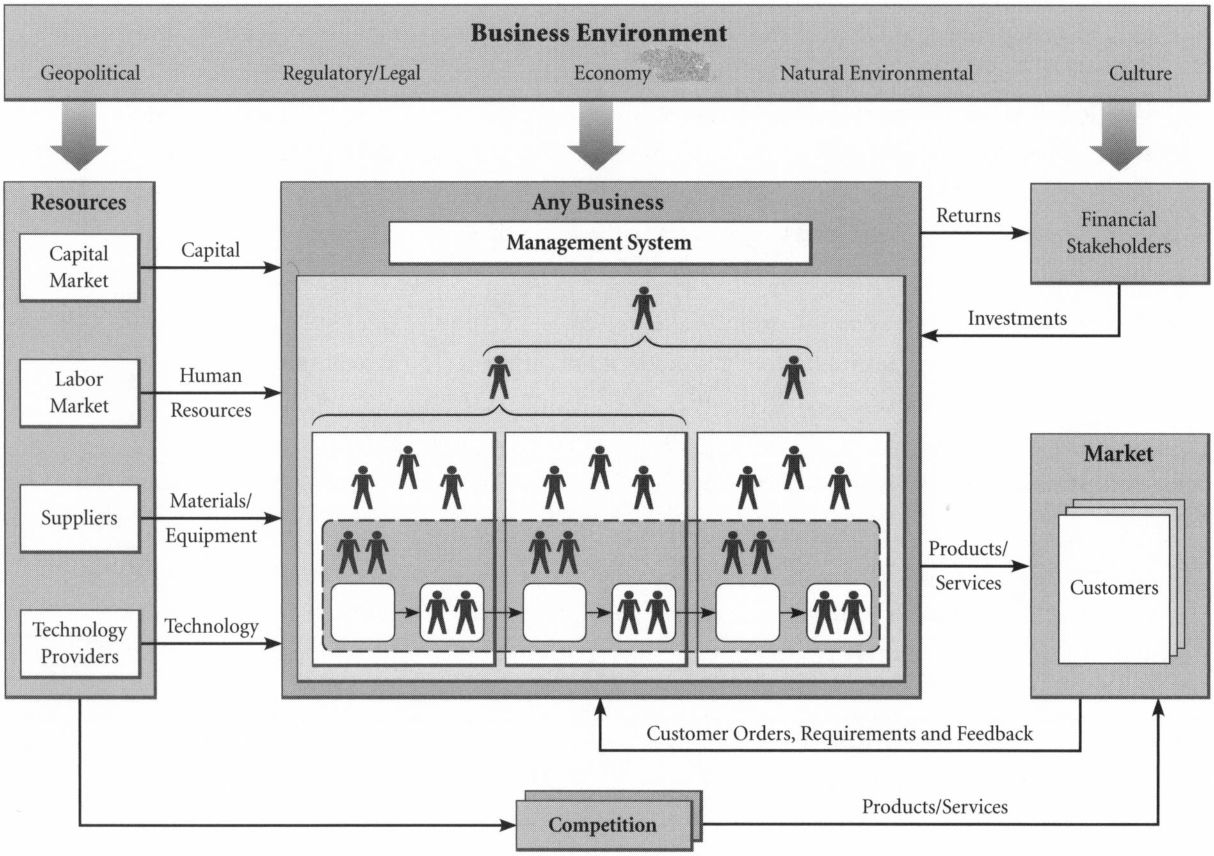

There are several corollaries to this assumption:

- Every organization is a gigantic processing system, composed of inputs, outputs, and internal processes that transform the inputs into valued outputs. Therefore, every process exists as part of a network of interdependent processes, each playing a role to produce value, manage the production of value, or support that transformative work. This means, among other things, that a single process cannot be effectively redesigned without a clear understanding of the other processes to which it is connected and to the organizational system of which it is only a part. And often, in order to address the deficiencies of a given process, we had not only to understand the larger system in which it resided, but to make improvements in the larger system.

- Every organization must be an adaptive system, continually monitoring the larger super-system and making small and large adjustments to be successful or even to survive in the long run. The critical business issues that were addressed by our process improvement projects at Motorola and other companies were all traceable to something in the super-system and the need for adaptiveness. The issue might be customer dissatisfaction with delivery times, poor product quality, the need to grow a market segment—the critical business issues were always an expression of the company's need to be more responsive to some changing condition or its own wish to change the competitive landscape.

2. Processes Are About Work

Process work is all about defining and managing work. The notion of "process" has turned out to be the best way to articulate the work done in organizations, and that is why it has outlasted its days as a management fad and now is a generally accepted concept for understanding and designing organizations.

3. Three Levels of Performance

In order to achieve sustained high performance, an organization has to plan, design, and manage performance at three levels: organization, process, and job. We focused on process improvement because we knew that processes (being all about the work) had the greatest leverage for change, yet they were the least understood, defined, or managed. But the implication of this assumption is that even though our process improvement work was aimed at the middle level, we well understood that process improvements had to be linked upward to organizational goals, plans, and structure, and downward to the daily activities performed by individual performers.

MILESTONES SINCE 1990

Since 1990, process has followed a trajectory that took us by surprise. In the 1980s, our heads were mostly down, doing this kind of work in a few companies because we saw the results yielded and we were personally convinced of the value. We didn't realize that the time had come for an explosion of interest in process.

In 1990, Geary Rummler and Alan Brache published *Improving Performance: How to Manage the White Space on the Organization Chart*.[3] The three levels of performance and the negative effects of functional silos were guiding themes of the book, and much of what had been learned at Motorola was contained in the examples. The book took off immediately, and our business grew phenomenally overnight, because we had about the only thoroughly developed process improvement methodology available. We were invited into many different industries and built up our own knowledge of process very quickly in the early 1990s as major corporations, especially those looking for innovative solutions, discovered us.

We were also discovered by competitors: other consulting companies began attending our public courses and then putting out their own offerings. Suddenly everyone was an expert in process. But generally it was an exciting and inventive period; many people realized the value of process thinking and began to explore the subject and contribute their own ideas. We were adding people to the staff from many different functional disciplines, because we were finding out that the arena of process is multidisciplinary, and that people from areas such as Finance, IT, Marketing, and Sales had as much to contribute to process improvement as the manufacturing and engineering folks we were used to working with. And so gradually, "process" evolved into "business process," and "process improvement" expanded to include ideas about "process management."

Reengineering

In 1993, Michael Hammer and James Champy published *Reengineering the Corporation*, and it hit the business world like a thunderclap.[4] Boosted by great attention in business magazines, reengineering became an overnight sensation; the world of process would be drastically affected.

For us, the early effects were mostly positive. We got a great deal of business from companies looking for "reengineering" help and knowing only that process had something to do with it. We had a reputation for providing solid methodology. We also got a lot of business from Hammer's dictate that one should simply rip up the current organization and start with a clean sheet. We were sought out by clients who had tried the clean-sheet approach and had gotten into deep trouble as well as by skeptical organizations that wanted a more thoughtful methodology. In reaction, we developed an early model of "process maturity" and argued that one should always understand the condition of an existing "is" process before deciding how much surgery is required.

The much greater—and worse—effect of the reengineering fad, however, was its eventual association with downsizing. Several prominent consulting firms began calling their work in cutting costs and headcount a "process improvement approach." One was known for a "brown paper" exercise that appeared to be similar to some of our techniques of mapping business processes on large sheets of paper and analyzing them with design teams. The truth, though, was that we rarely used process improvement for cost cutting or headcount reduction. Far more often, the critical business issue with our clients was business growth. Unfortunately, everyone in the process business for a time was tarred with the brush of the downsizing movement, and the field went into a negative tailspin.

Six Sigma

In the late 1990s, Six Sigma surfaced as another trend related to process. After Motorola won the first Malcolm Baldrige Award in 1988 and began hosting huge numbers of benchmarking teams from other companies, the Six Sigma approach was adopted by such companies as Allied Signal and GE. It was a gradual expansion, because Six Sigma requires a daunting amount of discipline and investment and could not spread nearly as quickly as the concepts behind reengineering.

Yet despite the obstacles to adoption, Six Sigma has evolved into perhaps the most widely accepted version of BPM practices of any available. A great many companies not involved in the process movement of the 1990s are now ardent Six Sigma practitioners. There are critics of Six Sigma, of course—those who have published research showing a high rate of long-term business failure among Six Sigma companies and those who suspect that Six Sigma can lead to organizational ailments like rigidity and loss of creativity. But it is hard to deny how powerful and widespread has been the impact of Six Sigma, regardless of its potential drawbacks.

We have thought it kind of a shame that the label of "Six Sigma" ever got attached to the methodology. Certainly, from the name, one would assume that it's all about statistics, and while that is certainly part of the story, the approach to process improvement that was practiced in the mid-1980s at Motorola, as we described earlier, was on addressing critical business issues and getting results.

But unfortunately, as practiced today in some organizations, Six Sigma doesn't look a lot like the original version. For example, today one of the chief goals of some versions of Six Sigma is to choose and certify a cadre of Six Sigma "black belts" to organize and conduct multiple improvement projects. The emphasis is on getting a project and getting certified, which leads to keeping the scope of projects small (seldom if ever taking on a large, cross-functional core process) and creating projects unconnected from each other and not driven by a strategic focus. One of the single big projects we conducted in the 1980s would likely be chopped up into several small projects today, with diminished results.

In addition, the practice of Six Sigma seems to have become a specialty and even a career choice. One supposedly has to be "black-belt" certified to do this work, which distances it from the people who perform the process or manage it. And the cloning of many black belts adds to that aura of needing a special class of people to do process improvement. Contrast that to the situation at Motorola. At one of the sites that Alan supported in the mid-1980s, there were three major business divisions plus five manufacturing organizations and two design engineering houses. The employees numbered about 5,000. They were supported by *one* statistician—who, by necessity, was an advisor, not a project leader. The improvement projects were performed by line people who were experts in their own processes. There are still organizations that approach Six Sigma in this fashion, but there are so many variations of Six Sigma today that it is hard to know what a company claiming to be a "Six Sigma organization" might be doing unless you can see them in practice.

Process Management/Governance

The concept of process management, or ownership, was described in *Improving Performance* as "someone is looking at and taking action to improve the performance of an entire cross-functional process."[5] Our notion was that process management is a senior management role, with a focus on addressing major "white space" issues. At Motorola the responsibility for process management was the same thing as responsibility for the performance of an entire business.

In the early to mid-1990s, it was rare to encounter an organization that had implemented process management, and if one did, it tended to be in the form of a council of senior managers, abetted by improvement specialists, that assumed collective ownership of the core processes and would meet occasionally to prioritize improvement efforts. But the idea gradually spread, and today many companies have adopted their own brand of process management. But never did we imagine how the concept could be misinterpreted.

We have been invited into some organizations that have appointed dozens of "process owners" for nearly every type of process, no matter how insignificant. The role is often assigned without any clear definition of the purpose or the responsibilities. In some companies, "process owners" are in reality staff employees who do process design and improvement efforts but are distant from the responsibilities of getting the work done. Inevitably, the concept either dies a quick but embarrassing death because nobody knows what to do, or it leads to turf battles between process owners and line managers over who is in charge of process performance (and performers).

We had never envisioned process management as a shadow "governance" structure laid on top of the line organization. Instead we had seen it as viable only if assumed as an additional role by a senior manager with existing responsibilities relevant to the process ownership role (for example, he or she was the manager of one of the key functional areas participating in the process). And we saw process ownership as necessary for only the big, core processes that deliver value to customers, but not for all the enabling processes and sub-processes.

The idea of process management still has value—and in fact, we think it is the very key to effective performance of an enterprise—but it needs to be cleaned up, redefined, and separated from all of the bad interpretations applied to it.

Process Documentation/Repositories

In a similar vein, the idea of mapping a business process has evolved into a cottage industry. There is no denying the considerable value to an organization of defining its processes, documenting them in some consistent fashion, and making the documents available for a variety of uses, such as training, measurement and management, and improvement. But we have run into organizations that have spent all of their efforts in documentation alone and have turned it into such a specialty (especially by applying hard-to-use kinds of modeling software) that nobody except the documenters understands or uses the process documents.

In one organization we visited, a special team of highly skilled engineers had devoted years of effort in creating some *5,000 pages* of process documentation in hopes of achieving a certain level in the CMMI process maturity scale. But in answer to the question, "Have you ever done any process improvement?" the answer was no—too busy creating the documentation. Furthermore, it turned out that the line departments weren't using those documents either; the documents were too cumbersome to access, read, or keep up to date. So the process maps did not represent the work at all.

In addition, we have seen a great deal of effort and money spent in trying to put this documentation into repositories so that the documentation can be accessed, referenced, and updated by others. Often these efforts engaged knowledge management professionals who brought techniques for cataloging and controlling the documentation. But despite these well-intentioned efforts we have seen little evidence of effective strategies to ensure the quality of documentation, encourage use by others, and identify and incorporate changes.

Advances in repository software capabilities have helped bring a much-needed hierarchical structuring to the process documentation. But organizing the documentation this way doesn't resolve one of the greatest fundamental challenges: the lower the level of documentation, the shorter the shelf life and the greater the maintenance requirements. So what we often find in organizations is a library of historical process documentation that almost always requires validation before it can be trusted as a statement of what is truly the current practice and is typically only referenced by a handful of "users."

What has tended to fuel this fixation on process documentation are the requirements of programs like ISO 9001 and its descendents, and CMMI and the burgeoning varieties of process maturity models. And to make this tendency worse, the powerful process modeling tools now available can make it relatively easy for people to create great mounds of process documentation—for some reason or other.

Don't misunderstand—we think you should define your processes, which means capturing the current practices and then designing the "should" version—but that means doing documentation with a purpose, and the purpose should shape what and how you document and should also dictate some requirements for usefulness.

Sarbanes-Oxley

Passage of the Sarbanes-Oxley Act in 2002 spurred a renewed interest in process long after the negative effects of reengineering and downsizing seemed for many companies to have taken a fatal toll on the whole concept. But "process" had never really disappeared, and when Sarbanes-Oxley was suddenly mandated—especially with its Section 404 requirement that CEOs and CFOs must certify that they have an effective system of internal controls over financial reporting and must report on the effectiveness of those controls at the close of each fiscal year— process mapping and management came roaring back. Many companies recognized that the best way to find out whether they had controls in place, and to design them in if they were lacking, was to employ a process approach.

Admittedly, much of the effort expended was in simply mapping processes as they existed, with very little improvement and very little questioning of business need, but Sarbanes-Oxley did serve to bring back an interest in process in companies where it had languished. And in companies where process thinking had never taken hold before, Sarbanes-Oxley was that critical business issue that generated an interest.

Automation

The biggest driver for process these days is the impact of information technology on process. Automation has always been there, of course, and has been one of the standard options for streamlining or improving a business process. Technology has generally been viewed as an "enabler" of performance, helping the human performer do the work more efficiently. But the acceleration of new developments in technology since the rise of the Internet in the mid-1990s is turning the integration of technology with business processes into a major strategic issue. Many companies today are increasingly relying on technology to provide their avenues to market, their distribution system, their supply management, their creative edge. And today some processes are so automated that it probably is inaccurate to think of technology as merely an enabler; it has become a performer of the work itself, sometimes alone and sometimes in support of human performers. There is hardly a process to be found that is not to some degree entwined with technology.

This development has pushed the CIO into a role of strategic thinker and collaborator with the CEO on how to engineer a successful enterprise. At lower levels, it has caused many IT organizations to become aware of their relationship to process, and, in some cases, to become the stewards of "process excellence" in their organizations.

There are some specific historical reasons why technology has become so prominent in the process space. We discuss a few of them next.

ERP Systems and Y2K

In the 1990s, ERP (enterprise resource planning) systems became widely popular, solving some vexing corporate problems while causing new ones. It made great sense for many companies to adopt a rigid, standardized set of software to execute their myriad everyday administrative processes; however, that same standardization was not such a hot idea when applied to the important processes in which competitive advantage potentially lurked—and who could know what processes were tomorrow's competitive edge? But ERP systems locked you into one way of performing a process—reversing the conventional wisdom that an organization should first design its business processes and then automate them. Nonetheless, the widespread adoption of ERP systems hastened the dependence of business processes on software systems.

The other factor to strengthen the process–software tie was Y2K, the supposed threat of catastrophic computer system failure at the end of the twentieth century that caused a mad scramble of organizations large and small to build in preventive measures to protect their computer systems from crashing. (Must have worked.) And it did make processes and systems that much more interdependent.

Workflow Modeling/BPMS

Workflow modeling tools have been available since roughly the 1980s, but it was not until the mid-1990s that the offerings became robust enough for business to pay attention. It has always been a dream of process designers to take all those sticky notes on rolls of paper and turn them into something easily navigated, changed, tested, and updated.

Some of the most prolific users of workflow models were Business Analysts, who used them to identify requirements as part of systems development efforts. This application of the toolset typically involved modeling the work that surrounded the system, a very worthy objective. But the resulting documentation was often referred to or confused with process models simply because the tools and the formats were the same. The assumption was that because we can document a work activity using workflow modeling tools, it must be a process.

Over time, an entire industry grew up to provide workflow modeling tools, and organizations of providers and users have been formed to agree on rules and conventions for their design. This has led to an increasingly robust but complex range of functionality and conventions that has resulted in a fundamental schism between the tool experts and power users who can build and interpret the models and the people who perform and manage the work (and ideally the users and maintainers of the models). This schism is a large barrier to institutionalizing the use of workflow models in organizations. Today's BPMS offerings do all kinds of valuable and attractive things; the issues today have to do with too much functionality, too much complexity, more bells and whistles than anyone really needs, and the basics—of creating, changing, and saving process maps—still too difficult. But progress continues, and we are hopeful that the usability of workflow models will improve.

GENERAL RESULTS

So where has the process/process management movement gotten? Despite some real results here and there, and despite our own role as practitioners, preachers, and believers, we think the movement has not reached its real potential. When you look critically at the current practice of process, you see challenges abound.

IT/BPM Challenges

IT has somewhat taken on (not always by choice) a leadership role in the process movement. But it is facing major obstacles:

- The approach that IT is taking to development of technology solutions is largely functionally focused. They respond to requests from Operations or Finance or Sales or Engineering, and they do their best to deliver functionality to meet the specific needs of the requesting organization. The problem is that the many different solutions don't add up to a coherent system of enabling technologies, but just a hodgepodge of applications and databases that become ever more complex and prone to breakdowns. Even so-called enterprise (ERP) solutions are functionally focused.

- There continues to be a fixation with bringing in the latest technology that fascinates the technologists, rather than starting with the organization's strategies and then figuring out how technology can enhance or improve the organization's ability to accomplish work and deliver results.

- Many IT organizations are not aligned effectively with the businesses they are supposed to be serving. For example, the role of Business Analysts is to play an interpretative role, bringing the requirements of business to the IT development specialists and helping them build solutions that meet business needs. Instead, some Business Analysts have been co-opted by the IT organization's own internal goals and practices, and they spend most of their time negotiating with business in an endless cycle of requirements rewrites.

Process Improvement Wars

Another issue preventing process and process management from reaching its potential is the battle for control of this discipline. We know of many instances of staff organizations fighting over leadership of process improvement. The reasons for these conflicts vary, but here are a few examples:

- A Fortune 50 multinational firm, with fifteen strategic business units and eighty additional business units, in operation for more than 100 years, had accumulated ten distinct internal consulting groups, including:
  - Supply Chain Management
  - PACE (an accelerated new product development and introduction process)
  - Six Sigma
  - Process Reengineering
  - Organization Effectiveness (OE)
  - Statistical Process Control
  - Strategy Development

In the beginning, these groups, housed in various headquarters staff functions, all worked independently and competed with each other for project work from the line organizations. It was not uncommon for three or four of these consulting groups to be simultaneously pitching their particular expertise to the same business unit. Then, after numerous complaints from line managers about the redundancy and confusion of all these consulting units, they were centralized under one corporate executive. This individual, however, uncertain how to proceed, made no effort to build a conceptual framework that would have provided a logic or rationale for distinguishing among the units, integrating any of their offerings, or consolidating them. As a result, nothing changed. The units remained self-supporting to some degree and continued to compete with each other. In fact, they got worse. Shortly after the reorganization, a big blow-up occurred when four units independently submitted proposals to help one business unit address an operational issue. Its frustrated general manager called representatives of all four proposing units to his office and told them he wanted nothing more to do with them until they returned with an integrated proposal. His rationale was that it wasn't his job to figure out the best solution to his challenge—that is what they were paid to do. But this kind of situation continued to happen again and again, until the budget of this centralized staff group became a highly visible target and the entire group was disbanded. A few survivors found work in specific strategic business units, but the company as a whole was robbed of the expertise that it needed and had been paying for but not getting.

- A large financial services company undertook a major effort to upgrade the company's entire technology, with the goals of eliminating dated and overlapping systems and integrating tools and databases for better employee performance. A prominent technology vendor was hired, and a program office was set up to oversee the initiative. However, inside Operations, work was already underway to meet Sarbanes-Oxley requirements and improve processes by mapping core processes. The IT vendor first got in the way of this effort by staffing up several internal teams and insisting that many of the business people involved in the Sarbanes-Oxley effort switch their attention to the technology transformation. Things were made worse when the IT vendor disparaged the tools being used to capture processes (that is, typical cross-functional process maps) and instead insisted on using its own IT-centric toolkit. It was a process notation war that went on for months and was settled only when the first technology release was so abysmal that the vendor was unceremoniously booted out and the business took over the transformation effort, blending it with the process improvement initiative. But meanwhile, the notion of "process" took a beating.

Big Crashes and Burns on the "Process-Managed/Process-Centered" Highway

As a long-term objective for a company, becoming "process centered" (or "process managed" or "process driven") is a laudable aim. We're not always sure what a given company might mean by the term, but our interpretation of becoming a process-managed or -centered organization means recognizing and treating processes as one of the most important components of the organization; processes are the means by which work is accomplished and value is created—in other words, processes are essential to any organization's purpose. So becoming process managed means carefully defining, designing, supporting, and managing one's processes. A fair number of companies we know have decided to become a process-managed/process-centered organization. What we haven't seen is much success in getting there. To wit:

- A consumer services organization created a large "process excellence" department, hiring dozens of people with strong experience in process improvement, Six Sigma, reengineering, and the like, and attending this activity with great hoopla and promises of good things to come. To get them all "on the same page," the new folks were sent individually or in small groups to a very well-known provider of seminars and certification in all things process. This action took place over months, at great expense. But meanwhile inside the new organization was utter chaos, with no coherent plan of action, no methodology for identifying clients or issues or areas of focus. So after months of embarrassing floundering around, the department was dismantled and its members disbursed to other areas or sent out the door. Result? The less said about that, the better.

Business Process Architecture Is a Good Idea, but . . .

Essential to becoming process managed is to define the organization's business process architecture. A business process architecture is a clear picture of an organization's business processes; their purposes and relationships in producing value; their link upward to organizational strategy, objectives, and requirements; and their link downward to human performers and supporting technologies.

In our early years of doing process improvement, when we focused largely on single cross-functional processes, we created pictures we called "process relationship maps" that would identify the process targeted for improvement along with its upstream and downstream processes, its enabling processes, and the management processes that provide guidance. So we always had a kind of "architecture" view, but in recent years we have come to recognize how important this view of the organization is. One cannot hope to transform a complex organization by addressing one process at a time (the exception being a small company that may have a single product or service and therefore a single core process that constitutes the guts of the organization). One has to comprehend the "organization as a system," which means understanding all of its processes; effective lasting improvement may require redesigning much or all of the process architecture. The ideal scale of this work has increased in our own practice, and we believe that improvement on this larger scale is the preventive to Hammer's message that "70% of reengineering projects fail." However, this is the current reality:

- There is very little evidence that companies have defined their business process architecture, and few see why it's of value to do so. This doesn't mean they are not doing process work; they are often madly generating process maps and doing Six Sigma projects, but they have not cast a net on all this activity with a picture of the business architecture—redesigning parts of the elephant without seeing the elephant.

- Where a business process architecture of sorts is being created, it is being done by the Enterprise Architecture function, so ipso facto it is a technology-oriented view, not a business view, and it is owned by IT, not the business leadership, so the value of such a picture is hard to grasp for anyone other than an Enterprise Architecture type.

BPM, but . . .

Somewhere along the way, process modeling software vendors adopted the term "business process management" for their wares, and they have invested so much in the term that a lot of people hearing "BPM" today automatically assume you are talking about the software.

But it is hard for us to see the *M* in BPM. Yes, today's BPM suites offer some amount of functionality to amass and report performance data, but they offer little of anything that could be called process management. The management work of planning and designing performance, providing and managing the resources and support to performers in the process, diagnosing variances and making critical adjustments, deciding whether a process should be improved, discarded, or replaced—all these chores can be aided with good tools that help make data readily available and easy to understand. But it is a major mistake to confuse the assistance with the management.

In a similar way, the ability to simulate process performance can be a very helpful aid in understanding how a process design will work once implemented, but the simulation capability does not by itself guarantee you a good process design—much less one that might be highly innovative and change the rules of a competitive game. Technology cannot substitute for human inventiveness and human intelligence applied to business problems—not yet, anyway, and probably not in our lifetime.

BPM would be better off calling itself what it is: business process technology. In this book, we try to be very clear about what we view as process management.

CLOSING POINTS

Process has most certainly evolved over twenty-five years, with great progress and impact in some respects but also with bumps along the way. Despite our admittedly dim view of some of the goings-on in the process world these days, we remain convinced that

1. Process/process thinking/process design/process management are essential to all organizations. We believe that, indeed, process is the most valuable insight into the nature of work and organizations in the past hundred years.

2. Process is here to stay, having outlasted its period of faddism and its many misapplications. It is now imbedded in business school curriculums as something every business professional should know. It has proven its worth.

3. There is, however, a better way to go about this work, a way that circles back to our original assumptions of the organization as a system, of processes being about the work, and the three levels of performance—but updated with numerous insights since *Improving Performance* was published.

4. What Motorola—and other practitioners that achieved large-scale successes with process improvement—were focused on was value creation. In hindsight we have realized that they understood that the business is fundamentally about serving customers in the most effective possible way with superior products and services, and that you cannot achieve that best-in-class service through downsizing, cost reduction, or other techniques that merely delay the inevitable.

The key questions for any process practitioner are (1) Where are you right now in your search for process excellence, and (2) where are you headed? We think that even if right now you may be buried down at the sub-process level where you may have little impact on business results, there is a pathway you can follow to move up the "process evolutionary path," if

Table 1.1 The Scope and Range of Process Work

Process Scope	Definition/ Documentation	Process Design	Process Redesign/ Improvement	Process Management System Design
Enterprise/Business Model				
Value Creation System				
Processing System				
Process				
Sub-Process/ Task/Sub-Process				

you will. That path is illustrated in Table 1.1, which moves up in scale from sub-process at the bottom to single process to multiple processes to the whole "value creation architecture" (a term we explain in Chapter Two) of a business to the entire business design. For the moment, the cells in this matrix are blank, but we will fill them in throughout the remainder of this book as we explain the approach we think can help you maximize the power of process in your own organization.

Process in a Value Perspective

In Chapter One, we asserted that despite a vast broadening of the language, concepts, and tools of "process," progress in transforming organizations into well-designed and managed institutions is still slow. We further argued that much of the momentum of the work of the 1980s that established process as a legitimate business concept has been followed by a trail of misfires and misapplications of potentially powerful techniques and tools.

In our view, the root cause of this lack of progress in process is that most people (practitioners and managers alike) still do not recognize and understand that organizations are systems and, consequently, don't realize the implications for how organizations should be planned, designed, and managed, which in turn means the value of process concepts continues to be misconstrued and misapplied. Despite lip service to "systems thinking," many practitioners of process improvement management don't get—in a practical, applied sense—that processes are part of a larger organizational system and therefore cannot be tinkered with in isolation. These individuals don't see the larger system context of particular processes.

This myopia is shared by managers and employees, many of whom are familiar enough with notions of process to talk about "their process" but don't see the connections of that process to a larger architecture of processes that must be designed and managed. As a natural course of being in a particular part of a given organization and possessed of a particular set of skills, they are fundamentally grounded in their own discipline or functional area (Engineering, Sales, Manufacturing, Customer Service, Product Development, Finance, HR, and so on) and tend not to look beyond their department boundaries. Nor are they encouraged and enabled to do so. And, if anything, technology has abetted their functional myopia. Alas, white space abideth.

The correction to this myopia is to return to the foundations of process work, to our underlying assumptions, and to how they have changed and expanded as we, and our clients, have learned more and more about organizations as systems.

BASIC PREMISE: THE ORGANIZATION AS A SYSTEM

Our starting point for understanding and characterizing any organization today is still to try to understand it as a system. But a system to do what? Answering that question is a helpful way of diagnosing what is happening in an organization and evaluating what needs to change in order to improve.

All organizations—public or private, large or small—exist to provide value. For all the activities and complexities of any organization, they must fundamentally produce something of value to someone other than themselves, or they will not be in business long. In short, a business is a system that exists to provide value to customers and financial stakeholders. A business must meet four key requirements to provide value to their constituents:

1. Understanding the value to be delivered to its dual constituency

2. Designing and maintaining a value-adding work system that has been engineered and optimized to produce the valued product/service

3. Resources to perform that work, which starts with capital and expense dollars that are converted into people, technology, equipment, facilities, and materials

4. Management of the integration of resources and the work system to produce the desired value

Figure 2.1 represents the ideal relationship among these four elements. What happens in many, if not most, businesses today is depicted in Figure 2.2. This is a picture of a system that is woefully out of balance.

Following is a summary of what has happened to the four requirements in many organizations.

1. Understanding the Value to Be Delivered to Its Dual Constituency

Many companies fail to manage a balance between the value delivered to customers and that delivered to financial stakeholders. Increasingly there is a short-term emphasis on delivering value to financial stakeholders (return on investment) versus value to customers. What seems to be lost is the inescapable fact that the return to financial stakeholders is ultimately dependent on the value (in the form of valued products/services) delivered to the customer. This shift away from delivery of value drives a corresponding shift in priorities within the organization: To satisfy the continual demand for short-term financial results, control of resources has become the primary internal priority.

Figure 2.1 The Four Key Requirements of a Business

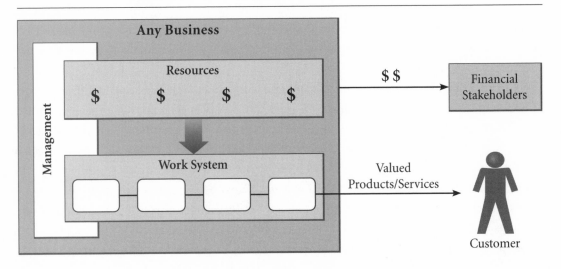

Figure 2.2 The Resources Fixation

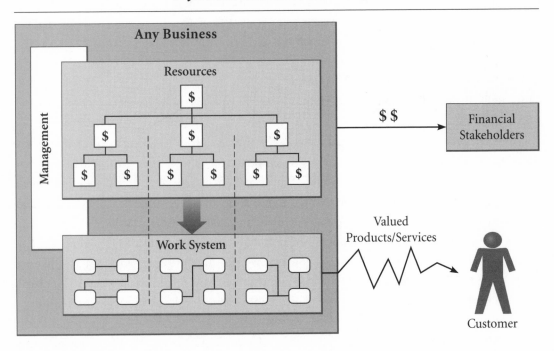

2. Designing and Maintaining a Value-Adding Work System to Produce the Valued Products/Services

A major reason the resource element is prominent in business is that, by contrast, the work and work system are virtually invisible to the human eye. With the exception of a few engineering drawings in a manufacturing or process operation, there is no agreed-upon end-to-end articulation of the value-adding work required to produce a valued product or service, from product/service inception, through marketing and selling, to delivery and support. Even when such a depiction may exist, it tends not to be a tool used by management to understand and guide the organization. Process understanding may reside at lower levels of the organization but not at the top.

Further, what little definition of the work and work system has been done tends to be confined to individual functional resource "buckets." The work specification is under the control of each function or department, constrained by their resources and their particular parochial view of the business. These costly work activities quickly evolve within the siloed resource buckets into what many organizational observers then call "culture," which is really many little individual, self-absorbed, rigidified cultures whose goal becomes self-preservation. In many cases these insulate functional resource buckets are further reinforced by legacy technology systems and applications provided by an ever-obliging IT organization. Thus, the IT organization reinforces a silo view of work, organizing itself to mirror the resource buckets on the organization chart. Then given its own fragmented understanding of the business, IT is unable to muster up a useful (to the business) end-to-end articulation of the value-adding work required to deliver a valued product or service. This myopia becomes particularly obvious when IT is tasked to create or install enterprise-wide systems (such as ERP). Its approach is to tackle the project functional area by functional area, the only approach it knows.

3. Resources to Perform That Work

Internally, the most dominant element in most organizations today has become resources, for several reasons.

One major reason we have already stated: the priority given the return to financial stakeholders. Resources is where the money is. This emphasis on value to financial stakeholders exacerbates a fundamental misunderstanding of cause and effect between our four requirements of a business shown in Figure 2.1. Many organizations behave as if there is a direct connection between resource management and returns to financial stakeholders. Perhaps there is in the short term. But the longer-term reality is this: when things are working as they should inside an organization, resources make their contributions within value-creating work systems that provide valued products and services to customers, which in turn results in earnings to be distributed to financial stakeholders. There is no viable shortcut to results by managing resources.

A second reason is the daily visibility of resources in any organization. The organization chart of a business is in most cases a high-level representation of the allocation of critical resources across the organization. Each function shown on the organization chart is a resource bucket, backed by a corresponding capital and expense budget. The visibility of the budget structure is understandable given that dollars are the lifeblood of a business, and in any well-run enterprise every nickel must be accounted for. The dollars are distributed at the beginning of the year and their utilization tracked and accounted for publicly every month. Heads roll if resource utilization doesn't tally with resource allocation at the end of the year.

A third reason is resource ownership represents status and power for executives and managers at every level of the organization. The bigger the resource bucket controlled, the greater the presumed value of the executive. And yes, there have been experiments in recent years with virtual teams and lateral promotions and managers without staffs, but clear away the rhetoric and we see that the power games regarding headcount have not changed.

4. Management of the Integration of Resources and the Work System to Produce the Desired Value

The relentless emphasis on resource management is predictable, given that resource utilization is critical but also relatively easy to monitor. (Who can't compare "actual versus budget"?) As ready evidence of this bias, note the annual planning and budgeting ritual, which easily extends over four to six months of a year and consumes a quarter or more of management time annually. Add to this the time spent monthly, quarterly, and annually at every level of the organization, examining "actual versus budget" and pursuing endless initiatives to close any gaps between the two, and you easily come up with 85% of management time focused on resource management. Add to that the untold hours of effort by numerous staff organizations assigned to crank out mountains of analyses and PowerPoint charts designed to protect the backsides of various and sundry managers, and you have organizations that barely get anything useful accomplished.

Meanwhile, the little attention paid to work and work systems is carried out within the functions and usually is focused on how to get more work with fewer resources. And all the while, the truth is that resources can be wisely managed *only* in the context of the value-adding work required to deliver valued products and services.

But how do we make this happen? How do we get "resources" back in balance with "work"? Resource management is front of mind for every executive or manager in any business. ("Who's paying for that? It sure as hell isn't coming out of *my* budget!") In contrast, the value-adding work required to keep the enterprise in business is invisible—buried in essentially independent functional resource buckets. Like Rodney Dangerfield, "work" gets no respect!

A starting point for rebalancing the management of work and resources is to *think differently about the contribution of work....*

THE VALUE MACHINE

Let's reorient ourselves to our picture of the ideal components of a business as shown in Figure 2.3. In that depiction, we start with the assertion that a business is fundamentally a value-producing machine (a Value Machine, for short) that exists to produce valued products and services to customers (1a) and a return to financial stakeholders (1b). When we look inside the machine, we see two fundamental components that must be managed in concert to produce the desired results:

- The end-to-end Value Creation System (2) that effectively and efficiently converts customer needs and desires into products and services that those customers value and will pay for. In this context, we are no longer viewing work as resource-consuming activities but

Figure 2.3 The Value Machine

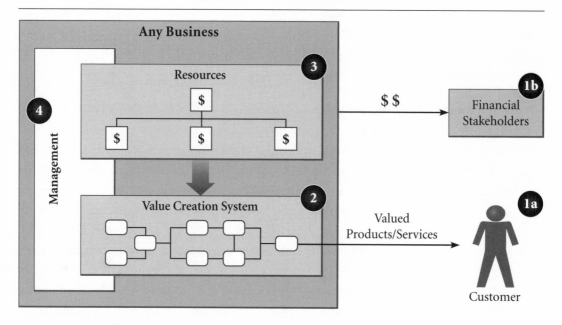

rather as a carefully designed set of value-adding outputs leading to valued products and services. This system of *value-adding* work is the backbone of the business. The business is only as good as this value creation system.

• The resources (3) necessary to fuel the value creation system.

The primary tasks of management (4) are to properly allocate and manage those scarce resources across the value creation system so as to effectively and efficiently produce the desired products and services.

Now we see that there are really two critical dimensions to business performance that must be managed in concert:

1. The **value creation dimension** (the system of value-adding work that delivers valued products and services to customers)

2. The **resource dimension** (the scarce resources required to perform the value-adding work of the enterprise)

Up to this point in modern management the world over, the management effort has been skewed in the direction of the resource dimension, with inconsistent results. There is ample evidence of this imbalance between resources and value creation, including:

• Endless cycles of reorganization that fail to work because the only thing being reorganized is the names on the functional resource buckets. There is seldom any change in the end-to-end value-adding work required to deliver the end product or service. In most cases, functional sub-optimization of the end-to-end work system continues unabated.

- Failed product/service launches because key functions can't or don't participate in the design, development, and proper preparation of the organization for the launch, because of their functional resource constraints and inward focus on their own activities.

- Customer outrage at companies that try to keep costs in line by skimping on resources (think of poorly staffed help desks and technical support) instead of properly delivering value.

- Downsizing death spirals as companies try to resource-manage themselves back to profitability. The resulting chaos in the value creation dimension is ignored by everyone but the customer.

It is time to begin managing both the value creation dimension and the resource dimension. Business performance most definitely is not a case of resources *versus* value. The only way a business is going to survive in the future is the wise allocation of critical, scarce resources *in the context* of the organization's unique value creation system. However, we are quick to acknowledge that this task is easier said than done. Forces driving an emphasis on resources are many, including:

- As acknowledged earlier, the functional structure of organizations, which is legitimate and necessary (As we describe later, there are workable ways to accommodate both resources and value within a functional structure.)

- The formal accounting, budgeting, and planning systems

- The desire for some accountability, which is easier to approximate with a resource bucket structure

And there have been many efforts over time to bring back some balance between value and resources. One such effort was the short-lived Activity Based Costing movement, born of the need to link resources to specific activity. Because it was a bolt-on, shadow management system, it quickly succumbed to the established accounting system. In something of a crude effort not to lose sight of the value creation system of an individual business, Gore, Inc., maker of GoreTex, among other products, has famously declared that they will not have a business of more than 300 employees. And in many businesses, the CEO calls out a half-dozen high-level initiatives for the year, in an attempt to impose some general value objectives on the already tightly resource-constrained organization. But to date, these and other approaches have not made a dent in the imbalance.

THE VALUE CREATION PERSPECTIVE

In the present context of work systems, the notion of process is frequently trivialized as "process improvement"—just another tool for cost reduction and productivity improvement.

But the need to recognize and manage the value creation system (along with resources) puts process in a different light, in a value perspective. For a business to achieve systematic, sustainable value creation, two things are required:

1. A sound value creation system—an infrastructure for delivering value
2. Management of the value creation system

Process is at the heart of both these requirements. Regarding infrastructure, a sound value creation system is nothing more than an effective and efficient network of value-producing processes. Thus process is the fundamental building block of a value creation system—a LEGO assembly of processes. With this understanding, we no longer look at processes as just a sequence of work activities to be modeled, improved, and managed in isolation. We see every process as a tightly woven component of a larger value creation *architecture*: a picture of the total value creation system. Every modeling, improvement, or management effort of a process must be seen in the context of the total value creation system of a business—as a contribution to that total value creation system.

Before a value creation system can be managed and improved, it must be articulated, made visible. Because process is the fundamental building block of the value creation system, process is the tool we use to systematically articulate the previously unarticulated, invisible value creation system of a business.

Thus the strategic contribution of process is to make the invisible visible and the unmanageable manageable.

OVERVIEW OF THE VALUE CREATION HIERARCHY

Historically, the organization chart has been the de facto organizing template for business. We argue that what is needed is a different view, against which proper resource allocation decisions can be made. Figure 2.4 is just that: a top-to-bottom framework for structuring the value-adding work in a business. We call it the *Value Creation Hierarchy*, or VCH.

As you can see from Figure 2.4, there are four levels of decomposition of the work carried out by the businesses making up an enterprise (the whole enterprise being at Level 1). And as you will see shortly, the VCH is more than just a documenting or decomposition scheme—every level is a work system structure and represents important decisions about work design.

Following is a quick overview of the five levels of the Value Creation Hierarchy represented in Figure 2.4. The VCH is explained in detail in Chapter Three.

Level 1: Enterprise/Business Model

The Value Creation Hierarchy sees any enterprise or business organization as a system, operating as part of a super-system that consists of markets, competition, resources, and the general business environment.

Figure 2.4 Value Creation Hierarchy

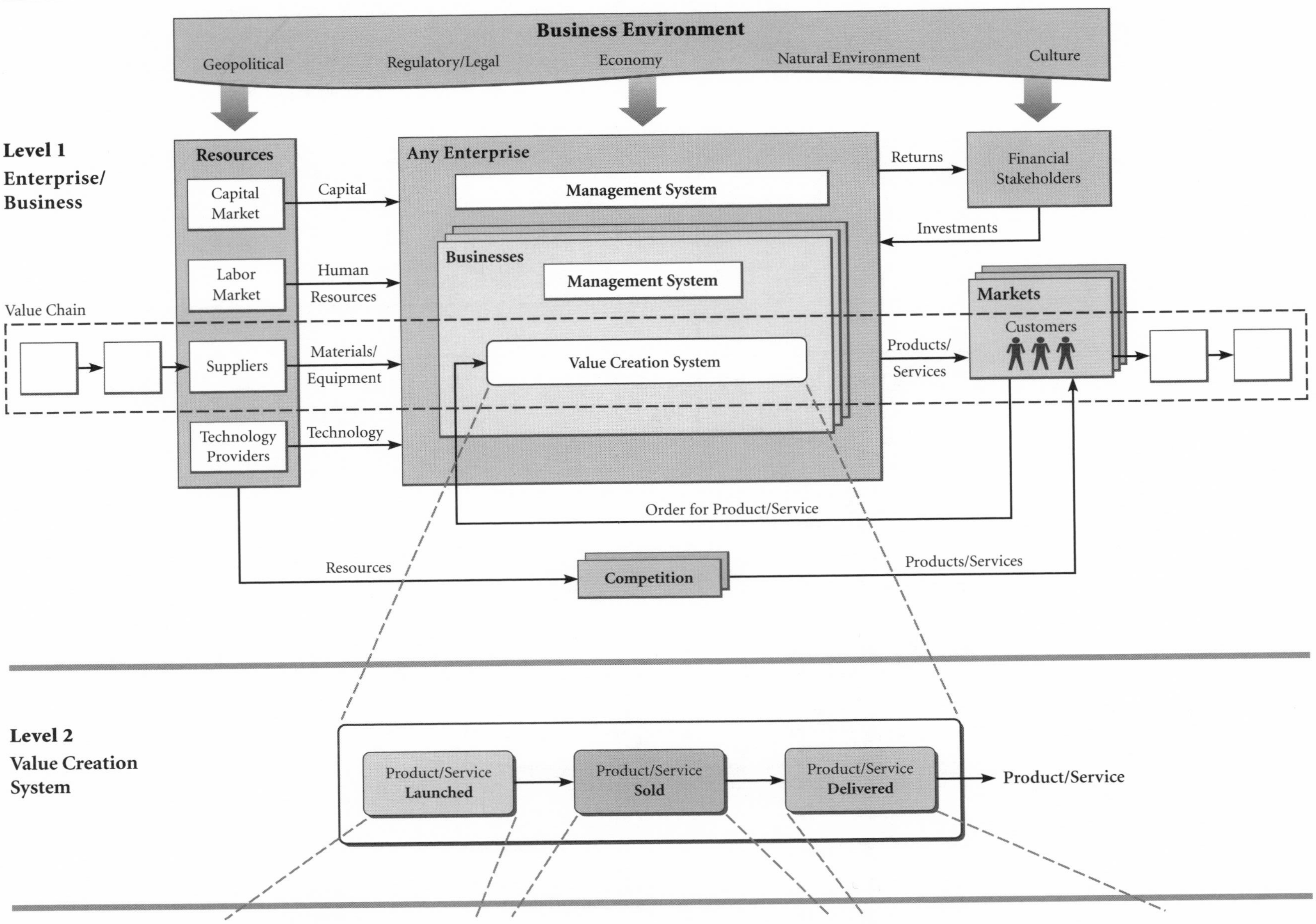

Business Environment

Geopolitical | Regulatory/Legal | Economy | Natural Environment | Culture

Level 1
Enterprise/
Business

Value Chain

Resources
- Capital Market
- Labor Market
- Suppliers
- Technology Providers

Capital
Human Resources
Materials/Equipment
Technology

Any Enterprise

Management System

Businesses

Management System

Value Creation System

Returns
Investments

Financial Stakeholders

Products/Services

Markets
Customers

Order for Product/Service

Products/Services

Competition

Resources

Level 2
Value Creation
System

Product/Service Launched → Product/Service Sold → Product/Service Delivered → Product/Service

Figure 2.4 *(Continued)*

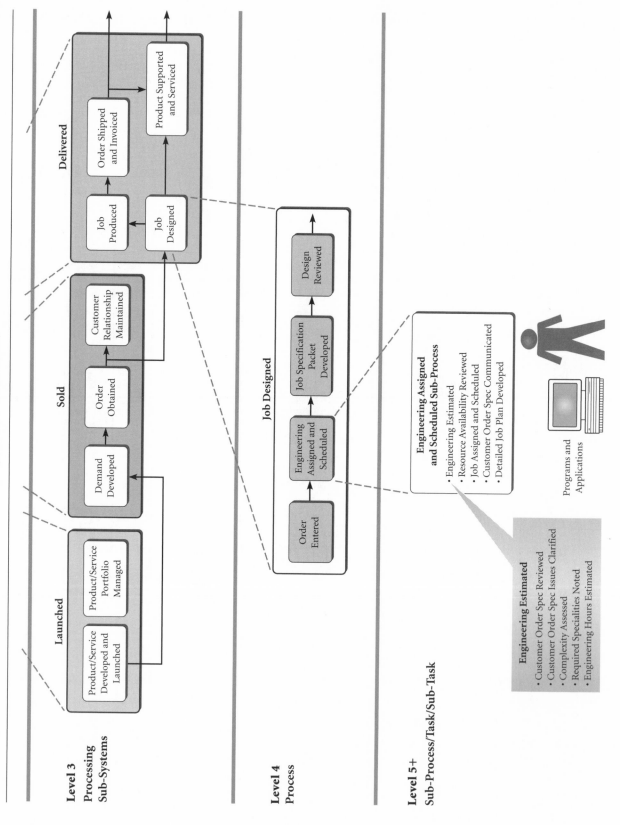

Level 3
Processing
Sub-Systems

Launched
- Product/Service Developed and Launched
- Product/Service Portfolio Managed

Sold
- Demand Developed
- Order Obtained
- Customer Relationship Maintained

Delivered
- Job Produced
- Job Designed
- Order Shipped and Invoiced
- Product Supported and Serviced

Level 4
Process

Job Designed
- Order Entered
- Engineering Assigned and Scheduled
- Job Specification Packet Developed
- Design Reviewed

Level 5+
Sub-Process/Task/Sub-Task

Engineering Assigned and Scheduled Sub-Process
- Engineering Estimated
- Resource Availability Reviewed
- Job Assigned and Scheduled
- Customer Order Spec Communicated
- Detailed Job Plan Developed

Engineering Estimated
- Customer Order Spec Reviewed
- Customer Order Spec Issues Clarified
- Complexity Assessed
- Required Specialities Noted
- Engineering Hours Estimated

Programs and Applications

The enterprise is made up of revenue-producing businesses that conceive, sell, and deliver valued products and services to customers. The enterprise business goals are achieved through the performance of the individual business units. The business units are the basic engines, or *Value Machines*, that deliver the value and generate the revenues for the enterprise. The decisions around identifying and structuring business units are the first level of decisions a business makes about the structure of work.

Inside each business Value Machine, there are two major systems required to deliver value to customers and financial stakeholders.

1. The **Value Creation System** (VCS), which is the structure of work required to create and deliver value (or, if you will, the "operating system" inside the Value Machine)

2. The **Management System**, which guides the creation of value

Level 2: The Value Creation System

Since our focus here is the structure of value-adding work, Level 2 starts with the drill-down into the components that make up the Value Creation System. (The Management System is examined in Chapter Five.) To provide value, a business must do three things, as represented by the three sub-systems that comprise the Value Creation System shown at Level 2.

1. Identify the customer's needs for a product/service and then find, conceive, invent, design or obtain a product/service to meet that need. (Typically, this involves activities we commonly think of as product development, product launch, and product life cycle management.) We call this processing sub-system *Product/Service Launched*. The major *output* is the "successful launch of the right product/service," as reflected by sustained sales and profitability of the product/service after launch.

2. Make customers aware of their need for the product/service and convince them that the business has the right offering available to meet that need. (Typically, this involves the activities we attribute to Marketing and Sales.) This processing sub-system is *Product/ Service Sold*, and the *output* is the "identification, capture, and retention of customers."

3. Deliver said product/service to the customer. (This typically includes all those activities involved in order processing, making ready for installation, installation, invoicing, servicing, and warranty management.) This is the *Product/Service Delivered* processing sub-system, and the desired *output* is the "efficient delivery, installation, and maintenance (to the customer's satisfaction) of the product/service."

The Value Creation System as a whole is a critical organization level, but it is seldom recognized and managed because of the highly visible resource dimension and the siloed ownership of functional areas that leaves nobody in charge of the entire Value Creation System. Yet the VCS goals are the direct connection to the customer and business. It is essential that the goals of the three sub-systems of Launched, Sold, and Delivered be aligned with the VCS goals and with each other, and that none of the sub-systems be allowed to sub-optimize the total VCS.

Level 3: Processing Sub-Systems

Each of the sub-systems of Launched, Sold, and Delivered in turn is made up of the work processes necessary to achieve the goals of the sub-system. The Value Creation Hierarchy in Figure 2.4 shows the processes for a product-producing business, but the Value Creation System applies just as readily to a service business or a government or nonprofit organization. We are adamant that, regardless of organizational type, you can always find the equivalent of Launched, Sold, and Delivered sub-systems. However, as you will see, we don't hold that there is a generic list of processes to describe the insides of each sub-system.

Level 4: Process

In Figure 2.4, the process-level example is an explosion of the "Job Designed" process shown in the Delivered sub-system. In this case, the process illustrated has four steps: order entered, engineering assigned and scheduled, job specs packet developed, design reviewed. Again, the steps in any given process should be unique to a business, appropriate to its industry, customers, and products. This is the level of end-to-end business processes—both those providing value directly to customers and those that support the value-adding processes. And at this level there are often differences in the design and execution of these processes by industry and by company.

Level 5: Sub-Process/Task/Sub-Task

The sub-process level is the link to the performer through the structure of work tasks and sub-tasks. An individual, a technology system, or a combination of the two ultimately performs the work of the organization.

For technology developers who create software systems and applications to enhance performance at Level 5, it is vitally important that the requirements on which they base their designs are appropriately driven by the organization's strategies, goals, and requirements, cascading down through the Value Creation Hierarchy.

KEY FEATURES AND BENEFITS OF THE VALUE CREATION HIERARCHY

Why is the VCH an important and useful model? Here are the reasons:

- Work/process definition starts at the top of the Value Creation Hierarchy with the business context. Each level of the VCH provides the critical performance context for subsequent levels. At each level, you make unique "organizing work" decisions to optimize performance at that level—but in the performance context provided by the preceding levels.

- All levels of process and process performance requirements are linked to customer expectations and business requirements (at Levels 1 and 2).

- If you start below the Value Creation System level (that is, below Level 2) when defining processes, most likely those processes will not be directly linked to customer or business requirements, and they will fall into the dangerous sub-optimization zone, where it is easy, and tempting, to maximize the performance of one sub-process and thereby sub-optimize the performance of the larger process or sub-system. And as we have pointed out, managers' tendency to focus accountability on the resource dimension drives them to do all they can to look good, even at the expense of the larger system (which they don't see anyway).

- The VCH provides a roadmap for process practitioners, helping answer the questions, "Where am I operating in the VCH? Where should I be operating if I want to improve process performance *and* organization performance?" For the process practitioner, the first question should be, "What organization performance needs to be improved?" followed by, "What process performance needs to be improved to achieve that end?"

The Value Creation Hierarchy makes it possible to align performance goals from the enterprise level to the performer level, as shown in Figure 2.5.

Figure 2.5 depicts how the goals of a fictitious company can be established at enterprise level and then cascaded downward to each succeeding level of the Value Creation Hierarchy.

- In the example, if a business had an annual revenue and profit margin goal (goal number 1), goals can be appropriately distributed down to each component of the Value Creation System, so there are sets of goals for the Launched, Sold, and Delivered sub-systems (goals 2, 3, and 4).

- Then goals can be cascaded down to processes inside each sub-system. For illustration, Figure 2.5 shows goals distributed for the processes inside Delivered (goals 4a, 4b, 4c, and 4d).

- Then it is possible to distribute goals down to each sub-process within the sub-system (goals 4a1–4), in this case the Job Designed sub-process.

- At the fifth level, goals are assigned to Engineering Scheduler (goal 4a2).

The result is a set of vertically derived performance goals that link the contributions of individual performers (in this example, the Scheduler) to a key goal of the enterprise (revenue and profit growth).

Figure 2.5 The VCH with Performance Goals

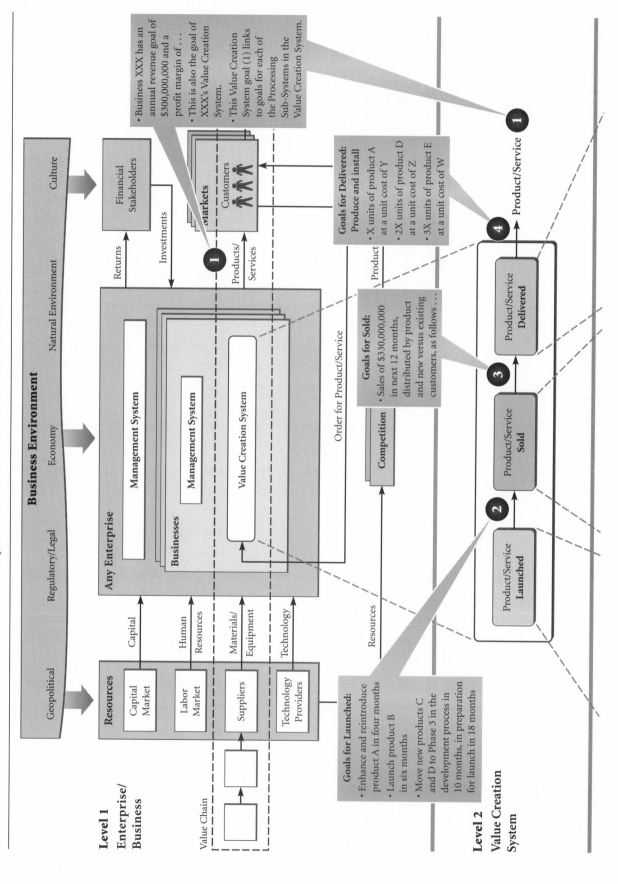

Figure 2.5 (continued)

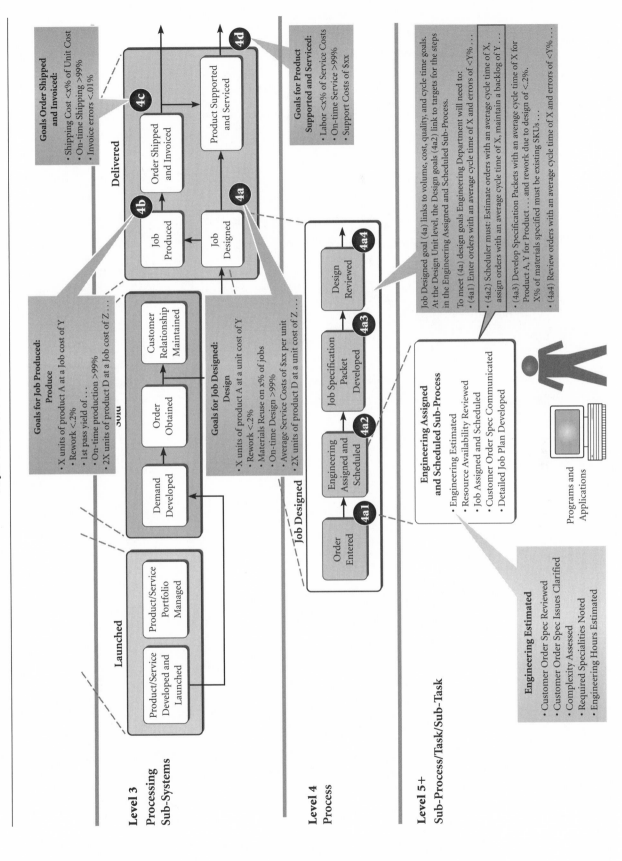

CLOSING POINTS

The Value Creation Hierarchy is the conceptual foundation for the remainder of this book. It is the lens through which we examine the future applications of process—of process in a value perspective.

The rest of this book is all about the Value Creation System and the role of process therein. Major topics include:

- The Value Creation Hierarchy, a generic framework for structuring the work required to create value in any business
- The development of a value creation architecture for a business
- Process management in the context of a value creation system
- A robust methodology for improving processes and designing process management systems in a VCS context
- Implications of the VCS for the role of the IT function in the future
- The journey to a process managed organization

Our forthcoming companion book for management addresses managing the value creation and resource dimensions in concert.

CHAPTER THREE

The Value Creation Hierarchy

In Chapter Two, we made the case for understanding the value-creating operating system of the business Value Machine. In this chapter we delve into the Value Creation Hierarchy (VCH), a framework for achieving that understanding. The VCH is a framework for structuring the work of conceiving, selling, and delivering valued products and services. This generic framework can be used by any business to guide the identification and articulation of its own Value Machine.

The Value Creation Hierarchy is our fundamental model for understanding how businesses organize, perform, and manage value-adding work. This framework makes it possible to understand, articulate, design, and manage the most complex of businesses.

At the end of Chapter Two, we provided a brief overview of the VCH. Now we circle back and take a more detailed look at how it works and what are the implications for process design and improvement and for business management.

A DEFINITION OF PROCESS

Before we begin our detailed examination of the Value Creation Hierarchy, we need to be clear what we mean by *process*. Just what is a process? Two things, as far as we are concerned.

First, as shown in Figure 3.1, a process has these components:

• Desired output

• An input that will be transformed into the desired output

• A system of work that accomplishes the transformation from input into output

Figure 3.1 The Components of a Process

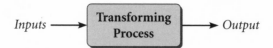

Processes have been described in many different ways, but these components show up in some manner in most definitions. A few we have used in the past include describing a process as "a series of planned activities that convert inputs into outputs," and "any repeatable set of activities." However, though accurate, these definitions lack a few things.

The second thing we mean by *process*, more fundamental than an emphasis on task sequence, is that it is really: *a construct for organizing value-adding work to achieve a business-value milestone in a way that meets three specific criteria*:

1. Effective and efficient performance

2. Effective management

3. Competitive advantage

Effective and Efficient Performance

First, a process is a construct for organizing value-adding work so that the work can be effectively and efficiently *performed*. Most everyone would agree with that. Most process improvement methodologies are focused on this attribute of process design.

Effective Management

Second, a process is a construct for organizing value-adding work so the work can be effectively *managed*. This is new. In the past, the major emphasis on organizing work has been effective and efficient performance of the work. Effective *management* of the work—the organization of work so that management has the ability to plan and track performance and fix accountability—has been overlooked. Take the assembly of an automobile engine as an example.

Engineers designing work processes would ordinarily group activities and parts into subassemblies that come together at critical points so that the process is both effective (high-quality output) and efficient (minimum cost and throughput time).

But if at the end of the process the engine fails to work as required, there are important questions to ask about the management of the assembly process: Why and where did the engine fail? Where in the assembly process is the cause of this failure? In what component? With what combination of components? Managers need to ask these questions and be able to find the answers. In addition to efficiency and effectiveness, the work must be designed and organized to give management *visibility* into the process and some *control* over its performance.

The need for management visibility and control can be challenging when the work is performed in multiple places, in different parts of the world, perhaps, or when the work has been outsourced. The design of an effective management system on top of such work processes is absolutely critical; it takes as much thought and creativity as design of the work itself.

On the other hand, when there is too much control built into processes, the management system can itself be a root cause of poor performance in work processes. A classic example is the product development process that is so burdened with project reviews and multiple sign-offs that the company fails to get its new products to market in time to beat the competition. Organizing work so that it can be effectively managed is a critical criterion for intelligent work design.

Competitive Advantage

Third, our definition of process means that, wherever practical, work should be organized within a business so as to provide that business with a *competitive advantage*. This criterion is adapted from the work of Michael Porter, who has said:

> "A company outperforms rivals only if it can establish a difference that it can preserve. Ultimately, all differences between companies . . . derive from the hundreds of activities required to create, produce, sell, and deliver their products and services."

> "The essence of strategy is in the activities—choosing to perform activities differently or to perform different activities than rivals."

> "Competitive advantage comes from the way . . . activities fit and reinforce one another."[1]

In the context of the engine assembly example, Ford Motor Company, for example, should design and organize its engine assembly process in a way that is difficult for its competitors to duplicate without years of effort and expense.

There is an important assumption underlying our definition of process: that a process is not some God-given sequence of work that is chiseled in stone. Yes, the process engineers (or their equivalent) laid out a sequence of steps that meet the "work effectively and efficiently performed" criterion. The process may make sense to them, but this isn't the only criterion for organizing work. There are countless work activities required to produce any valued output, and, in most cases, there are options as to how that work is designed and organized. In addition, it is important that we recognize that not all outputs are valued equally. In the eyes of a business, some outputs may also be seen as key milestones in creating value for the business.

VCS MILESTONES

The Value Creation System is a framework for structuring the value-adding work required to produce valued products and services. That work can be described in various ways, but most commonly it is defined by activities or processes. However, we can also describe the work required by the VCS not by activities or processes but by the value produced by those activities and processes.

The VCS is comprised of three sub-systems, each of which results in a value milestone: at the end of the Product/Service Launched sub-system of processes, we have a product/service that has been designed and is ready to be launched into the marketplace. At the end of the Product/Service Sold sub-system, we have a product/service that has been packaged, promoted and marketed, and successfully sold; and by the end of the Product/Service Delivered sub-system, the product/service has been produced, readied for shipment, transported, and received by the customer. Once you get beyond the level of sub-system value milestones, subsequent value milestones will vary by industry, business, and business strategies.

The value milestone concept is a very useful notion when trying to get agreement among various parties on the definition of a "process." For example, four departments, plants, or branch offices are required to agree on one "order entry" sub-process. The first thing the meeting facilitator (or whoever is responsible for producing this agreement) discovers is that each party means something quite different by "order entry" process, and each is in love with theirs. They each involve different activities carried out by different performers (both human and technology). And in each of the four locations the "order entry" processes all relate to other processes to different degrees and in different ways. The place to start such a discussion with the interested parties from the four locations is to get agreement on the value milestone of the group of activities roughly referred to as "order entry." Once there is agreement on the value milestone (which might be expressed as "Order Formatted and Ready for Processing"), the discussion can move to the work required to achieve the milestone and the best way to organize that work (think "three criteria"). The next discussion is about who performs that work, and if appropriate, how. Not necessarily an easy set of discussions, but a lot easier (and quieter) than trying to engineer agreement without the value milestone concept.

NOW, A SECOND TRIP DOWN THE VCH

Now let's take a closer look at the Value Creation Hierarchy, the foundational model of this book (Figure 3.2). The VCH is a top to bottom framework for organizing work in a way that meets all three of our criteria for organizing work.

The VCH is also a scalable model. It can be depicted as a hierarchy of processes:

1. The business at Level 1 is a process, transforming customer needs into products/services that meet those needs.

2. The Value Creation System at Level 2 is a process, transforming specific customer needs and business requirements into products/services that will meet customer needs and generate the necessary revenue and profits to meet financial stakeholder needs.

3. The Product/Service Delivered sub-system at Level 3 is a process, transforming a sales order into installed communication hardware, operating to customer specifications.

Figure 3.2 Value Creation Hierarchy

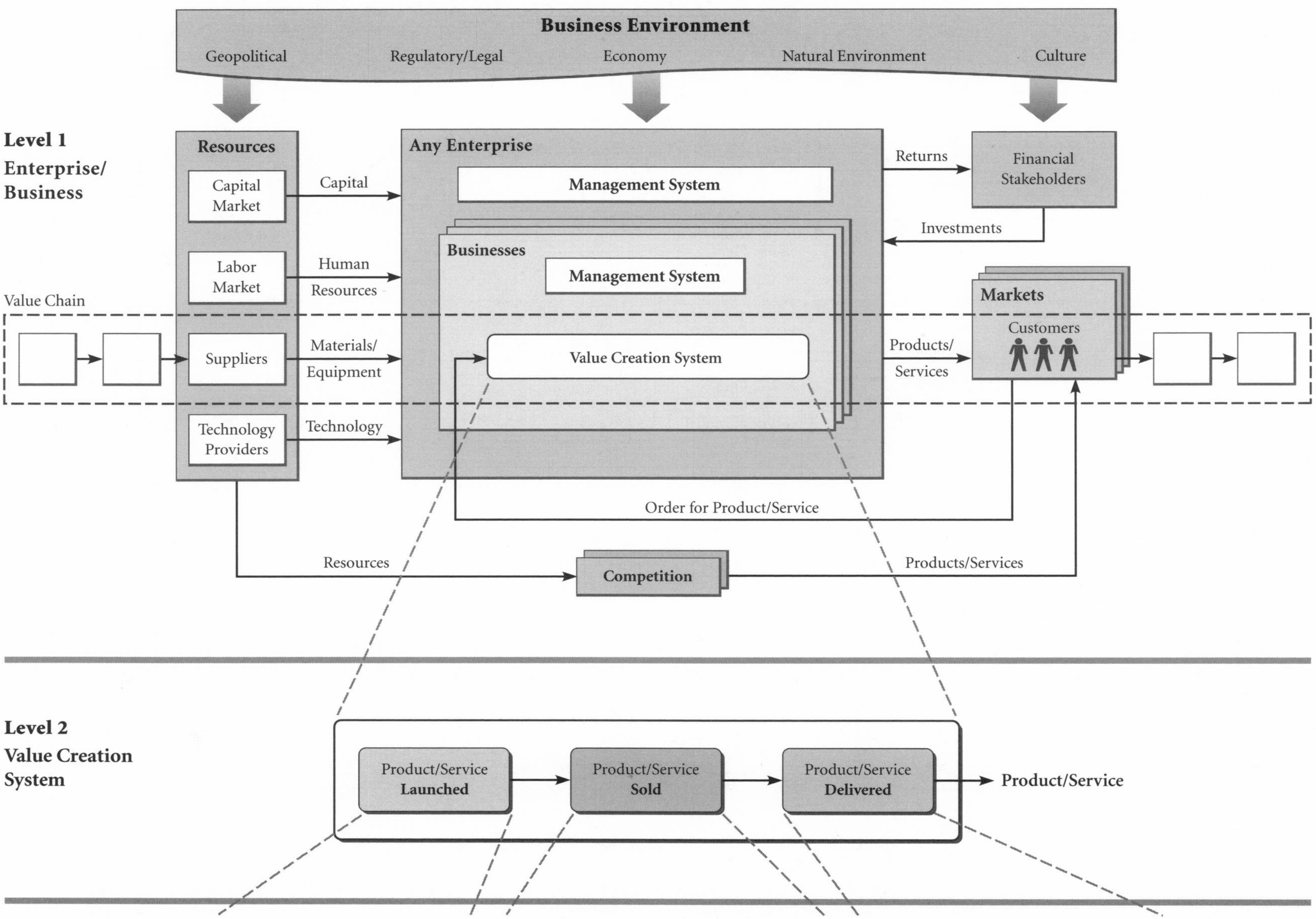

Figure 3.2 (Continued)

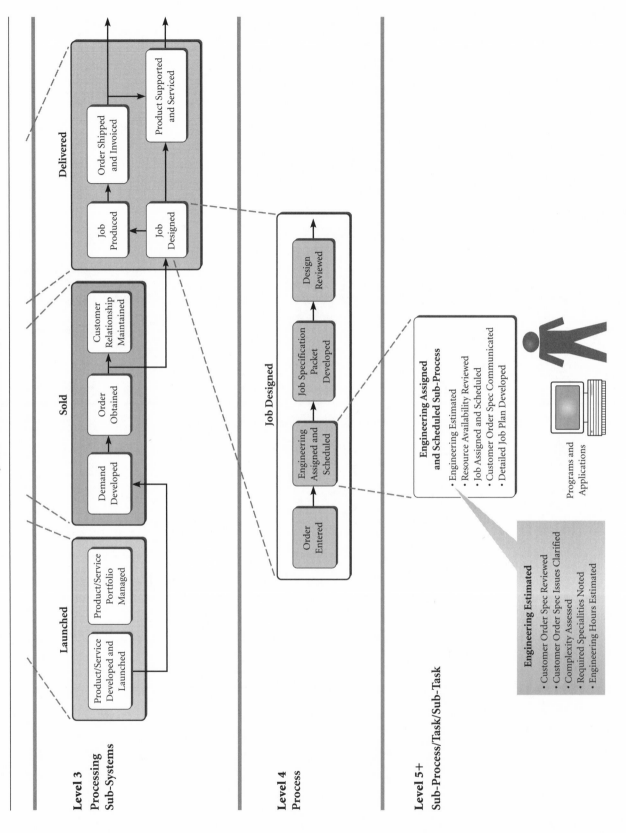

Level 3
Processing Sub-Systems

Launched

- Product/Service Developed and Launched
- Product/Service Portfolio Managed

Sold

- Demand Developed
- Order Obtained
- Customer Relationship Maintained

Delivered

- Job Produced
- Job Designed
- Order Shipped and Invoiced
- Product Supported and Serviced

Level 4
Process

Job Designed

- Order Entered
- Engineering Assigned and Scheduled
- Job Specification Packet Developed
- Design Reviewed

Level 5+
Sub-Process/Task/Sub-Task

Engineering Assigned and Scheduled Sub-Process
- Engineering Estimated
- Resource Availability Reviewed
- Job Assigned and Scheduled
- Customer Order Spec Communicated
- Detailed Job Plan Developed

Engineering Estimated
- Customer Order Spec Reviewed
- Customer Order Spec Issues Clarified
- Complexity Assessed
- Required Specialities Noted
- Engineering Hours Estimated

Programs and Applications

4. The Job Designed process at Level 4 is a process, transforming the sales order into a Job Order that specifies how the product is to be built.

We use as an example the fictional Belding Engineering Services, Inc., to describe the VCH in detail. This will serve two purposes:

1. Demonstrate our point that the VCH is a useful template for quickly understanding a fairly complex business
2. Provide an example of the work structuring decisions at each level of the VCH

Important background to our example is the organization chart of Belding Engineering in Figure 3.3, which is a decidedly resource dimension view of the company. As we make the second trip through the VCH, we will uncover the value dimension of Belding Engineering.

Figure 3.3 The Belding Engineering Organization

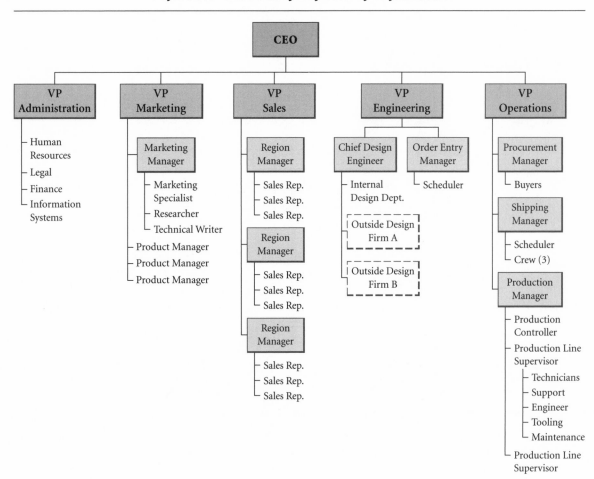

LEVEL 1: ENTERPRISE/BUSINESS

Figure 3.4 depicts Level 1 of the Value Creation Hierarchy as an elaboration of the notion of an organization as a system. The starting point is the box at the center labeled "Any Enterprise." Those boxes external to the "Any Enterprise" box constitute what we call the *super-system*, in which the enterprise (or "organization system") resides. Every organization system has two further system characteristics: an *adaptive system* and a *processing system*.

Organizations Are Adaptive Systems

The "Any Enterprise" organization system must continuously adapt to changes in its super-system, including changes in:

- The consumer marketplace
- The capital marketplace
- Competition
- Resources/supply chain
- The general business environment of
  - The economy
  - Culture
  - Natural environment

Figure 3.4 The Value Creation Hierarchy: Enterprise Level

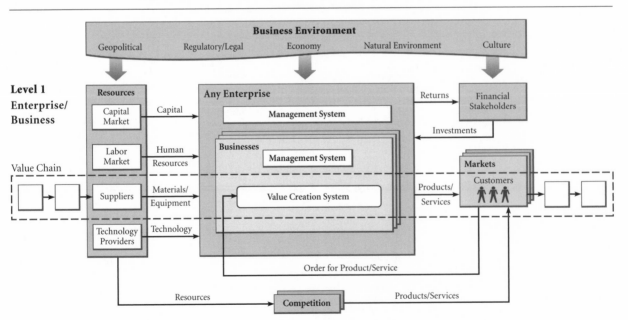

○ Governmental/regulatory

○ Geopolitical circumstances

This super-system that surrounds the organization system is the ultimate performance reality and performance context. Bluntly put, every business must adapt to the reality of its super-system or die.

Organizations Are Processing Systems

Next, let's shift our focus to the inside of the "Any Enterprise" box in Figure 3.4. We argued in Chapter Two that every business is a processing system or Value Machine that takes in inputs (that is, customer needs) and converts them or transforms them into outputs *valued* by customers. In so doing, the business consumes or utilizes key resources such as capital, technology, human resources, materials, and equipment.

Any Enterprise is made up of revenue-producing businesses that conceive, sell, and deliver valued products and services to customers. The enterprise business goals are achieved through the performance of the business units. The business units are the basic Value Machines that deliver the value and generate the revenue of the enterprise.

Although we can think of the entire enterprise as a giant Value Machine, the businesses are really the starting point for serious process thinking. The business unit provides the business context for processes and is the first link in the connection of process results to organization results.

Now let's begin to apply the VCH framework to Belding Engineering Services, Inc. In this example, Belding is one of several businesses that make up a company we will call "Corporate," which is the enterprise. Belding is the Value Machine we are going to look at through the VCH lens.

Belding Engineering is part of its own extended value chain (from suppliers to customer's customers) and has its own management system and super-system, including markets, competitors, resource requirements (and, possibly, sources), and business environment (particularly legal and regulatory requirements).

Because each business unit operates in its own super-system, each requires its own strategy to determine how it will successfully compete in its market given the dynamics of its ever-changing super-system.

Determining exactly how to organize businesses around products, services, and markets (that is, determining a business model) is the first set of decisions regarding the organization of work. Those decisions are, in fact, all about how to organize the work of the enterprise so that it can be *performed* effectively and efficiently, can be *managed* effectively, and offers the potential for a sustainable *competitive advantage*. Failure to design an effective business model is a fundamental strategic misstep that cannot easily be overcome through subsequent tactical adjustments and maneuvers.

Level 1 Key Points

- Belding Engineering/Any Enterprise is a system, adapting to the continuing changes in its super-system and creating value for its customers and financial stakeholders.

- Belding Engineering/Any Enterprise must be connected to its super-system, clearly understanding the constraints and opportunities therein.

- Belding Engineering/Any Enterprise must understand the value expected by the customer and have worked through the trade-offs between customer desires and business realities.

- The business unit provides the business context for processes and is the first link in the connection of process results to organization results. Failure to make this connection is the most common mistake made by process practitioners, leading directly to the increasingly frequent lament, "We aren't getting the return we expected from our process work."

Tool: Super-System Map

A tool we use to help clients track and understand their critical relationship with their super-system is the *super-system map*. (See the Belding Super-System Tool in Figure 3.5.)

This diagram can be used by management teams to perform systematic strategic reviews or do planning. The tool can help to facilitate year-to-year reviews of trends by working the team through all key components of the super-system to analyze current state and predict future scenarios. At Belding, rather than rely on a rather arbitrary "threat/opportunity" exercise, an annual super-system review is used to align the executive leadership team on a common view of the next three years. This review becomes input to the annual strategy review exercise: "Based on what has happened and we believe will happen in the next three years, what changes should we make regarding our strategy?" The annual super-system analysis also becomes input to the subsequent update of the running three-year operating plan: "Based on what is happening and likely to happen in our super-system, what changes must we make to the design and resource allocation of our Value Creation System?"

LEVEL 2: THE VALUE CREATION SYSTEM (VCS)

In the traditional, resource-oriented worldview, if you were to lift the lid off any of the business boxes in Figure 3.2, Level 2, the first level of work detail you would see is the organization chart or "resource buckets." In applying the Value Creation Hierarchy lens to Belding, the first thing we see inside Belding (and any business) at Level 2 are the three processing sub-systems that work together to create valued products and services. These constitute the *Value Creation System* (VCS). Every business has some approximation of the *Launched, Sold,* and *Delivered* sub-systems as depicted in Level 2, usually largely invisible and not well managed. (Hard to manage something you can't see.)

Figure 3.6 shows the nonlinear relationship among Launched, Sold, and Delivered. The table at the bottom of the figure provides more detail on the three sub-systems that comprise the Value Creation System.

Figure 3.5 The Super-System Map

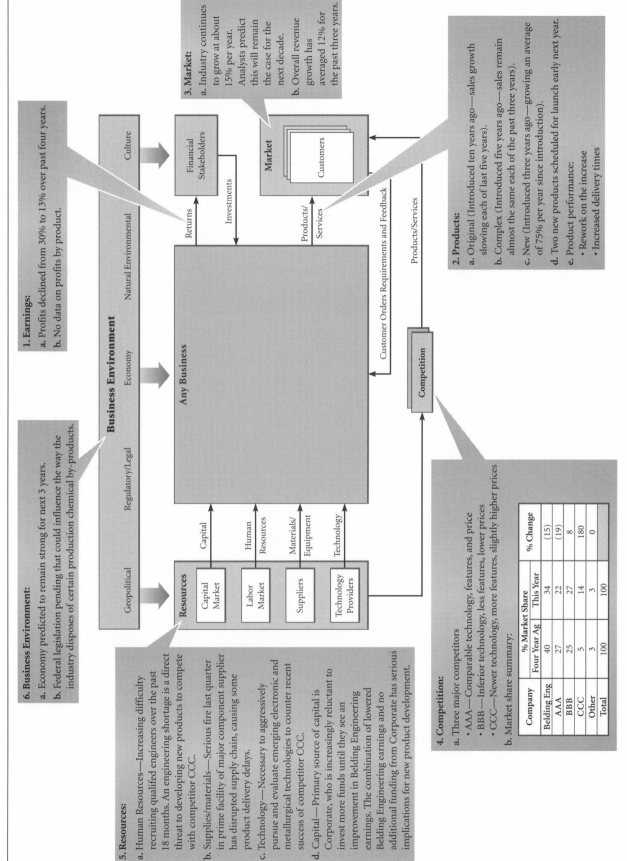

1. Earnings:
a. Profits declined from 30% to 13% over past four years.
b. No data on profits by product.

3. Market:
a. Industry continues to grow at about 15% per year. Analysts predict this will remain the case for the next decade.
b. Overall revenue growth has averaged 12% for the past three years.

2. Products:
a. Original (Introduced ten years ago—sales growth slowing each of last five years).
b. Complex (Introduced five years ago—sales remain almost the same each of the past three years).
c. New (Introduced three years ago—growing an average of 75% per year since introduction).
d. Two new products scheduled for launch early next year.
e. Product performance:
• Rework on the increase
• Increased delivery times

6. Business Environment:
a. Economy predicted to remain strong for next 3 years.
b. Federal legislation pending that could influence the way the industry disposes of certain production chemical by-products.

Business Environment

Geopolitical   Regulatory/Legal   Economy   Natural Environmental   Culture

Financial Stakeholders

Market

Customers

Returns   Investments   Products/Services

Any Business

Customer Orders Requirements and Feedback

Products/Services

Competition

Capital   Human Resources   Materials/Equipment   Technology

Resources

Capital Market   Labor Market   Suppliers   Technology Providers

5. Resources:
a. Human Resources—Increasing difficulty recruiting qualifed engineers over the past 18 months. An engineering shortage is a direct threat to developing new products to compete with competitor CCC.
b. Supplies/materials—Serious fire last quarter in prime facility of major component supplier has disrupted supply chain, causing some product delivery delays.
c. Technology—Necessary to aggressively pursue and evaluate emerging electronic and metallurgical technologies to counter recent success of competitor CCC.
d. Capital—Primary source of capital is Corporate, who is increasingly reluctant to invest more funds until they see an improvement in Belding Engineering earnings. The combination of lowered Belding Engineering earnings and no additional funding from Corporate has serious implications for new product development.

4. Competition:
a. Three major competitors
• AAA—Comparable technology, features, and price
• BBB—Inferior technology, less features, lower prices
• CCC—Newer technology, more features, slightly higher prices
b. Market share summary:

Company	% Market Share		% Change
	Four Year Ag	This Year	
Belding Eng	40	34	(15)
AAA	27	22	(19)
BBB	25	27	8
CCC	5	14	180
Other	3	3	0
Total	100	100	

Figure 3.6 The Primary Processing Systems of an Organization

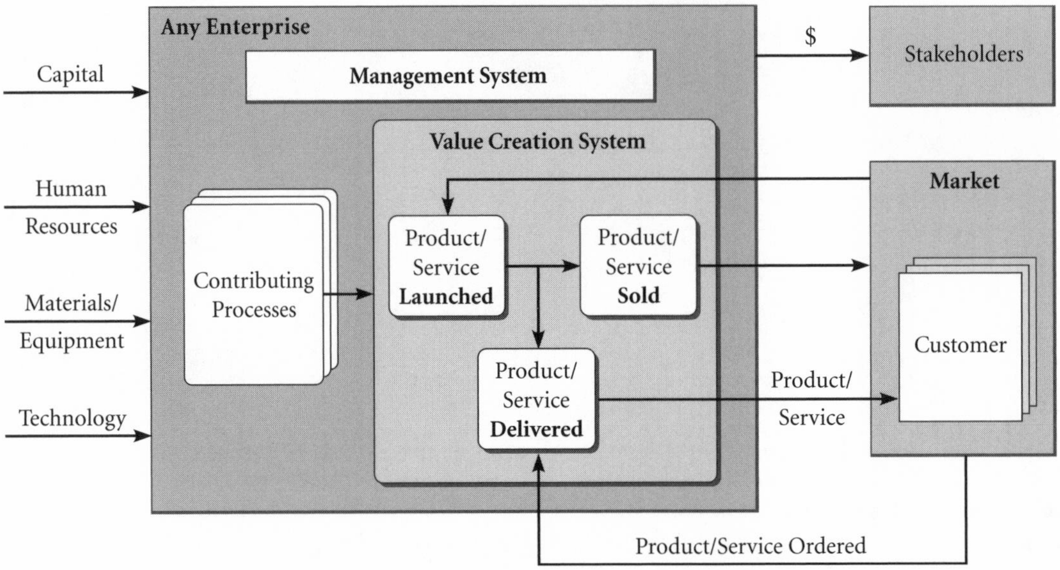

Primary Processing Sub-Systems	Input	Output	Description
Product/Service Launched (Product/Service Life Cycle)	Customer need to be satisfied	Product/Service/ Offering ready to be Sold, Delivered, and Supported	Two parts: 1. Finding or inventing and launching a Product/Service/ Offering that will satisfy a customer need 2. Managing the Product/Service/Offering life cycle
Product/Service Sold (Customer Life Cycle)	A Product/Service/ Offering ready to be Sold to potential customers	An order for a Product or Service	Three parts: 1. "Demand Generated": Creating demand for the Product/Service, usually done by Marketing. Output is usually a "lead." 2. "Customer Committed": Frequently requires a Sales organization to convert "interest" into a commitment to purchase. 3. "Relationship Maintained": Enhancement and mainte-nance of the customer relationship
Product/Service Delivered (Order Life Cycle)	Product/Service available to deliver Customer order	Delivered Product/ Service ready for use by customer	At least two parts: 1. Processing the Order, from "Order entered" to "Payment received" and "Warranty administered" 2. If a Product; making and delivery. If a Service; custom-izing and delivering. May also include installation and servicing

Note that each sub-system has its own life cycle, all of which have to be integrated at some level:

- Product/Service Launched is about the ***product/service life cycle***, which runs years and extends from product/service conception through enhancements and modifications, to eventual "sun setting."

- Product/Service Sold operates on a ***customer life cycle***, which may run years, from the time the customer is initially aware and attracted to the products/services of the business through committing to a purchase and remaining a satisfied, loyal customer.

- Product/Service Delivered operates on an ***order life cycle***, starting with the receipt of an order through delivery and servicing of the product/service.

As at Level 1, we are making work definition and structural choices at Level 2, using our three process definition and design criteria. A key decision in any business has to do with the number and structure of the Value Creation Systems. This decision can affect the performance of the Value Creation Systems, their manageability, and whether they offer a competitive advantage. For example, let's look at Belding's VCS choices. The company currently has ~~four~~ three major product lines, which might be treated as follows (see Figure 3.7):

1. A single Value Creation System used by all three product lines
2. Separate lines of business with alternative dedicated Value Creation Systems for each
3. A common Launched for each product line, but dedicated Sold and Delivered for each
4. Common Launched and Sold for the lines of business, but dedicated Delivered for each

You can see the VCS variations that can be developed, depending on product and market characteristics, the elements Belding wishes to optimize, and our three work organization criteria. For example, does the VCS structure:

- Provide effective and efficient ***performance*** of the value-adding work?
- Lend itself to sufficient and efficient ***management*** control?
- Provide some ***competitive advantage***?

At Level 2, we have our first opportunity to link the value and resource dimensions. We do this via the Value-Resource Relationship Map in Figure 3.8. For purposes of illustration, this graphic assumes Belding has just one VCS and juxtaposes the vertical functions as represented by the Belding organization chart in Figure 3.2 and the three sub-systems composing the VCS. According to this graphic, the Product Launched sub-system involves all the Belding functions except Shipping. The Product Sold sub-system involves only Marketing and Sales. And you can see who is involved with Product Delivered.

Figure 3.7 Value Creation System Choices of Belding Engineering

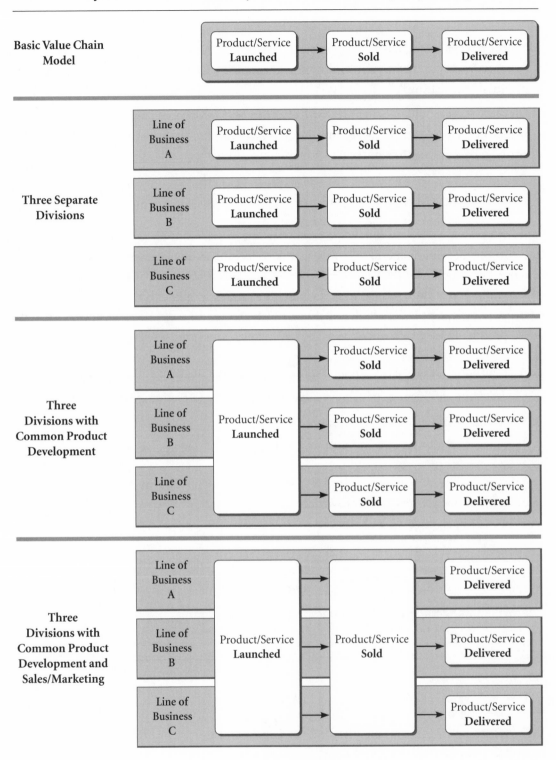

There are several points to notice in this Value-Resource Relationship Map:

First, it makes it very clear that there are two dimensions of a business that must be managed in concert. As you look at Figure 3.8, imagine that the VCS sub-systems of Launched, Sold, and Delivered had not been made visible by that graphic, and you'll be able to see why an organization trying to manage solely by the resource buckets is bound in the long run to fail. They have no organized way to get their hands around the work required to systematically and efficiently create valued products/services.

Second, it makes it clear that managers are going to have to learn to simultaneously manage in both the value and resource dimensions (a supportive management system can help with this task, as you will see in Chapter Five). The map in Figure 3.8 also provides insight into the multiple tasks to be performed by key functions. When asked, "What is your major area of responsibility?" most every Sales executive will tell you it is "selling." But Figure 3.8 shows that at Belding, Sales contributes to all three VCS sub-systems—and its contribution to each is not trivial (although frequently unmanaged). Obviously Sales is a major player in the Sold sub-system. But it is also a critical player in Launched, where its market intelligence and customer knowledge are essential to new product selection and design. And finally, the accuracy of their order specifications as Step 1 in Delivered has a huge impact on subsequent product quality and customer satisfaction. The Value-Resource Relationship Map makes it

Figure 3.8 Value-Resource Relationship Map

Belding Engineering Value-Resource Relationship Map

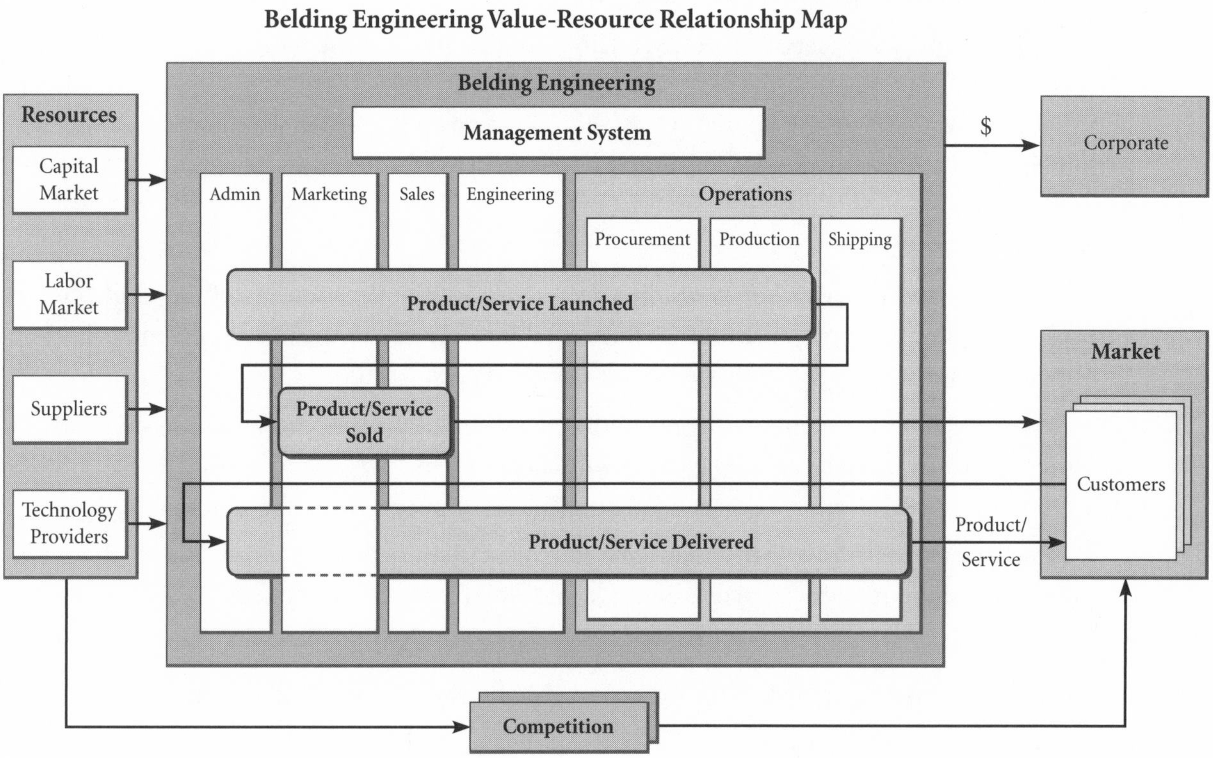

very clear that Sales must support all three of the sub-systems, and resources must be allocated accordingly, or the VCS will be corrupted. The Relationship Map also makes it clear that the *functions (resource buckets) exist to perform and support the work of the Value Creation System*.

You can see that the decision about how to structure work at the Value Creation System level (Level 2) often implies designs for both the value *and* resource dimensions. For example, in order to achieve effective and efficient performance of the process, you might decide you need rapid communication of customer order requirements between departments. A human resource solution might be to structure a cross-functional team; a technology resource solution might be to buy or build a real-time customer order tracking system.

In 1990, Geary and Alan Brache wrote about the need to "manage the white space between the boxes on the organization chart" in *Improving Performance*. The concern at that time was that functions were managed, but that the critical gaps *between* functions (the "white space") were not. The remedy proposed for management of processes that cut across the various functions was to manage that "white space." But with the introduction of the Value Creation System as a way to better understand and organize value-adding work, we now see an even more dangerous and insidious white space: the gaps between the three sub-systems. We all have experienced these gaps, which are revealed by management comments such as:

- "We continually invent products (services) we can't sell!"

- "We sell products (services) we can't deliver!"

- "We design products (services) we can't deliver on time and we lose money on every sale!"

These statements are all symptoms of the failure to manage the white space among Launched, Sold, and Delivered—the failure to manage the Value Creation System.

Level 2 Key Points

- The design and management of work at Level 2, the Value Creation System level of the Value Creation Hierarchy, is critical. If this isn't done properly, all the process and management work at subsequent levels are forever compromised.

- This is the last level to connect directly to the customer. If the connection is not made here, there is no way it can be accomplished at subsequent levels.

- It's at Level 2 that critical decisions about the resource buckets ought to be made. The Value Creation Hierarchy helps managers to make rational optimization decisions about how to position resources in the Launched, Sold, and Delivered sub-systems.

- Alignment of the Value Creation System is essential.

  ○ The VCS must be aligned with customer expectations and business requirements.

  ○ Sub-system goals must be aligned with the VCS goals and with each other.

- Sub-systems must not be allowed to maximize or optimize their performance at the risk of suboptimizing the total VCS.

- Don't let resources trump value.

- Despite the preceding points, in most organizations the Value Creation System is largely invisible and seldom managed in total. For years, organizations have spent time and money chasing disconnects in processes at Level 4 of the Value Creation Hierarchy, while potentially fatal disconnects among Launched, Sold, and Delivered go unmanaged. (A notable example is the high-tech pharmaceutical company that surprised their VP of Sales with a requirement to hire and train 1,500 new sales reps in the next six months to handle a new product introduction.)

- The three sub-systems of Launched, Sold, and Delivered constitute a three-block model, which is a powerful framework for guiding critical management decisions (addressed in detail in our companion book for executives and managers). For example:

  1. Systematically comparing your Launched, Sold, and Delivered sub-systems with those of a key competitor to see where in the basic Value Creation System

     - Your competitor has a competitive advantage.
     - You have the potential for a sustainable competitive advantage.

  2. Systematically comparing your Launched, Sold, and Delivered sub-systems with those of a potential acquisition to understand what parts of the Value Creation System can be effectively integrated and which should remain as separate entities

  3. Evaluating the potential impact of outsourcing various processes on the effectiveness of the Value Creation System. How would this decision impact:

     - The performance of the VCS?
     - The ability to effectively manage the VCS?
     - The potential for a competitive advantage in the VCS?

The Value Creation System (Level 2) is the missing link in strategy implementation. The Value-Resource Relationship Map in Figure 3.8 makes it clear why strategies are seldom successfully implemented. Historically, in a "resource dimension-only" world, once a strategy has been determined, the implementation tasks are doled out to individual functions for relatively independent implementation. Each function focuses on the work assigned its function. And the overall organization results are seldom what was intended. (The sum of the parts is way short of the anticipated "whole.") Figure 3.8 points out the step that is missing. You can't go from an organization-level strategic goal directly to functional goals. The necessary sequence is:

1. Organization strategic goal to VCS goal

2. VCS goals to goals for each of the processing sub-systems: Launched, Sold, and Delivered

3. Launched, Sold, and Delivered goals to the coordinated goals of functions

In short, you implement a strategy through the integrated management of the value and resource dimensions, not through the resource dimension alone.

Tool: Value-Resource Relationship Map

The Value-Resource Relationship Map shown in Figure 3.8 can be used as a tool to do the following:

- Contrast the "is" value-resource relationships with a "should" picture. The Belding Map in Figure 3.8 is a "should" depiction, showing the ideal participation of all functions except for Shipping in Product Launched. However, the reality of "is" in many businesses is that Launched activities are usually confined to the Marketing Department with token (and reluctant) participation by Engineering (or the reverse). For various reasons, Sales and Production sit on the sidelines, ready to criticize the new product/service. Presenting the executive team with contrasting "is" and "should" Value-Resource Relationship Maps is a good start in recognizing and managing the VCS.

- The CEOs of several of our client organizations have used the "should" relationship map to align their leadership teams around their accountability for managing both the value and resource dimensions of the business.

LEVEL 3: PROCESSING SUB-SYSTEMS

The next level of value-adding work in the Value Creation Hierarchy is *Processing Sub-Systems*. Each of the three processing sub-systems in turn is made up of the value-adding work processes necessary to achieve their respective goals. The process goals and requirements of the individual processes within each processing sub-system must be aligned with one another to accomplish the goals of the entire processing sub-system.

Again, at this level, we are structuring and organizing the work according to our three process criteria. We are defining and designing the system of processes within each processing sub-system so that:

1. They can perform together effectively and efficiently.

2. They can be effectively managed.

3. They can, either individually or in a unique combination, offer the potential of a competitive advantage.

Those processes making up the processing sub-systems at Level 3, Figure 3.2, are from our Belding example. Unlike Level 2, where we hold that the Launched, Sold, and Delivered template applies to all businesses, at Level 3 we don't suggest that there is a generic list of processes for each processing sub-system. On the contrary, per our third criterion (competitive advantage), we expect and encourage some process uniqueness. For sure, the processes making up the Launched processing sub-system will necessarily vary by industry (retail, petroleum, financial, telecommunications). At the level of detail shown in Figure 3.2, the three processes making up the Belding Sold processing sub-systems probably hold for most businesses (until you go to the next level). The processes within the Belding Delivered processing sub-systems are representative of a classic manufacturing operation and do not apply to other types of businesses.

Figure 3.9 presents an expanded version of the Value Creation Hierarchy. Starting with Level 3, we show two types of processing sub-systems:

1. On the right, we continue to show the decomposition or drill-down of the *transforming* or *primary* sub-systems and processes that constitute the core VCS and directly touch the customer or customer buying process.

2. On the left, we now show the decomposition of what we are calling *contributing processing sub-systems*.

Contributing processes are comparable to what others call "enabling" or "supporting" processes. We are calling them "contributing" processes because we want to make it clear that they are key contributors to the overall VCS, not "second-class citizens." But they make their contribution through the services they deliver to the primary processes and processing sub-systems.

The major reason for making this distinction between contributing and primary processes is to clarify the working relationship between the two. As shown in Figure 3.9, Level 3, Belding's "Human Capital Available" sub-system contributes to the Product Delivered sub-system. (In fact, it contributes to all three processing sub-systems.) This means that the goals and process requirements for the Human Capital Available sub-system come from the primary processing sub-system that is directly connected to the customer (through the VCS). The practical point is, if you are attempting to improve a contributing process or processing sub-system, you need to understand that the requirements on that process or processing sub-system come from the primary processes or processing sub-systems. Failure to do so is a too common mistake: designing a contributing process to internally driven requirements. Improving a contributing process starts with determining the requirements of the primary processes it serves.[2]

Tool: Cross-Functional Value Creation Map (CFVC)

The value-adding work at the processing sub-system level of an organization can easily be captured in a format we call a Cross-Functional Value Creation Map, such as that shown in Figure 3.10 for Belding Engineering.

This format incorporates the same horizontal swimlane convention frequently used to capture processes that are performed by multiple functions. It provides a high-level summary of all the value-adding work performed within a total Value Creation System, from Launched through Delivered. Any process box can be "double-clicked," as appropriate, to show detailed process maps. Note that these processes are all nested in the performance context of the next higher

Figure 3.9 The VCH with Contributing Sub-Systems

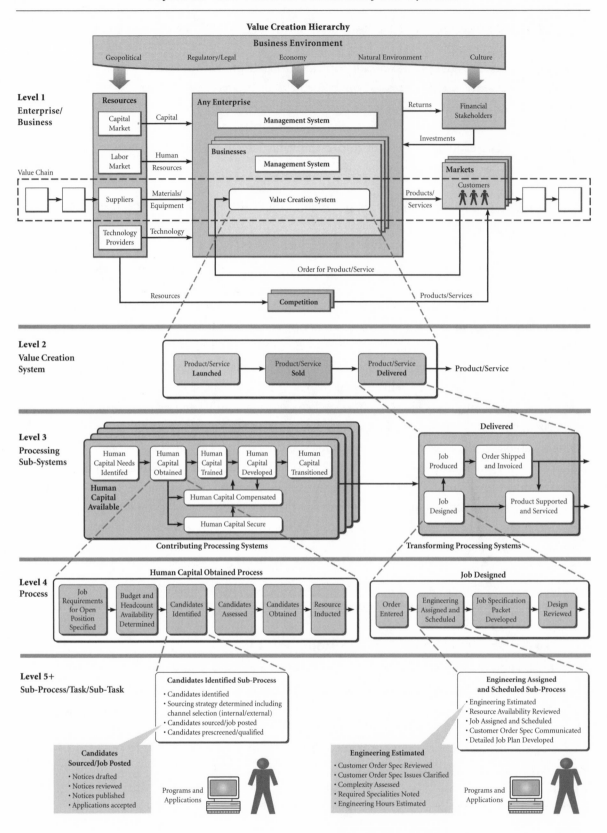

Figure 3.10 Cross-Functional Value Creation Map

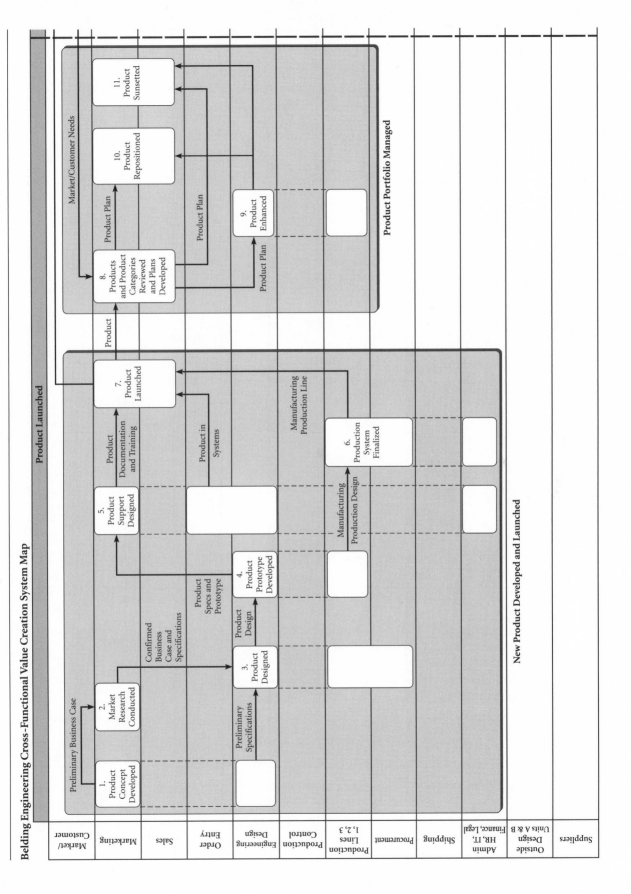

Figure 3.10 (*Continued*)

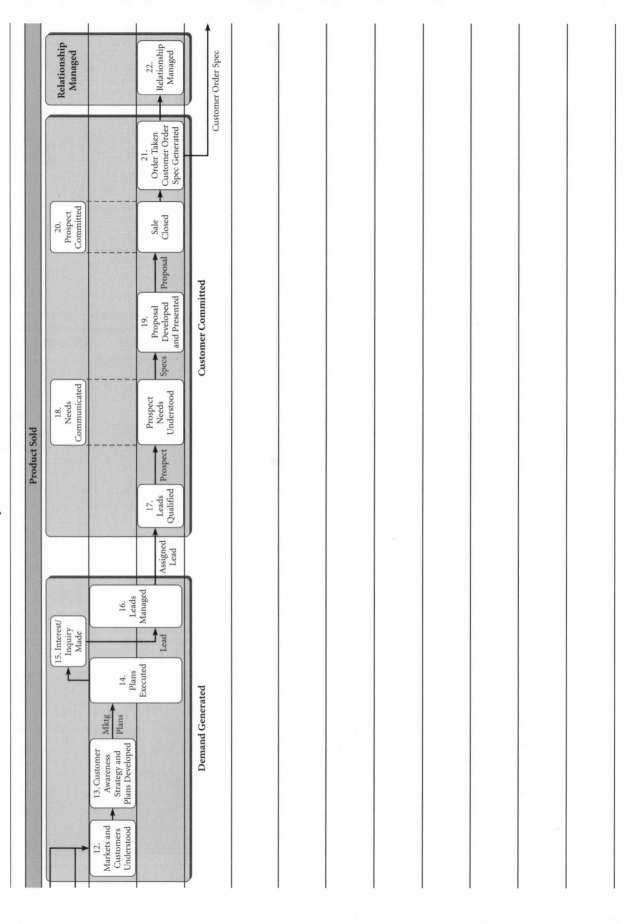

Product Sold

Relationship Managed

22. Relationship Managed

Customer Order Spec

21. Order Taken Customer Order Spec Generated

20. Prospect Committed

Sale Closed

Proposal

19. Proposal Developed and Presented

Specs

18. Needs Communicated

Prospect Needs Understood

Prospect

17. Leads Qualified

Customer Committed

Assigned Lead

15. Interest/ Inquiry Made

16. Leads Managed

Lead

14. Plans Executed

Mktg. Plans

13. Customer Awareness Strategy and Plans Developed

Demand Generated

12. Markets and Customers Understood

Figure 3.10 *(Continued)*

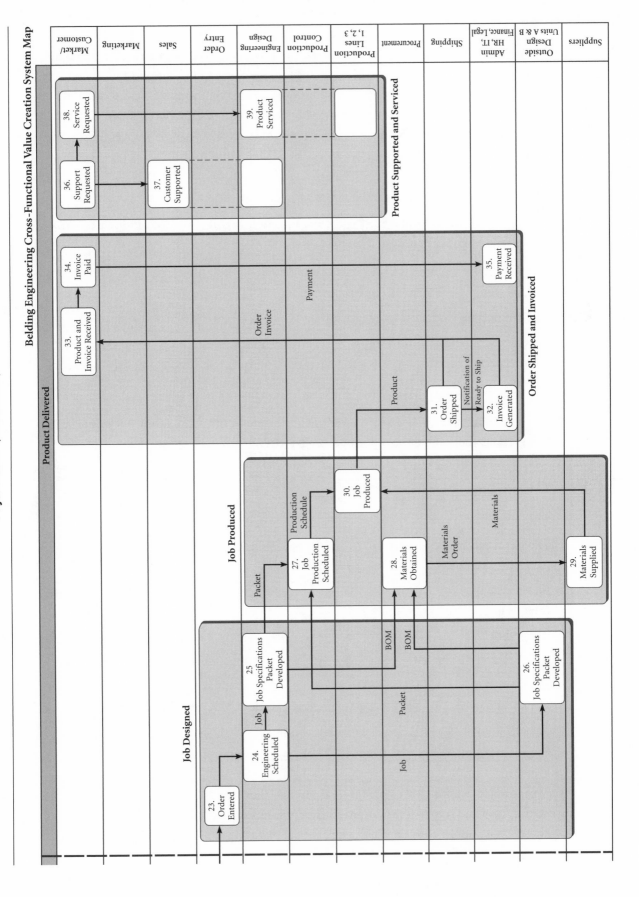

Belding Engineering Cross-Functional Value Creation System Map

level, starting with the Launched, Sold, and Delivered sub-systems and the VCS. At no point are the processes working in a vacuum, separated from the VCS connection to the customer. Note also that at a macro level, the value-adding work of the VCS is now linked to the functional resource buckets shown along the vertical axis. The Cross-Functional Value Creation Map is a powerful tool for beginning to manage the Value Creation System for several reasons:

- It captures on one page:
  - The work necessary to produce value for the customer
  - The work that must be managed if the organization is going to successfully meet customer (and, eventually, investor) requirements.
- It highlights for executives:
  - Critical hand-offs (potential white space) that must be managed
  - Likely points for performance measures
- It provides a framework for helping the executive team in systematically "troubleshooting" poor VCS performance, rather than engaging in nonproductive "finger pointing" between functions.

The Cross-Functional Value Creation Map also helps point out some subtle but important points regarding the Launched, Sold, and Delivered sub-systems. In particular, the map accommodates the different life cycles and time horizons of the Launched, Sold, and Delivered sub-systems.

- Within Launched:
  - The New Product Developed and Launched process of Belding Engineering may encompass a two- to four-year cycle for a given product.
  - In contrast, the Product Portfolio Managed process operates on a multiyear timeline that extends until a product is "sunsetted."
- Within Sold:
  - The Demand-Generated process is potentially a multiple-year time horizon for a given product.
  - The Customer-Committed process (from lead to order taken) may run several months.
- Within Delivered:
  - A variety of different cycles, for the Job, for Inventory Management, and so on.

One final point that the Cross-Functional Value Creation Map helps to make clear: There is more to the Launched sub-system than meets the eye—more than the typical notion of "product development and introduction." Focusing on the New Product Developed and Launched process on the map in Figure 3.10, note the number of Belding functions that must participate in this process for a successful product launch. Also note that the Launched sub-system includes the design (boxes 5 and 6) of all necessary product support, including preparation of the sales force to sell the product and assistance to Production to make the product. In contrast to the earlier example of the pharmaceutical firm, there is no designing a product and throwing it "over the transom" for Sales to figure out how to sell it and Production to figure out how to produce it. One of the requirements on the Belding Launched sub-system is "organization prepared/enabled" to support the new product/service in every way. From our experience, the Launched sub-system provides the greatest opportunity for improvement in most organizations.

Level 3 Key Points

- At the Processing sub-system level, the focus is the unique organization of the value-adding work of a business so that it can be effectively performed and managed and provides the potential for a competitive advantage. As a result, process definition (that is, the organization of work) should be driven by the specific strategies, goals, and competitive challenges of the individual business as you move down the Value Creation Hierarchy.

- It is essential that the processes within each sub-system be aligned with the goals of the sub-system and each other. A primary management task is to be sure no process sub-optimizes the performance of the sub-system whole.

- Management of the processing sub-systems is more critical than management of a single process. We suggest a processing sub-system management team first and foremost, then single-process management teams as necessary to oversee processes with broad functional interdependency. We discuss this more in Chapter Five.

- Effective ongoing alignment and management of the processing sub-systems requires a solidly designed and implemented management system. The Cross-Functional Value Creation Map makes the process integration management task very visible.

LEVEL 4: PROCESS

The next level of value-adding work captured in the Value Creation Hierarchy is the *Process* level. Figure 3.9 depicts both a Belding primary and a contributing process exploded from the Processing sub-system level. Although on the surface, the Job Designed process in Figure 3.9 might look like a typical "order entry" process, it is essential that the process steps are unique to the business, reflecting its industry, customers, and products.

The value-adding work at the Process level of the Value Creation Hierarchy is captured in the cross-functional process map format shown in Figure 3.11.

This is essentially a drill-down of a portion of the Product Delivered sub-system portion of the Value Creation map shown in Figure 3.10. In more detail, we see what resources are

Figure 3.11 Cross-Functional Process Map

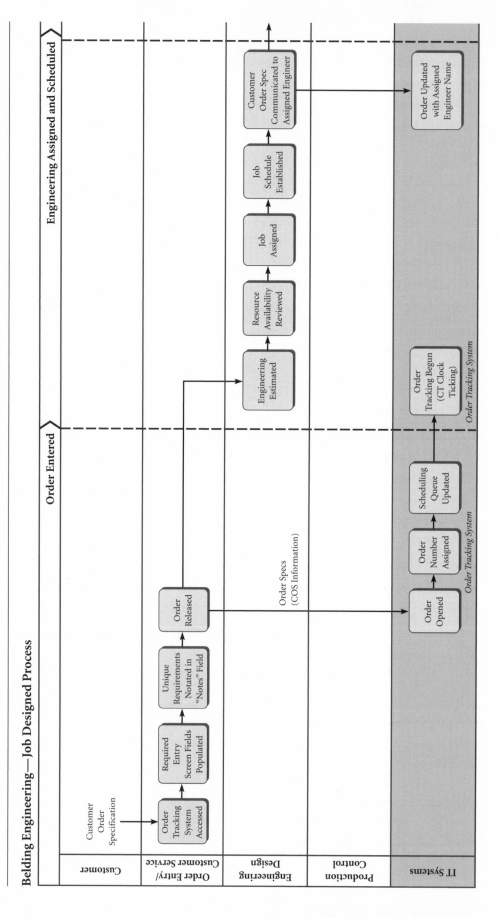

Figure 3.11 (Continued)

	Design Reviewed	Job Specifications Packet Developed

Customer

Order Specifications Clarified

Order Entry/ Customer Service

Engineering Design

Design Released ← Design Accepted and Marked "Approved" ← [COS Requirements Met?] —yes→

[COS Requirements Met?] —no→ Job Specification Packet Returned to Rework

Engineering Design Reviewed ← Job Specification Packet Released for Review ← Detailed Job Plan Developed ← Order Specifications Clarified ← [Information Complete and Clear?]

[Information Complete and Clear?] —no→ Order Specifications Clarified

[Information Complete and Clear?] —yes→ Detailed Job Plan Developed

Customer Order Spec Reviewed for Clarity and Understanding → [Information Complete and Clear?]

Production Control

IT Systems

Job Packet Updated as "Approved"

Job Packet Stored with Order File

required of what functions to deliver the valued process outputs. Figure 3.12 shows another level of technology specification that can be captured using the Cross-Functional Process Mapping tool. Note that the fifth swimlane in Figure 3.12 shows the role of technology as part of the value-added work system. The Cross-Functional Value Creation and Process Maps are essential tools in making the value dimension of businesses visible and manageable.

Level 4 Key Points

- You cannot look at a Level 4 process in a performance vacuum. Whether primary or contributing, an individual process has requirements and goals that should be determined by sub-system requirements and goals and ultimately by VCS requirements and goals. Failure to make these connections leads to the increasing grumbling that process improvement work does not affect organization results and raises the disturbing (but not unwarranted) question, "Is BPM a fad?"

- As before, we adhere to the three process definition and design criteria when organizing work at this level:

  1. Can the process be effectively and efficiently **performed**?
  2. Can the process be effectively **managed**?
  3. Does the design of the process offer the potential for a **competitive advantage**?

Tool: Cross-Functional Process Map

In our experience, the Cross-Functional Process Map shown in Figure 3.11 is one of the most useful tools available for analyzing, designing, improving, and managing processes. It has two very useful features:

1. It allows you to capture reality, in that most any process of consequence is cross-functional (or minimally, cross-performer). This makes it easy to see the cross-functional (or cross-performer) hand-offs, which is the "white space" leading to many process performance issues.

2. Every process step and performing entity is seen in the larger, total process context.

As you will see in Chapter Seven on methodology, we use the cross-functional process map format to:

- Capture an "is" process
- Validate an "is" process
- Record a "should" process
- Communicate the "should" process to all parties that must perform and manage the process
- Specify requirements for systems

Figure 3.12 Process Map with Technology Swimlanes

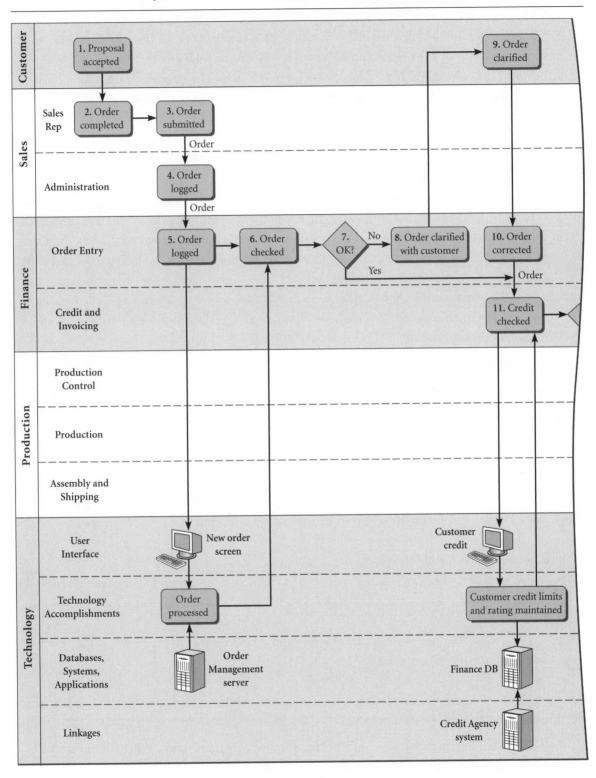

LEVEL 5: SUB-PROCESS/TASK/SUB-TASK

The *Sub-Process* level is the link to the performer through the structure of work tasks and sub-tasks. An individual, a technology system, or a combination of the two ultimately performs the work of the organization. There are important tradeoffs to be made at this level between the human and technology performers, balancing the flexibility and adaptability of the human against the consistency and control of technology. In Chapter Six we present a powerful framework for integrating human and technology performers with process design as part of a process design/improvement methodology.

Tool: Cross-Functional Process Map

We continue to use the Cross-Functional Process Map to organize and understand the structure of work at Level 5, as it displays the relationships among performers executing tasks. When there is just one performer, the map is really just a flowchart. But very often, there are at least two swimlanes: one for the human performer and one for the technology that supports the people performing the tasks.

In addition, we often use two other tools at this level, where we are most definitely designing or trying to understand both what the work is and how the resources are being used to do the work. These tools are

1. Role-Responsibility Matrix

This tool is used to add explanatory information about the roles performed in a given process. The process map is usually a cursory identification of the various steps in the process, but a Role-Responsibility Matrix can provide more information on exactly how steps are performed and who is doing what, especially when a given step is performed by more than one performer.

In Table 3.1, the Role-Responsibility Matrix reveals that it takes two different roles (order entry and production control) to complete the order assignment.

2. Technology Enabler Chart

To specify exactly what an existing or proposed technology would do to support a given process, we often use a tool called a Technology Enabler Chart, a sample of which is shown in Table 3.2.

Table 3.2, developed in most cases for a proposed or redesigned process, provides the following information:

- Identifies and names each technology (systems, databases, applications) imbedded in a process

- Describes the characteristics of the technology—in business terms, What should the technology accomplish or how does it support the work process?

Table 3.1 Role-Responsibility Matrix

Function	Order Entry/Customer Service	Engineering Design	Production Control	IT Systems
Process Steps				
Order Entered	The Customer Order Specification (COS) is entered into the Order Tracking System. All required fields are populated. Unique requirements are notated in the "Notes" field.			
1. Order Opened: • Number assigned • Schedule queue updated			Orders and schedule updates reviewed. Adjustments made if needed based on "Notes" field.	Order numbers assigned sequentially as received. Production schedule updated based on order delivery date.
2. Engineering Scheduled		New orders scheduled for detailed engineering. Order assigned to specific engineer for completion.		
3. Order Tracking Begun (CT clock ticking)				Order tracking initiated. Cycle time captured and available for reporting.
4. COS Reviewed		Order specifications evaluated for clarity and understanding.		

Table 3.2 Technology Enabler Chart (excerpt)

Technology Item	Desired Characteristics	Related Design Details Documents	Technology Status
Automatic order routing system includes triage rules	Upon submission of order, triage rules applied to auto-route to appropriate Engineering queue Extensive business rules validate completeness of submissions	3.5.2. *Order submission* 3.5.3. *Engineering queue accessed*	Technology does not exist in the organization today, but it does exist in market and is a mature technology Requires creation of new service module Requires additional infrastructure

- Describes the current state of the technology:
  - *Brand-new concept:* Does not exist today
  - *Available but not owned:* Can be purchased on the market but the company does not own it today
  - *Owned:* Can be used as it exists today in the company

- *Needs upgrade:* Is owned but would require upgrading or improvement to be used for this process purpose
- Identifies any existing documentation that might further describe the desired technology (for example, use cases, activity diagrams, product specifications)

Level 5 Key Points

- The majority of process improvement work done in organizations today is at Level 5, the sub-process level, buried within functions. (This is especially true for process definition and improvement work initiated by the IT function.) The major flaw is that the "improvement" work starts at this level, absent any performance/requirement context provided by Levels 2 through 4. The results are:
  - The organization can't see the impact of the change on organization or business results.
  - There is high risk of maximizing the performance of one sub-process or function but sub-optimizing the performance of the Value Creation System.
  - In the case of participation by the IT function, the risk of planting more technology legacy land mines.
- At the root of the tendency to start process improvement work at Level 5 is the failure to understand that there are two dimensions to a business, as illustrated in Figure 3.13.
  1. The top view depicts the organization chart or *resource view* of a business. If that is the prevailing view of an organization, there is a great bias to identifying processes (in reality, usually sub-processes) as operating nearly exclusively within functions. When viewed this way, there is no way to connect a functional silo-constrained sub-process to organization results without a lot of accounting hocus-pocus.
  2. The bottom diagram shows the typical relationship between the *value* and resource dimensions of a business. This view of an organization illustrates the reality that most processes (and even sub-processes) are cross-functional, link to one of the three processing sub-systems, and must be analyzed and designed or improved as a whole.

POTENTIAL PITFALLS IN CURRENT PRACTICES

In Figure 3.14 are two alternative views of the internal workings of a business as a Value Machine. The left view is what you see of the Value Creation Hierarchy if you focus on just the resource dimension. You see the business at Level 1, and then the performers at Level 5. Levels 2–4 are invisible. The right-hand view is the full VCH.

Using this as context, we provide some observations and insights about current BPM and management practices:

Figure 3.13 Resource-Centric and Value-Centric Approaches to Process Definition

Resource-Centric Approach to Process Definition

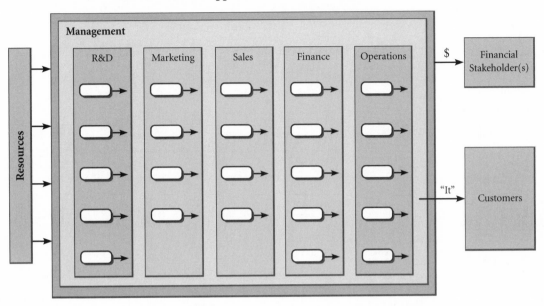

Value-Centric Approach to Process Definition

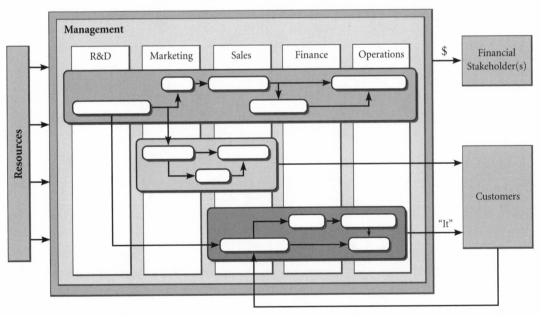

Figure 3.14 Alternative Views of Business as a Value Machine

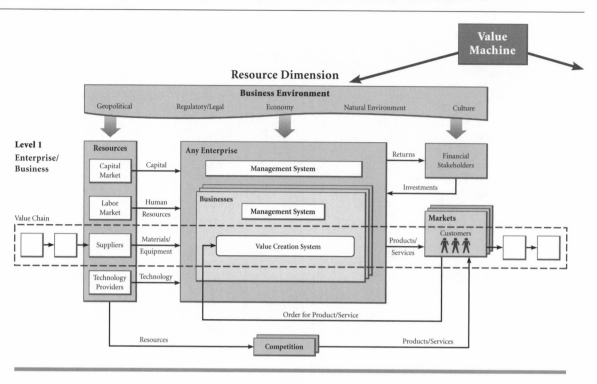

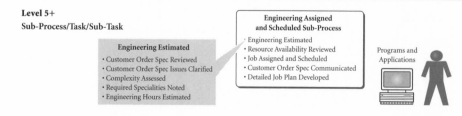

Figure 3.14 (*Continued*)

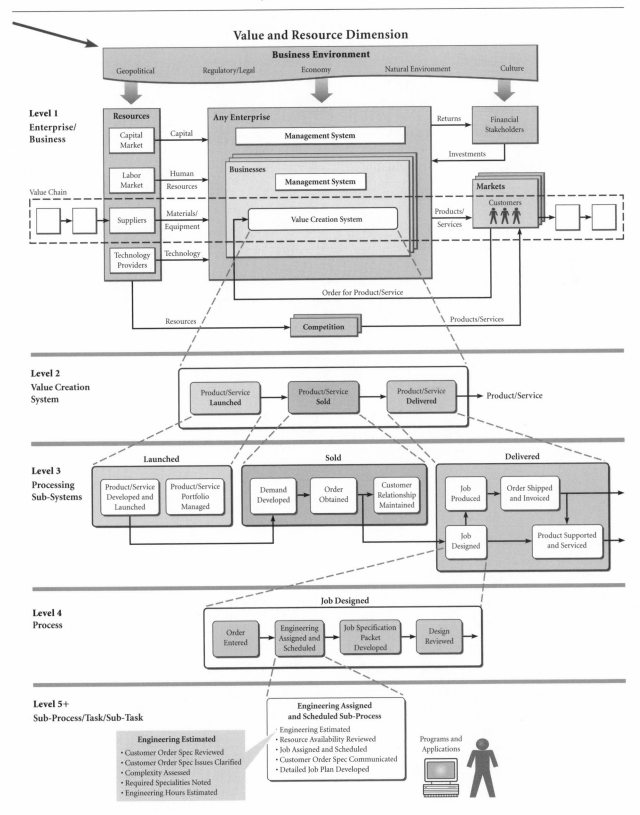

Current BPM Practices

Process Identification Pitfalls

- Too often, process identification starts in a vacuum, at Level 4 or 5, in functional silos. This means the process/sub-process is disconnected from the requirements of the business, its Value Creation System, and processing sub-systems.

- Adopting a generic list of processes or a reference model rather than articulating and understanding their organization's potentially unique VCS at Levels 2 and 3. This ignores our third process design criterion of "Look for a competitive advantage."

Process Improvement Pitfalls

- If processes are not linked to the VCS and the Launched/Sold/Delivered processing sub-systems, subsequent process improvement efforts have these problems:
  - The criteria for selecting processes for improvement are not tied to specific business needs.
  - Process improvement results are not linked to organization results.
  - There is no "natural" maintenance of process improvements because there is no obvious connection to valued business results.
  - Process improvement efforts gravitate toward less relevant process improvement goals such as maturity model levels.
  - No clear responsibility is defined for process improvement.

Process Management Pitfalls

- When processes are defined from the bottom up (Levels 4 or 5), they are disconnected from the business; the subsequent process management system is disconnected from the business management system.

- If, in the preceding scenario, process owners are assigned, there can be confusion and hostility among the roles and contributions of the process owner and the existing functional management structure.

Technology Pitfalls

- At the process level (Level 4), there is a growing potential for conflict between unique requirements of a process versus available off-the-shelf software applications.

- In the case of the example in Figure 3.11, the unique requirements of an effective Order Entry and Job Design process could be greatly compromised by the installation of an off-the-shelf order management system software application.

- Software packages offered at the process level can lead to unfortunate hard wiring and premature "hardening of the arteries" of an organization's VCS.

Management Practices

In a resource dimension mind-set (left side of Figure 3.14), these problems often surface among management:

- Executives, working at the business level (Level 1), see only one thing to manage to achieve business results: the resources at Level 5. The intervening structure of the value-adding work necessary to produce valued products/services is not visible. As a result:

- In many cases, executives do not properly understand how value is delivered to customers and financial stakeholders. They don't see the process levers to push to affect value.

- They continue to press on the "talent" and technology levers, hoping the desired valued products/services will somehow occur.

In contrast, with a value-and-resource-dimensions mind-set, as shown in the right-hand view in Figure 3.14, there are these benefits:

- Executives working at the business level have a complete blueprint or schematic of the Value Machine operating system. They see the value-adding work required to consistently create value. As a result, they can:

  ○ Influence the design of this work

  ○ Manage this work (more in Chapter Five)

- Making the Value Creation Hierarchy visible enables management to:

  ○ Identify key leverage points to manage

  ○ Understand who is responsible for what

  ○ Determine what variables and metrics must be understood in order to optimize and align the Value Creation System

  ○ Link organization, process, and people results (see the goal alignment example for Belding Engineering in Figure 2.5)

  ○ Quickly troubleshoot the organization at the appropriate level

- Management's understanding of the critical nature of Level 2 (the Value Creation System and Launched, Sold, and Delivered sub-system level) is the point of greatest executive leverage in the entire Value Creation Hierarchy. Only senior executives can oversee the proper alignment of the Launched, Sold, and Delivered components of the VCS. Without this alignment, there is not much hope for the remaining levels of the VCH.

- With the view that Level 2 provides, senior executives can make sound decisions about the allocation and alignment of resources across the processing sub-systems rather than leave it to the functional silos to make those decisions from their naturally biased, narrow viewpoints. Restructuring, when it does happen, can only be accomplished rationally, at the VCS level.

In retrospect, it was the understanding and management of the Launched, Sold, and Delivered level by Motorola executives in the early 1980s that made their efforts so successful. And why we saw the potential of "process" as a management tool.

CLOSING POINTS

From time to time during the past fifteen years, people have misinterpreted our enthusiasm for "process" to mean we were anti-function/department and that we advocate organizing a business around processes. Let's be very clear: Organizing a business around processes is a *bad idea*.

As we pointed out in Chapter Two, and as quite clearly showed in Figure 3.8, there are two critical dimensions of a business that must be managed in concert. The Value Creation System spells out what value-adding work must be done by whom to produce valued products and services to customers efficiently and effectively. The functions/departments (better described as "centers of excellence") hold the scarce resources necessary to perform that value-adding work. These centers of excellence are the best device to date for organizing the scarce resources of a business. Functions/departments/centers of excellence are an efficient way to acquire, develop, support, and manage these necessary groups of expertise or "talent."

So until something better comes along, functions and departments are fine. The issue isn't functions as such; it has been how to allocate the resources across the functions so that the Value Creation System can perform effectively. There has not yet been a way to manage the interface of the value and resource dimensions. But help is on the way. Through the process work described in this book and the Value Creation Management systems presented in our companion book, we have an effective way to manage resources in a value context.

That ends our detailed look at the Value Creation Hierarchy. In Chapter Four, we show how the graphic templates at each level can be woven together to provide a picture of the total Value Creation Architecture of a business—a management-friendly wiring diagram/operating schematic of the Value Machine.

CHAPTER FOUR

Developing the Value Creation Architecture of a Business

In Chapter Three, we introduced the Value Creation System as a framework used within the Value Creation Hierarchy for structuring the work required to produce products and services. That work can be described in various ways, but most commonly activities and/or processes are used. However, we describe the work required by the VCS not by activities or processes, but by the *value* produced by those activities and processes.

MAKING THE VALUE DIMENSION VISIBLE

If a business is going to consistently, systematically create value for its customers and financial stakeholders, it is essential that the leadership of the business knows precisely how value is created, so that they can:

- Understand and leverage the Value Creation System
- Redesign and improve the effectiveness and efficiency of the VCS as necessary
- Manage the VCS to be adaptive and agile

In this chapter, we demonstrate how the Value Creation Hierarchy (VCH) presented in Chapter Three can be applied to any business to provide a practical, management-friendly view—or "architecture"—of the business. We discuss:

- The components of the Value Creation Architecture (VCA) and the templates available to develop one
- The benefits of having a VCA

- How a business can use a VCA
- Strategies for developing a VCA and who should develop it
- Critical success factors for a VCA

We use several terms and acronyms in this chapter; here are some distinctions to keep in mind:

- The *Value Creation Hierarchy* (VCH) presented in Chapter Three is a model for understanding the levels that compose an organization, from total business at Level 1, through multiple levels of processing, to Level 5, where the performer resides.
- The *Value Creation System* (VCS) refers to the three middle levels of the VCH, all of which depict processes at greater and greater levels of granularity. So the term "VCS" is shorthand for the processes of an organization that collectively produce value.
- The *Value Creation Architecture* (VCA) is the structure of the processes of a given business. In this chapter we show you the set of documents that can be used to depict the VCA of a business. When you are interested in seeing, understanding, designing, improving, or managing the VCH of a business, you would develop a set of VCA documents. Got it? Yeah, took us a while too.

There are two critical audiences for these topics: (1) executives and senior managers, and (2) process practitioners.

Executives and Senior Managers

From the outset we must stress that a Value Creation Architecture is a vital management tool. In the context of a business as a Value Machine, the VCA is the schematic of the operating system of that machine. Without a set of documents to represent that schematic, the organization, and what goes on inside it, is just a sealed black box. But with this schematic, management:

- Can quickly assess the capabilities required to support strategic options
- Knows where to insert measures to monitor performance
- Can systematically troubleshoot poor machine performance and trace the cause back to contributing system components
- Can wisely allocate resources to improve the performance of critical machine components
- Knows where and how to change out components of the Value Machine's operating system to respond to changing customer and business requirements—in short, to be agile

In short, the VCA provides management with insight. The development of a VCA for a business requires input from a variety of sources, under the guidance of trained internal process practitioners. But ideally the development of the VCA schematic is directed by the executives and managers accountable for the performance of the Value Machine. The final product of that developmental work—that is, the operating schematic of the business—must be a tool that is effective for business management.

Process Practitioners

Process practitioners should be significant participants in the development of a business's Value Creation Architecture—either leading the development or making major contributions. By process "practitioner," we mean any of the wide collection of organization jobs/roles that are involved in analyzing, designing, improving, implementing, maintaining, or managing work processes. Individuals performing these roles may be part of any line or staff organization, most particularly IT, Quality, or Process Excellence groups.

Process practitioners should be major users and beneficiaries of the VCA once it is built, because this is the tool that can guide them to choose the right improvement efforts. The process practitioner—on the business or IT side—should never again look at or think about a sub-process or process in isolation. He or she should see every process as part of a network of value-adding processes that make up the Value Creation System.

Minimally, when redesigning a process, the VCA-wise process practitioner will scope out the larger system as part of understanding the "is" situation and determining performance requirements.[1] (More about this in Chapter Six.)

Ideally, the process practitioner will not have to scope the larger system from scratch for every improvement effort. He or she will start the "is" analysis of a given process by examining the documentation for the existing VCA and immediately seeing the performance and requirements of the process in question. The VCA provides a roadmap for the process practitioner in developing performance requirements.

A CLOSER LOOK AT VALUE CREATION ARCHITECTURE

What exactly is a Value Creation Architecture? It is the Value Creation System of a business, represented by a set of linked documents that depict the work required of a business to produce its valued products and services.[2] One creates VCA documentation by looking at the business through the Value Creation Hierarchy lens and applying the documentation templates available for every level of the VCH to articulate that business's unique value creation system.

The core documentation template set for depicting a VCA, linked to the appropriate VCH level, is summarized in Figure 4.1. The functionality of each template is summarized in Table 4.1. You saw many of these templates for the Belding Engineering Services example in Chapter Three. The documentation we introduced in Chapter Three can be linked together to form the core of a VCA.

As a way to provide a quick, closer look at a VCA, we recap why and how Belding Engineering built their VCA.

Figure 4.1 Templates Used for Value Creation Architecture

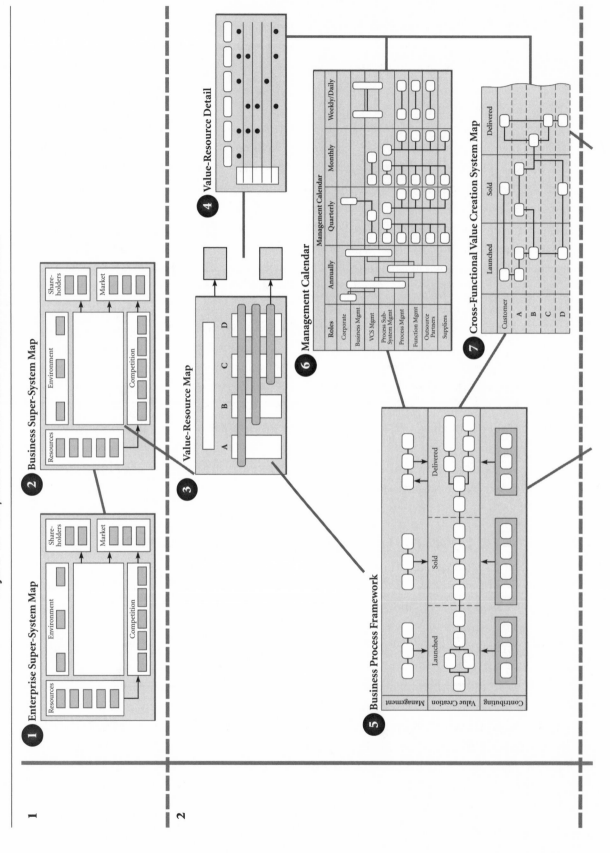

Figure 4.1 (*Continued*)

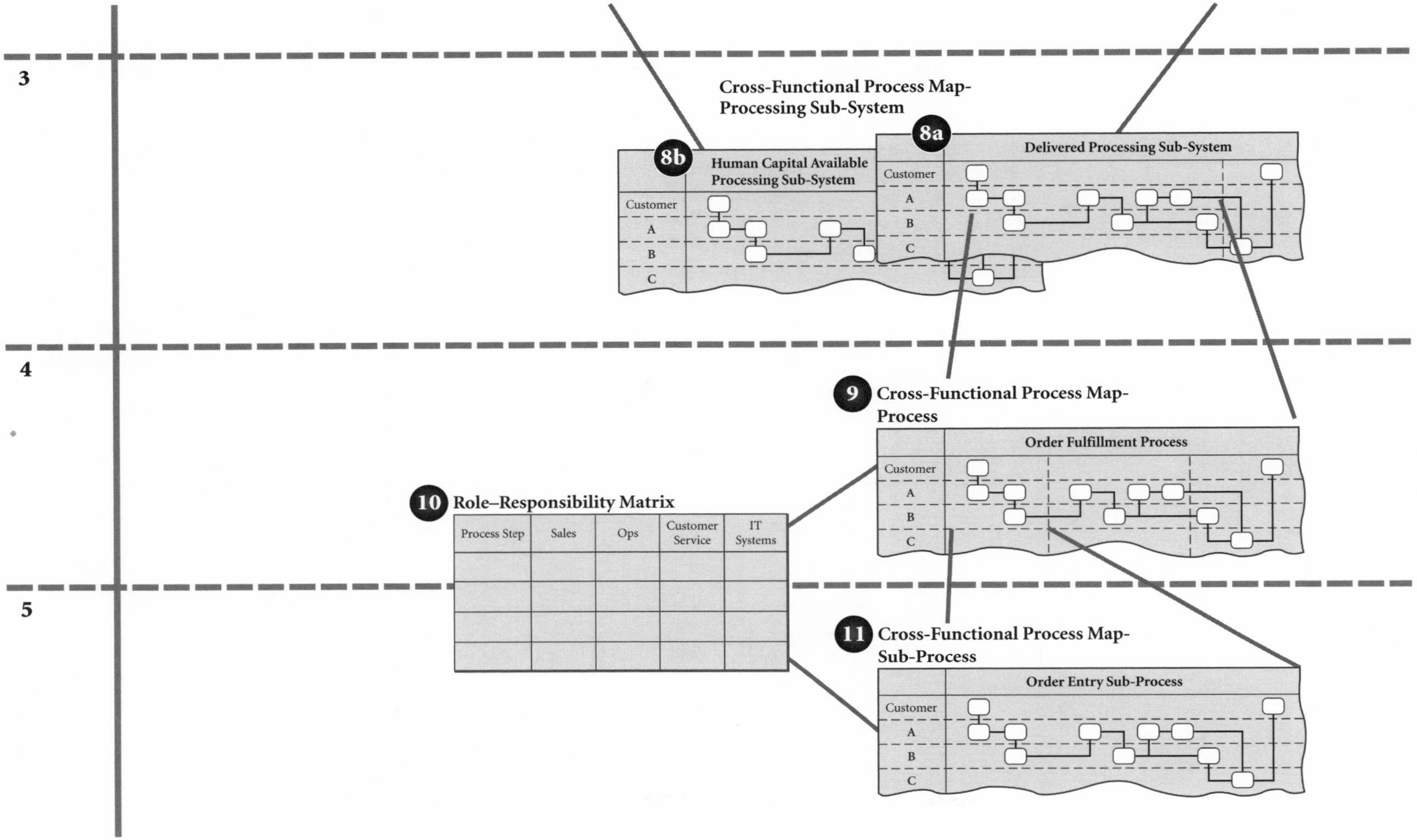

Cross-Functional Process Map-Processing Sub-System

Delivered Processing Sub-System

Customer	
A	
B	
C	

8a

Human Capital Available Processing Sub-System

Customer	
A	
B	
C	

8b

Cross-Functional Process Map-Process

Order Fulfillment Process

Customer	
A	
B	
C	

9

Cross-Functional Process Map-Sub-Process

Order Entry Sub-Process

Customer	
A	
B	
C	

11

10 Role–Responsibility Matrix

Process Step	Sales	Ops	Customer Service	IT Systems

3

4

5

Table 4.1 VCA Tool Set

VCH Level	VCA Tool	Tool Features	Tool Benefits
Level 1 Enterprise/ Business Model	Enterprise Super-System Map Template 1	Describes an enterprise's products/services and markets Describes the variables that can influence enterprise Provides a macro view of the enterprise's lines of business	At a high level, identifies the value a business delivers to its market Identifies external factors that can affect business performance and need to be monitored and acted upon as necessary to stay adaptive/competitive Can be used to identify current facts, trends, and/or future predictions for the variables and the business in question Is a one-page "essence of the business" view
	2. Business Super-System Map Template #2	Is a sub-set of an Enterprise Super-System Map Describes the external variables that influence a single line of business Treats the larger enterprise as part of the super-system for that business	
Level 2 Value Creation System	Value-Resource Map Template 3	Provides a macro view of the business's value creation system and functional resources that participate in the VCS	Puts both organizational dimensions (value and resources) in one picture
	Business Process Architecture Framework Template 5	Identifies all the key processes and their interrelationships for a given business in three categories: 1. Management processes 2. Value-creating processes 3. Contributing processes	Helps in identifying and naming the important processes of a business Distinguishes between three important but very different types of business processes (that is, value creating versus management versus contributing) BPA provides jumping-off point for doing process design, improvement or management
	Management Calendar Template 6	Is a cross-functional view of management calendar	Identifies, names, and puts into sequence the major events of the management calendar Also identifies the management participants in the events of the calendar
	Cross-Functional Value Creation System Map Template 7	Is a cross-functional view of the processes that together create, market and sell, and deliver valued goods and services to the market	Identifies, names, and puts into sequence the major value-creating processes and tasks of the business Also identifies the participants in the value-creating processes
	Value-Resource Detail Matrix Template 4	Provides a summary listing of the resources (human and technology) distributed across the value-creating processes)	Is a quick way to assess how resources are allocated to value creation in a business Can show gaps, redundancies, and illogic in resource allocation Can be used to plan for future technology, HR hiring, competency building, and so on
Level 3 Processing Systems	Cross-Functional Map–Processing Sub-System Templates 8a and 8b	Provides a view of a set of related processes (for example, all of the Launched processes)	Helps for focusing on a sub-set of the Business Process Architecture
Level 4 Process	Cross-Functional Process Map–Process Template 9	Depicts the tasks, participants, sequence of work, supporting technology, and performance data (for example, cycle time, cost, resources) for a single business process	Provides a detailed understanding of how a given process works (that is, "is" version) Can be used to design an improved future-state process (that is, "should") Can be the basis for requirements for technology development
	Cross-Functional Role-Responsibility Matrix Template 10	Describes the roles (for example, performers, approvers, advisors, input providers) of participants in a given business process	Adds detail about how a process is performed, how contributing functions are involved in supporting a process
Level 5+Sub-Process/ Task/ Sub-Process	Cross-functional Process Map–Sub-Process or other tools Template 11	Depicts the tasks, participants, sequence of work, supporting technology and performance data (for example, cycle time, cost, resources) for a sub-process or even a single task within a business process	Provides procedural information about how a portion of a process is performed Can be used for design of a "should" sub-process Can be content for procedures manuals, training programs/documents Can provide requirements for technology development

THE BELDING ENGINEERING VALUE CREATION ARCHITECTURE

Background

Some background facts on Belding Engineering relevant to the development of its Value Creation Architecture are:

- Belding is a developer and supplier of sophisticated electronic communications equipment.

- Its organization chart appears in Figure 3.3.

- Belding has been in business fifteen years and was acquired by Corporate eight years ago.

- Revenues continue to grow, but at a rate less than the overall growth rate of the industry for the past two years.

- Profits have been in a worrisome decline over the past three years. This reduced profitability has begun to hamper plans for future growth.

- Production has sporadically been required to perform "rework" on customer orders during the past year. Sales reports a corresponding jump in customer complaints, having to do with missed delivery dates.

- The last new product introduction (a year ago) has been termed a "disaster" and has contributed to the decline in profits.

- In response to the declining profit picture, Belding underwent a 10% across-the-board budget cut three years ago and a similar across-the-board 15% cut six months ago.

- Executive morale is at rock bottom.

- Three months ago Corporate replaced the incumbent CEO, who had been with Belding since its inception.

- The new CEO is S. K. Owens.

S. K. Owens has been with the Corporate organization for ten years. In his previous Corporate assignment, he successfully turned around the Sterling Publishing subsidiary, applying some innovative process improvement and management strategies.

Owens is expected to stop the profit slide in two quarters and get Belding profits "back to par" in six quarters. It has been suggested by his Corporate liaison that he consider a reorganization of Belding as a means of "shaking up" the staff and finding some efficiencies.

During his first two months at Belding, Owens has learned the following:

- The VPs assume he will be reorganizing the company and are waiting for "the next shoe to fall."

- The normal functional silo/fortress mentality has been heightened due to the inability to figure out how to stop the slide in profits. One-on-one meetings with his new staff have been informative and productive, but full staff meetings have quickly become ugly, with much finger pointing.

- One of the major contributors to the failure of the last product introduction was that there was very limited input to the design of the product from the Sales and Production functions because the staffs of those two organizations had been cut back to the bone in the two downsizings. For example, there weren't any resources Production could spare to address the "manufacturability" issues with the new product. And as a result, there were plenty of manufacturability issues.

Based on his experience working with an outside consultant while heading Sterling Publishing, Owens had come to believe that a business is fundamentally a Value Machine. And further, what is required for the successful management of any such Value Machine is a schematic of its operating system. Within his first eight weeks at Belding, Owens concluded that neither he nor his direct reports had a firm understanding of the value-adding work required to consistently produce profitable products that customers would value and buy.

Even if he wanted to cut more costs, Owens didn't know where he could effectively do so. And even if he thought a reorganization would be valuable, he didn't want to start tinkering with the Belding Value Machine without the benefit of the operating system schematic.

Owens started his third monthly Leadership Team meeting with his direct reports by announcing he wanted immediately to commence an effort to document the Value Creation Architecture of Belding Engineering. Owens then introduced a member of the Corporate Performance Support Group whom he wanted to head this project. The goal was to develop a first working approximation of the VCA documentation in twelve weeks. The work would be done by what Owens labeled the "Insight Team," consisting of the consultant from the Corporate Performance Support Group, who would be the team lead, and two senior Belding staff. The Insight Team would do the development work; the Leadership Team would review, evaluate, and make decisions.

VCA Development

Using the summary of templates in Figure 4.1 as a roadmap for the VCA development project, CEO Owens and the Insight Team followed the sequence summarized in Table 4.2.

Phase 1: VCA Documentation for VCH Level 1: Enterprise/Business

The Insight Team started by gathering pertinent data from appropriate Belding functional areas and then developed an *"is" Business Super-System Map*, shown as Template 2 in Figure 4.1. (The team decided that since Corporate is really a holding company, a Super-System Map of Corporate would provide little value.)

The Insight Team then facilitated a two-day meeting of the Leadership Team, in which the "is" Super-System Map was used to guide discussion of the critical variables affecting Belding. The Leadership Team reached agreement on:

- The current reality of all five critical components of the Belding super-system

- The assumptions regarding trends over the next three years for each of the five super-system components

Table 4.2 Insight Team Project Summary

Phase	Templates	Activities	Duration
1. VCA Documentation for VCH Level 1	2. Business Super-System Map	Gathered pertinent data from all Belding functions and other resources to populate an "is" Belding Super-System Map Facilitated a two-day review of the "is" SSM with the Belding Leadership Team	Two Weeks
2. VCA Documentation for VCH Levels 2 and 3	3. Value-Resource Map 4. Value-Resource Map Detail 5. Business Process Framework 6. Management Calendar 7. Cross-Functional Value Creation Map 8a. Cross-Functional Process Map–Processing Sub-System	Gathered data on how Belding currently developed, introduced, sold and produced their three product lines Displayed data using appropriate Level 2 and 3 templates. Facilitated a two-day review and validation of the draft Levels 2 and 3 VCA with the Extended Leadership Team	Seven Weeks

For the time being, Owens and the Leadership Team decided to continue with the idea that Belding has just one line of business and one Value Creation System, accommodating all three of their current product lines. They recognized, however, that this could change if they chose to alter Belding's strategy to respond to potential threats or opportunities in the market and competition.

Phase 2: VCA Documentation at VCH Level 2: Value Creation System and Level 3: Processing Sub-Systems
The Insight Team gathered data on how Belding currently was developing, introducing, selling, and producing their three product lines. Based on these data, the Insight Team developed the following:

- *Belding Value-Resource Map* (using Template 3 in Figure 4.1). The Team developed both "is" and "should" maps. The "is" map was a powerful picture, showing the lack of participation of key functions in the critical Product Launched sub-system of Belding's Value Creation System (one explanation for the failure of the previous new product introduction).

- *Belding Value-Resource Detail Map* (using Template 4). This document assesses how resources are currently allocated to value creation at Belding (the "is") and how they should be allocated to meet value creation goals. This map provided clear specifics about the "is" and "should" allocation of resources across the value creation system.

The application of Templates 5–9 was an iterative process, but followed this initial sequence:

- *Business Process Framework* (Figure 4.1, Template 5). The BPF is a high-level "roll-up" of the data captured in Templates 6, 7, and 8. It shows all the significant process (that is, value creation processes, management processes, and contributing processes) of Belding and their systemic interrelationships. The BPF provides Belding executives and employees with a common view of all the major processes of the business, on one page. The document is a concise summary of the value-adding work that must be performed and managed to provide products/ services to customers. The picture is a work-centric picture and does not reflect who does the work; the primary focus of dialogue, troubleshooting, and decision making stays on the work and on the creation and delivery of value. At any point, the process boxes summarized on the BPF map can be examined more closely by going to Template 6, 7, or 8, which make it abundantly clear who is expected to perform what work.

- *Management Calendar* (Figure 4.1, Template 6). The Insight Team developed an "is" Management Calendar showing the current management meetings and other activities designed to manage the business.

- *Cross-Functional Value Creation System Map—Primary* (Figure 4.1, Template 7). This document captured the major processes making up the three processing sub-systems of Launched, Sold, and Delivered. This "is" document captures, on one page, all the processes and functions that must work together to deliver valued products to customers. It is a critical management tool. The map was annotated to note where the three product lines differed in the course of the value creation system.

- The one template not used was the *VCS Contributing Process Map* (Figure 4.1, Template 8b). These maps were not developed at this time, pending a later prioritization of contributing processes by the Belding Leadership Team.

- *Cross-Functional Processing Sub-System Map* (Figure 4.1, Template 8.a), one each for Launched, Sold, and Delivered. These maps are drill-downs of the processing sub-systems shown in Template 7.

The Insight Team facilitated a two-day retreat with the Extended Leadership Team (VPs and direct reports) to review and validate Maps 3–8. The agenda included:

- A detailed walk-through and validation of the "is" maps
- With the help of the Insight Team, identification of major disconnects (deficiencies) in the current value creation system and prioritization of processes to be documented at Level 4
- Prioritization of contributing processes for future documentation
- Development of high-level future-state design concepts

Participants gained many insights during the walk-through of these documents at the retreat, but there were three that were considered most significant.

First, while comparing the "is" versus "should" Belding Value-Resource Map and Detail Map (Templates 3 and 4), Sales and Production executives and managers suffered some embarrassment when it became clear that they had failed to provide adequate input and support to the previous product introduction—contributing greatly to its eventual disaster. CEO Owens used this opportunity to start a constructive discussion of how resources needed to be allocated to functions in the future so that they can adequately support the total Belding Value Creation System.

Second, the Business Process Framework (Template 5) triggered extensive discussion about the notion of a Value Creation System with the three primary sub-systems of Launched, Sold, and Delivered. One participant said, "We thought we had a coordinated Launched, Sold, Delivered sequence to get profitable products to market, but nobody really had a coherent view of it. Executives and managers only saw their individual functional silos." To another participant, the most valuable insight was the need for aligned goals: "We never had anything like total VCS goals or aligned Launched, Sold, Delivered goals. Our only goals are established within functions, never across functions."

Finally, the Cross-Functional Value Creation Map (Template 7) and Cross-Functional Process Maps (Template 9) revealed the complexity of the business, to some participants for the first time: "This really is a complicated cross-functional business—but manageable once you see all the parts." Many also noted that the Launched sub-system is particularly cross-functional, but it is largely invisible and unmanaged. Said one executive, "Most every one of our current operating problems is cross-functional in nature and can't be adequately addressed by a single VP or function." Another pointed out, "I have to admit I never really 'got' this process stuff until now. I've read some of the articles and heard the preaching, but it seemed to me it was just borrowing things that belong in Manufacturing. But with these maps, I can see the entire business, and I can see how processes are woven into everything we do, not just in Production. It's an eye-opener."

Phase 3: VCA Documentation for VCH Level 4: Processing Sub-Systems

For this phase, the Insight Team developed *Cross-Functional Process Maps* down to the sub-process level for those primary and contributing processes identified in the Extended Leadership Team Meeting. They also provided a list of disconnects and preliminary recommendations for improvement for each process mapped.

The Insight Team then facilitated a one-day middle management meeting. The agenda focused on a review of the Level 4 Cross-Functional Maps and related disconnects and recommendations. The Insight Team also provided a summary of the insights and conclusions reached through the Extended Leadership Retreat. A major conclusion was that the insights were valuable enough that the documentation should be institutionalized. To that end, the following was decided:

- A hard copy of the Belding Super-System Map and related assumptions, and the results of Templates 5, 7, 9, and 11 would be permanently displayed on the CEO's conference room walls, for reference in all Leadership Team meetings.

- The Insight Team would continue in place for two months and develop a system for archiving the documentation and keeping it current.

- Redesigning would begin with the Order to Cash process (a significant part of the Delivered sub-system) and the Launched sub-system, the two most critical components of the Value Creation System. The former was critical to improving customer satisfaction and short-term profitability and the latter to long-term success. CEO Owens would approach the Corporate Performance Support Group for resources for this work.

The CEO said he had some thoughts on how the VCA work that had been done could be used to help the Leadership Team manage Belding in the future. He would present these ideas at the next Leadership Team meeting.

WHY BOTHER DEVELOPING A VCA?

It may seem as though we are talking out of both sides of the mouth: warning against unnecessary process documentation and then urging companies to develop a Value Creation Architecture. But there is a big difference (real and perceived) between an initiative to "articulate our Value Creation System" and one to "document our processes." In today's increasingly competitive world, one ought to be able to build a business case for the value of the former. The latter initiative sounds so "yesterday." In many organizations "documenting our processes" has already been done, often badly and with no good business reason. (We know several organizations in which, to this day, executives and mid-managers alike break out in hives at the mention of "ISO-anything.") There are two generally good reasons for investing in documenting a VCA:

1. To provide the foundation for a Value Creation Management System—a system to manage the Value and Resource dimensions in concert.
2. To address some critical business issue. Once the investment has been made in such a VCA, the foundation is in place to begin moving toward a Value Creation Management System. The Belding project just presented is such a case as is described in Chapter Five.

But don't start a VCA effort because it is the thing to do. Without a clear critical business issue or mission and a supporting business case, it can end up a highly visible disaster—of no benefit to either executives or process practitioners.

The following are several examples of VCA efforts initiated in response to critical business issues:

- Shortly after the Sarbanes-Oxley Act was passed, a financial services company underwent its annual internal financial audit and discovered that it had several serious control deficiencies that, if not fixed quickly, would have to be reported to regulators. Senior executives stood in some legal jeopardy, and the company's stellar reputation was also at risk. The company decided that the best way to improve its internal financial controls was to take a process approach to understanding the effectiveness of controls that were already in place as well as any that would have to be created from scratch. At the direction of executives, a SOX team developed an "is" VCA down to Level 3, identified those processes in which financial controls were critical, evaluated the adequacy of existing controls, and determined where controls were lacking. Once the set of desired controls was identified, multiple teams were established to build those controls down to Level 5, test them, and implement them across the company's operating units. The result was a second audit that was passed without a single material deficiency.

- A highly matrixed high-tech company was experiencing extreme turnover at a very critical engineering management level in the business. Young product managers were unable to successfully negotiate across the "old boy" functional silos to bring new products to market. It was massive resource power bases against a completely invisible value dimension. The organization developed Level 2–3 VCA documentation that made the VCS sufficiently visible to clarify roles and responsibilities among functions and the product managers and to provide a roadmap for Product Managers for negotiating the complex Value Creation System.

- A small manufacturer of executive aircraft received substantial funding to support an aggressive five-year growth plan. The underlying assumption for the growth was extensive outsourcing of the work making up the Delivered sub-system of the Value Creation System. The Executive Team directed the development of a Value Creation Architecture to Level 3 for Launched and Sold and Level 5 for Delivered. The Level 5 detail for Delivered was necessary to assure successful transfer and management of the required value-adding work to outside resources. The Level 3 detail for Launched, Sold, and Delivered was necessary to assure the goals and operations of all three components of the company's value creation system remained aligned during this critical period of growth.

DEVELOPING THE VCA

Given that Value Creation Architecture documentation is generated by systematically applying the templates shown in Figure 4.1, there are three questions that need to be answered:

1. Who should develop the VCA?
2. How should it be developed?
3. What are the critical success factors in its development?

Who Should Develop the Value Creation Architecture?

This is an important question to answer for two reasons: first, it is important to understand what a powerful management tool the VCA documentation can be. For that reason we believe the VCA documentation effort needs to be driven by business executives. The effort can be staffed by a variety of people, but the product of the effort must meet the criterion of "usable management tool."

Second, for some years now, IT organizations have been producing documents called "business process architectures," "enterprise architectures," and so on, that are frequently described as "models" of the business. However, these documents generally show some aspect of the *technology architecture* of a business and do not model how a business works—or how value-adding work is done to create valued products and services. Yet the labeling of these tools as "enterprise architectures" implies much more than technology, and they have served to confuse many people, including, it sometimes seems, their creators. So when we talk about creating "architectures," there might be confusion about what kind of architecture we are referring to and who should develop it. We believe the documentation of an organization's Value Creation Architecture, as we define it, should be developed by a team or task force of individuals who possess a good understanding of all facets of the business, under the direction of senior executives. And members of the IT organization are valuable members of this team.

Approaches to Developing a Value Creation Architecture

There are several different approaches, depending on variables. Here are some major distinctions to consider:

1. First, is documentation of the Value Creation Architecture:
   - A top management mandated or sponsored initiative?
   - An IT sponsored initiative?
   - A low profile, bottom-up effort being informally promoted by the Process Excellence Group or its equivalent?
2. Second, if it is a mandated initiative, is the objective to create a:
   - Current state VCA view?
   - Future state VCA view?
   - Both?
3. Third, regardless of whether current or future state, is the resulting VCA documentation to be:
   - The basis of a management system, as was the case with Belding?
   - A management reference tool on the wall primarily to facilitate management decision making and provide a helpful framework for future process improvement efforts carried out by both the business and the IT function?

And here are some development guidelines for approaching each set of circumstances.

Low Profile, Bottom-Up Effort

Usually the idea here is to get as many members of the informal "process community" to agree on the value of having a common, comprehensive set of VCA documents to help in properly scoping design or improvement projects. (More on the value of this in Chapter Six.) The next step is to get participants to agree on a framework for describing and linking the disparate processes they will each encounter as they go about their project work. Of course, we think the Value Creation Hierarchy would be a great organizer for the effort. If the VCH were adopted, then probably a good next step would be for some folks in the Process Excellence Group to begin roughing out what they believe to be the process structure of Launched, Sold, and Delivered (Level 2), perhaps using the cross-functional value creation format of Template 7 (Figure 4.1). Every process encounter by the Process Excellence Group for the next year or more is used to learn more about the high-level Value Creation System of the business. And at the same time, every project conducted by members of the process community is input to completing the process network puzzle at some VCH level.

This is Phase 1: documenting the current-state VCA. To move to a future-state VCA view, the Process Excellence Group needs to enroll a senior business executive as client or sponsor for the effort. Then the group could coordinate development of the future-state or "could be" VCA picture using the resources of the process community.

Mandated

Regardless whether the VCA documentation is a current-state or future-state effort, the project sequence should not vary that much. The team will do data gathering and model building using appropriate templates and validation sessions for Levels 1–5, much as was done in the Belding example and summarized in Table 4.2. Whether the objective of developing a VCA is in response to a critical business issue or as the foundation of a management system, the project sequence should be the same. The exceptions are

- The future-state engagement will require more time than the current-state project. Data-gathering time shouldn't be that different, but modeling time and validation time (including consensus-building time) will be considerably more, as executives and managers are involved in thinking outside the box.

- The current-state project may be followed by a future-state project, which would take more time but may definitely be worthwhile.

- The initiative is IT sponsored. The path forward depends on the objective of the initiative. If the goal is developing a technology-centric architecture for the exclusive use of the IT community, then IT should do what is required to achieve that goal. However, if the goal is to attempt to model the business as a way of aligning business and IT requirements, two things are needed: business executive ownership of the initiative and deployment of a methodology (such as the VCA methodology described here) that models the business in a way recognizable to business executives.

In every case, we recommend a team of individuals who possess a good understanding of all facets of the business under the direction of a senior executive. And you might include an external consultant who has done this work before.

Critical Success Factors

There are three factors that we feel are critical to developing an effective Value Creation Architecture: your choice of starting point, your definition of value milestones, and meeting our three familiar criteria for organizing work.

Starting Point

Most efforts (and tools) employed to model the work of an organization start with the resource dimension. That is, the first level of work organization is within the functional "resource buckets" (for example, Marketing processes, Sales processes, Engineering processes, and so on). And all subsequent decomposition continues within each functional silo. Such a process architecture is fundamentally flawed for two reasons:

1. It does not properly recognize the cross-functional nature of most significant processes. Processes are artificially truncated into sub-processes to fit into the functional structure.

2. It misses altogether the notion of work being part of an end-to-end, cross-organizational value creation system.

In contrast, the approach described in this chapter starts by modeling the *value dimension* of a business. This generates a multilayered picture of the total, end-to-end Value Creation System, showing the critical relationships among types of work required to produce valued products and services. Once we understand this value-adding work, we can link to the functional resource buckets via our Value-Resource Maps (Figure 4.1, Templates 3 and 4). A Value Creation Architecture created this way is true to its name; it is a structure of the work required to create value.

Value Milestones

In Chapter Three, we introduced the notion of the value milestone for use in organizing and structuring work; the Value Creation Hierarchy has a high-level value milestone structure at each level.

Figure 4.2 contains a portion of the Belding Business Process Framework that has a value milestone structure embedded. The levels of work structure shown in the Value Creation band of this framework are

- Processing sub-system (Launched)
- Value milestone
- Processes

Figure 4.2 Example of Business Process Framework

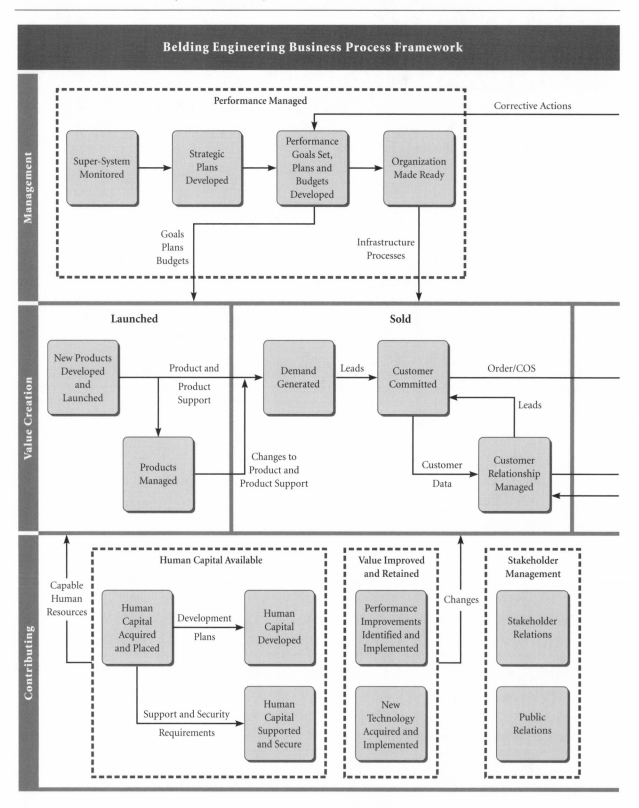

Figure 4.2 (*Continued*)

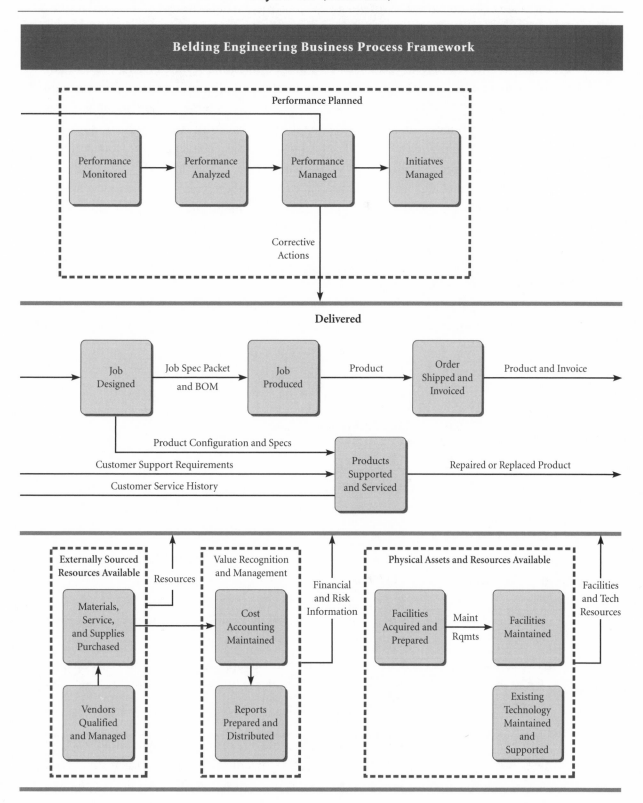

Belding Engineering Business Process Framework

The value milestone concept is useful for the construction of both current-state and future-state Value Creation Architectures. For current-state projects, when trying to organize a lot of data from different sources, with different perspectives, the challenge is to establish an overall process structure. The first step is to determine a value milestone or outcome logic for each of the processing sub-systems (Launched, Sold, and Delivered). Each value milestone represents a likely process or sub-process. Working with these value milestone labels or "headlines," you can quickly get agreement from participants on the basic structure of processes and sub-process for Launched, Sold, and Delivered. The next step is to get agreement on the work required to achieve each sub-process and process value milestones.

For future-state architecture design, this is a "clean sheet" exercise. You build a structure or logic of value milestones within each processing sub-system, for processes, sub-process, sub-process steps down to tasks. This should constitute a draft future-state Value Creation Architecture.

Definition of a Process

You already know the third critical success factor. As you establish the value milestone logic and specify the sequence of work to achieve those milestones, don't forget our three criteria for organizing work:

1. The work can be **performed** effectively and efficiently.
2. The work can be effectively **managed.**
3. There is the potential for a **competitive advantage**.

Applying these three critical success factors should put you on your way to the development of a superior Value Creation Architecture.

CLOSING POINTS

So that's a look at Value Creation Architecture: what it can look like and how it can be developed. In general, the utility of a VCA is

- As the basis for a value creation management system. We discuss this in detail in Chapter Five.
- As a roadmap for process design or improvement. This application is addressed in Chapter Five, as part of a management system, and in Chapter Six, as part of a process improvement methodology.

If process is to have significant impact on business performance (or, put another way, if business is ever going to properly leverage process), organizations need to understand their Value Creation Architecture—the process "big picture." Businesses need to understand and emphasize the entire Value Creation System rather than focus on isolated components (that is, processes) of the system in a vacuum.

In our view, Value Creation Architecture is the future of process. Without the process big picture as a roadmap, it will be very difficult for the notion of process, now buried in functional silos, to rise above the sub-process level. A Value Creation Architecture is also the future of sound management. Without understanding the value-adding work to be managed, management activities quickly degenerate into counterproductive turf wars.

CHAPTER FIVE

Process Management in the Value Creation Context

In Chapter One, we discussed current practices in process management: in the past, we process practitioners defined and improved processes in isolation (at Level 4 of the Value Creation Hierarchy); our efforts were frequently disconnected from customer expectations and business requirements. In those rare instances when a process management system was developed for those processes, the management systems were also developed in isolation and subsequently were disconnected from the real business management system (thus the drift to Maturity Models and Governance Systems). The promise of BPM software aside, the result frequently has been ineffective process management systems. Yet as we pointed out in our definition of process in Chapter Three, one of the three key criteria for good process design is that it can be managed effectively.

But "process in a value creation context" provides a different perspective. In the future, we can look at process management as a fully integrated component of the enterprise value creation management system. And most important, the value creation management system is the integrated management of both the resource and the value dimensions of the business.

Here we limit the discussion of value creation management systems to the illustration of what a "fully integrated" process management system looks like and what the implications are for process practitioners of this alternative to today's flawed definitions of process management. The design, implementation, and operation of the value creation system of a business are the focus of our companion book for managers and executives.

To do this, we introduce two basic management models and then describe the evolution of a process management system by returning to our Belding Engineering Services example.

PERFORMANCE MANAGEMENT MODELS

The basic performance management model shown in Figure 5.1 consists of three components:

1. *Performance Planned:* Goals and plans are set and communicated to the "performer."

2. *Performance Executed:* The "performer" (who can be an individual, a process, or an organization entity—for example, a company division, plant, or department) delivers the desired performance/results prescribed in the goals and plans.

3. *Performance Managed:* Actual performance is monitored against the goals and plans, and if a negative deviation is detected, there may be a "change" signal sent to:

   a. The "performer" to change the execution in some way and/or

   b. To the Performance Planned component to either change the goals or the plans to accomplish the goals

Put another way:

- Performance Planned = "Plan"

- Performance Executed = "Actual"

- Performance Managed = Action to close the gap between "plan" and "actual"

Figure 5.1 Performance Planned and Managed System

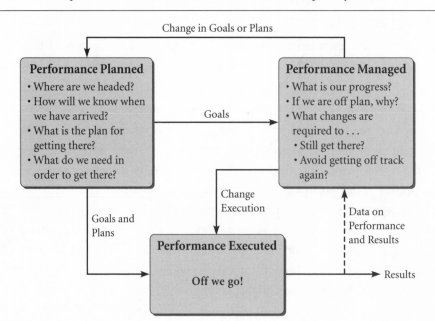

Performance Executed—the individual, process, or entity that performs the work—is always a visible component of this fundamental performance system. On the other hand, the *Performance Planned* and *Performance Managed* components, which constitute the "brains" or intelligence of the performance system, tend to be invisible and flawed. This Performance Planned/Performance Managed combination (which we refer to as the "Performance Planned and Managed System") makes it possible for the performance system to adapt to external changes and react to execution failures. It is the mechanism whereby the performance system is both an effective processing system and an adaptive (learning) system.

Figure 5.2 provides more detail about the functioning of the Performance Planned and Performance Managed components. In addition to providing goals (direction) and plans to Performance Executed, the Performance Planned component makes available the necessary resources (financial and other) to achieve the goals.

Linking together the components of Performance Planned and Managed to Performance Executed at each level of management forms a total management system. (See Figure 5.3.) Each level of management sets plans and reviews performance of the next level down in the management hierarchy. In this context you can see why most process management designs fail (you need to link the *work processes* with Level 2, via Level 3) and why technology alone won't help.

Finally, addressing process management in a value creation context enables us to understand and address the reality of managing both the value and resource dimensions of an organization (resources in the context of the value dimension, as shown in Figure 5.4).

Figure 5.2 Detailed Performance Planned and Managed System

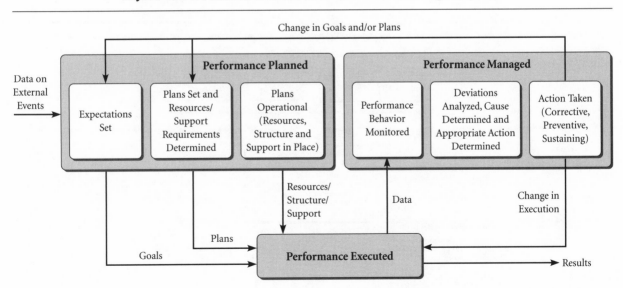

Figure 5.3 Work/Work Management System

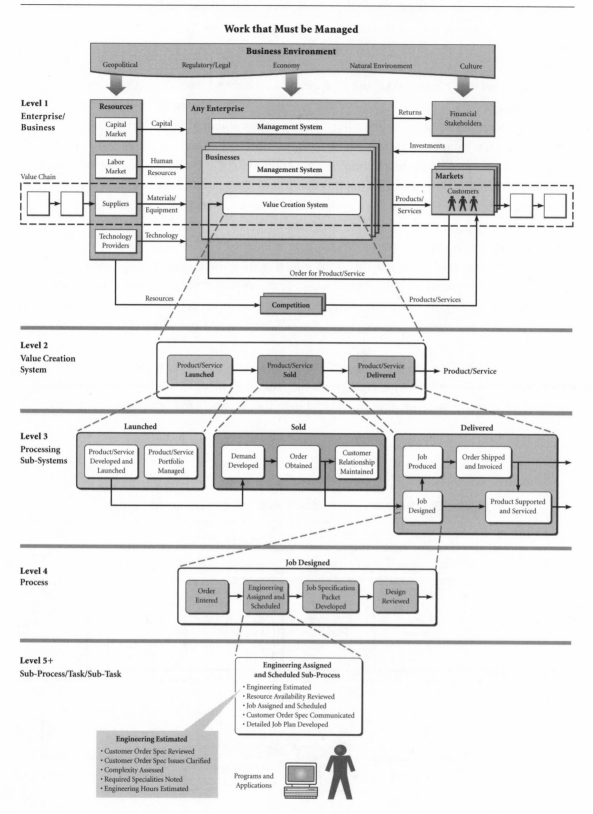

Figure 5.3 (*Continued*)

Corresponding Work Management System

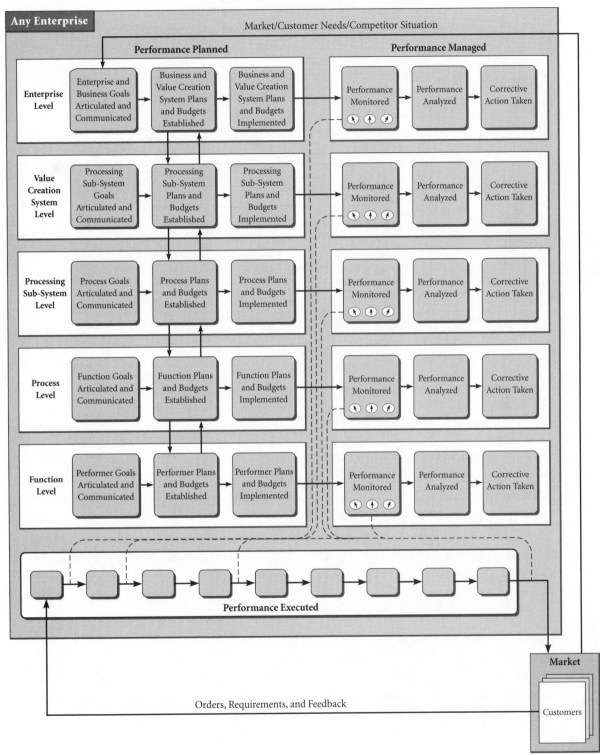

Process Management in the Value Creation Context   **101**

Figure 5.4 Managing Two Dimensions

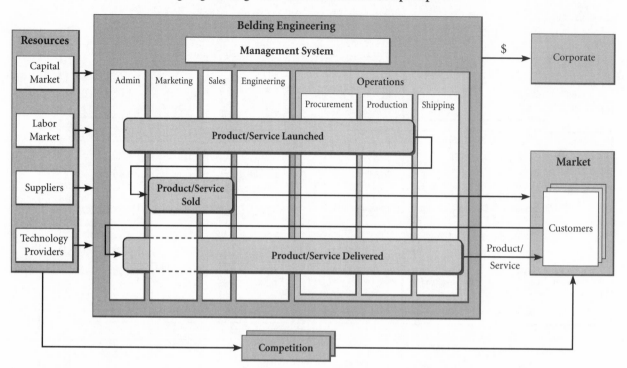

Belding Engineering Value-Resource Relationship Map

When you understand process management as part of a total performance system that links organization goals, plans, resources, and actions to processes, functions, jobs, and performers, you can see that it can't succeed simply as an additional staff responsibility within an existing system. Process management is the critical element in making a management system effective, for it links performance and results to organizational vision, mission, and strategy by defining what is needed from the processes (Levels 2–4) and integrating management controls throughout those processes. Achieving such an integrated performance management system is far more than a technology project: it is the design and management of both critical dimensions (value and resources) of any organization. Technology can help such a design and management effort, but it is no substitute for the accountability, judgment, and decision making of executives.

Now, again using Belding Engineering, we show you two approaches to process management in a value creation context. Let's start with a quick overview of the Belding management system before S. K. Owens became the CEO.

BASELINE BELDING ENGINEERING SERVICES

Before the new CEO's arrival, Performance Planned at Belding Engineering consisted of an annual planning process completed over a four-month period. The major steps were

1. Belding CEO received earnings guidelines/expectations from Corporate.

2. CEO and the Director of Finance met individually with VPs to discuss operating and budget goals for each function for the next year.

3. VPs and their functions prepared draft budgets for the next fiscal year (total and by month). These proposed budgets were sent to the Director of Finance, who consolidated them into a draft Belding budget.

4. The CEO and Director of Finance then met individually with each VP to bring each proposed budget "into line."

5. The Finance Department published the final Belding budget.

The Performance Managed system consisted of the following:

1. The previous CEO held a monthly Operations Review with the VPs and occasionally a quarterly one-day "retreat."

2. The agenda included a review of company budget, sales performance, and shipments. Gaps between planned and actual performance were discussed, along with possible corrective and preventive actions.

3. Follow-up meetings were held with individual VPs as appropriate.

The function performance measures at the monthly operations review are summarized in Table 5.1.

Belding Management System: First Iteration

As described in Chapter Four, the CEO Owens launched a Value Creation Architecture initiative after two months with Belding. A major management issue that he continues to see is that executives and managers are managing resources without any value creation context, which results in function maximization and total organization performance system sub-optimization. Owens is concerned about the value delivered to customers (products on time that work) and Corporate (earnings). The vice presidents are primarily concerned with meeting their resource goals.

One outcome of the VCA effort was identification of the Order to Cash process (that is, Belding work activities from the time the customer agrees to order a product until Belding receives payment for the order) as a core process that was in dire trouble and needed to be articulated, redesigned, and managed.

With the assistance of the Corporate Performance Support Group, Belding designed an Order to Cash process and corresponding Order to Cash Process Management System. The process and management system were implemented simultaneously. (The process design and process management system design methodology followed by Belding is described in Chapters Six through Ten.)

A major prerequisite for establishing process management for the Order to Cash process was first gaining agreement and understanding that Order to Cash is in fact a primary cross-functional process that requires a cross-functional management system. That may seem obvious, but it is not an easy concept to grasp if an organization has not learned how to think about itself in process terms. Further, it was challenging for managers to understand that in order to achieve an effective process management system, Belding was imposing a horizontal value creation process (Order to Cash) on the vertical resource management structure of the business (see Figure 5.5).

CEO Owens went about this by appointing an Order to Cash Process Management Team consisting of the VPs of Sales, Engineering, Procurement, Production, and Shipping (and supported by functional managers as required). The

Table 5.1 Director of Finance Function Performance Measures

Finance	Marketing	Sales	Engineering	Operations	Procurement	Production	Shipping
Admin budget (Plan/Actual)	Marketing budget (Plan/Actual)	Revenues (Plan/Actual) Sales budget (Plan/Actual)	New product development projects (Plan/Actual) Engineering budget (Plan/Actual)	Units shipped (Plan/Actual) Cost per unit shipped (Plan/Actual) Operations budget (Plan/Actual)	Materials costs per unit shipped (Plan/Actual) Procurement budget (Plan/Actual)	Production cost per unit shipped (Plan/Actual) Production budget (Plan/Actual)	Shipping cost per unit shipped (Plan/Actual) Shipping budget (Plan/Actual)

Figure 5.5 Belding Engineering Value Versus Resource Dimension

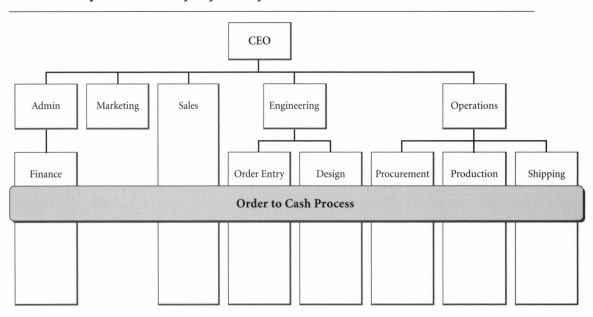

team was chaired by the VP of Operations and supported by a Performance Architect from the Corporate Performance Support Group. (More on the performance support group and performance architect in Chapter Ten.) The Process Management Team is accountable for ensuring that the Order to Cash process meets the goals that have been established for the process and for aligning those process goals to function goals. This means that the appointed functional VPs are accountable for two sets of goals: the usual functional resource (that is, budget) goals *and* the cross-functional Order to Cash process (that is, value creation) goals. The CEO signaled his performance priorities by establishing the following bonus compensation policy:

- Quarterly bonuses (as has always been the policy)
- VPs' bonus compensation was weighted (new):
  - 60% for Order to Cash process performance (value management)
  - 40% for achieving functional budget performance (resource management)

- Even if functional budget goals were met during a quarter, that bonus was not paid if the Order to Cash goals were not met. (*new*)

Performance Planned Process

The new Performance Planned process was constructed as follows (see Figure 5.6):

- Belding financial and customer satisfaction goals set.
- Belding financial goals converted into appropriate function financial and operational goals (first approximation of a budget).

Figure 5.6 Performance Planned Process

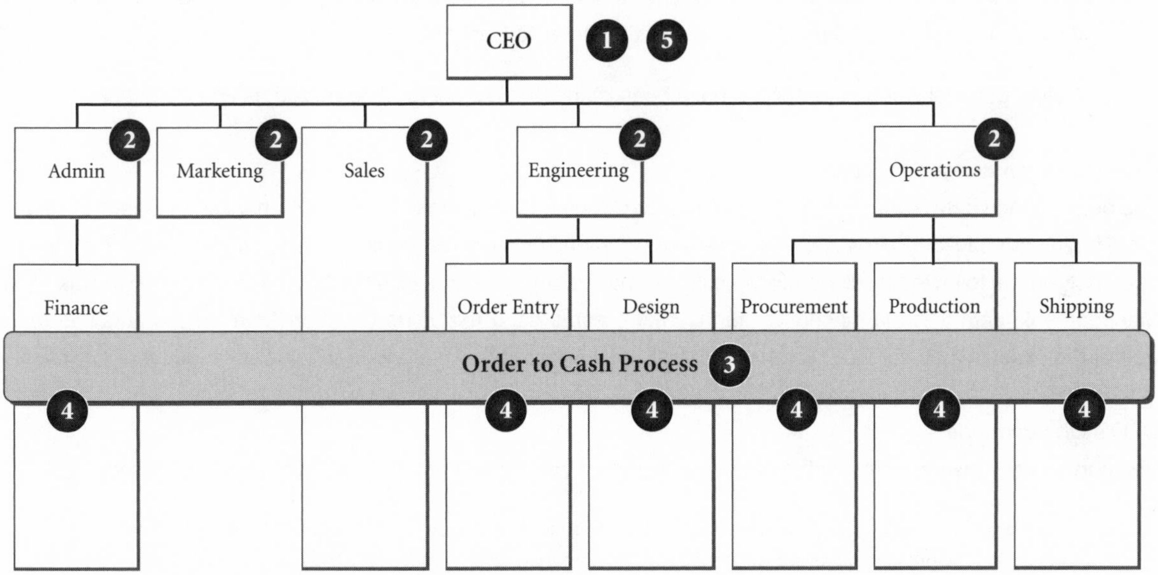

1. Belding financial and customer satisfaction goals set
2. Belding financial goals converted into appropriate function financial and operational goals (Approximation One)
3. Belding and customer satisfaction goals converted into Order to Cash process goals, including:
   - On-time delivery
   - Order/Job profitability
   - Rework
     - Number of jobs
     - Total cost
4. Using the Cross-Functional Order to Cash Process Map:
   - The Process Management Team specifies what they need from participating functions.
   - FMT negotiates budget-performance trade-offs with the PMT.
5. The Belding annual budget is finalized.

- Belding financial and customer satisfaction goals converted into Order to Cash process goals, including:
  - On-time delivery
  - Order/job profitability
  - Rework
    ◦ Number of jobs
    ◦ Total cost

Using the Cross-Functional Order to Cash Process Map, the Order to Cash Process Management Team determines what performance it needs from each participating function to meet the Order to Cash process goals set by the president. Each function VP then assesses the impact of the Order to Cash demands on his or her "first approximation" budget. The function VP negotiates budget-performance trade-offs with the Process Management Team. The result is some combination of the following:

- Modification in the goals of the Order to Cash process

- Modification in the demands made by the Order to Cash Process Management Team on various functions

- An increase in total function budgets by the president or the redistribution of resource monies between various functions to accommodate the requirements of the Order to Cash process

Once all negotiations and adjustments have been made, the annual Belding budget is finalized.

Performance Managed Process

The performance data available to manage Order to Cash process performance is summarized in Figure 5.7. Note that there is data on end-of-process performance and on each sub-process within Order to Cash. The performance management routine followed by all participants is summarized in the matrix in Table 5.2. Both the Order to Cash Process Management Team and the functional management teams used the Value Creation Architecture documents on the wall of the executive conference room to troubleshoot poor performance and identify root causes for correction.

CEO's Observations

Six months after the Order to Cash management system was implemented, the CEO's observations were

> We are making progress. It took two months for the Process Management Team to isolate the problems impacting rework and customer satisfaction. We determined which products, which engineering groups, which sales regions and which production lines were contributing to the problems. Having performance goals, our previously developed value creation architecture and good performance data made the difference. And there were no bonuses paid out in the first quarter, which provided some extra motivation. It took another three months to make the necessary changes in how the process is executed. We have already made modifications on how the planning interface between the Process Management Team and functions will work in the next annual planning cycle. And maximum bonuses were paid out at the end of Quarter Two.

A big issue that Owens had hoped to address with this change was the lack of cross-functional collaboration. Asked whether any progress had been achieved on this front, Owens said,

> I have sat in on several of the monthly Process Management Team meetings and both quarterly meetings. The level of collaboration and communication that has evolved between participants is extraordinary. The team uses the same conference room I use for my monthly Leadership Team meetings and I am pleased to see how

Figure 5.7 Order-to-Cash Process Performance Data

Function Indicators for Product Delivered	Administration	Engineering	Operations	Procurement	Production	Shipping	Process Measures
Job Designed		• Design meets spec • Rework due to Design • Failures due to Design • Jobs designed on time • Design costs • Job costs					• Production errors • Failures due to Production • Failures due to Design • Invoice errors • Products shipped on time • Customer order spec to ship cycle time • On time service/replacement • Cycle time to completed service/replacement • Cycle time to issue resolution • Job costs • Warranty costs • Service costs • Customer service costs
Job Produced				• Materials available on time • Inventory	• Product meets spec • Rework due to Production • Failures due to Production • 1st pass yield • Jobs produced on time • Production costs • Job costs		
Order Shipped and Invoiced	• Invoice timeliness • Invoice accuracy • Cycle time invoice to cash • Late payments due to errors					• Jobs shipped on time • Shipping costs	
Product Supported and Serviced	• Cycle time to issue resolution	• Customer service costs • Warranty costs • Cycle time to issue resolution	• On time service	• Service costs—materials	• Service costs—labor • On time service or replacement • Cycle time to completed service or replacement		

Table 5.2 Performance Management Routine

Component	Activities per Time Period			
	Daily/Weekly	*Monthly*	*Quarterly*	*Annually*
Process Management Team		Review monthly process performance Review issues Ask questions Take/recommend action Update database	Review quarterly process performance Review issues Ask questions Change goals and/or resource allocation as appropriate Update database	Review annual process performance Set process improvement goals for next year Establish process goals and resource requirements for next year
Process Performance and Management Database	Database updated	Database updated	Database updated	Database updated
Function Management Team	Monitor process and job performance as appropriate Take action as necessary Raise issues with the Process Management Team as appropriate Update database	Implement changes as directed by the Process Management Team	Adjust goals and/or resource allocation as appropriate	Recommend process improvements and resource requirement modifications to the Process Management Team
Performance Architect	Monitor process performance Respond to requests for help Conduct research for improving process performance Make recommendations to the Process Management Team as appropriate Update database	Support implementation of changes recommended by the Process Management Team	Support implementation of changes recommended by the Process Management Team	Recommend process improvements to the Process Management Team

they rely on the value creation architecture documentation to clarify what they are talking about. In their case, it is clearly true that "a picture is worth a thousand words."

Pros and Cons of the Belding Engineering Management System

Pros   Performance of the Order to Cash process is essential to Belding's performance. The Process Management System designed for the Order to Cash process achieves linkage between this Level 4 process and Level 2 of the business, where customer expectations and enterprise requirements are visible. Process management for Order to Cash has become a part of enterprise management, linked through the enterprise Performance Planned and Performance Managed systems.

Cons   Having a process management team for the Order to Cash process could be viewed as a "bolt-on" addition to the existing Belding management system, and after some period of time, Owens began to worry that this was what he had inadvertently created. He had no other mechanism for getting the VPs of the various functions that participated in the Order to Cash process to talk with each other and make collaborative decisions, and this team created a venue for such management activities. But many of the real decisions were still being made back in functional silos. So eventually, Owens had to move to something more far-reaching to truly integrate process management into business management at Belding.

There currently is no mechanism in Belding Engineering to see that the Launched, Sold, and Delivered sub-systems are aligned. Because of the emphasis on a single (although essential) process, the allocation of resources to the Order to Cash process could negatively affect other essential performance goals, such as new product development and market development. Thus, the Order to Cash focus could be contributing to the sub-optimization of the total Belding performance system. There is no good way to ascertain this without a broader approach to process management.

The bottom line is that while it is beneficial to link up one important process—Order to Cash—to enterprise goals and customer expectations, there are still so many unlinked activities and so many opportunities for sub-optimization that this achievement is far from the true goal of enterprise-wide performance management. *In truth, there should be no such thing as "process management"—just management.* An effective enterprise performance management system would link all levels of the Value Creation Hierarchy, thus ensuring that the work done at all levels inside the organization results in production of the goods and services that customers want, at a cost and profit level that the organization desires.

Current Belding Management System

Note: The management system described in this section is the focus of our forthcoming companion book for managers and executives. We will provide a high-level overview below, as it provides context for the design of a process management system, but the details of designing an entire management system will be found in the other book.

It has now been four years since S. K. Owens arrived at Belding Engineering Services as its new CEO. Based on the organization's success in managing value creation and resource allocation in concert for the Order to Cash process, the president decided to extend that management notion to the entire company. In the context of the Value Creation Hierarchy, the president has embarked on the design of a management system that will link all five levels, from enterprise to performer.

With the continuing help of the Corporate Performance Support Group, Belding updated its documents of the Belding value dimension. Specific documents that are continually used in the management of Belding include many of the documents created to define its VCA—in particular, the Super-System Map, Business Process Framework (BPF), and Cross-Functional Value Creation Map. (Templates of these appear in Figure 4.1.)

The management structure for managing the total Belding Value Creation System is intended to fully integrate value creation management with the existing business management team structure without creating burdensome bureaucracy. The CEO's direct reports, overseeing all Belding functions, are accountable for achieving financial and operating goals through management of the Value Creation System.

Executives on the Leadership Team (one each for Launched, Sold, and Delivered) have been assigned as the key links to functions as regards performance planning and management. This level is the link between value and resource management. Each of these three executives heads up a cross-functional management team. (The Order to Cash Process Management Team morphed into the Delivered Management Team.)

Process management teams were also formed for sizable cross-functional processes making up Launched, Sold, and Delivered that cannot be adequately managed by a function. For example, the Customer Committed process (that is, the sales process) can most likely be managed by the Sales function, without the need for a separate process management team. By contrast, the Product/Service Released process within the Launched sub-system involves several functions to produce the necessary outputs and could likely benefit from a process management team, reporting to the Launched Management Team. The Leadership Team was careful not to allow an uncontrolled growth of "process management teams" for processes that did not warrant it.

The Leadership Team also regarded one of its most important tasks as ensuring that process initiatives served to strengthen Belding's competitive advantages. They took to heart Michael Porter's dictum that all organizational "activities" (that is, processes) should fit and reinforce the company's strategy, so a large part of their role was to look at proposed improvements in light of strategic fit and overall impact on Belding's entire Value Creation Architecture.

Performance Planned Process

Performance planning is about aligning and allocating vertical resources to the horizontal Value Creation System. Process goals are set first. Then resource goals are set to support accomplishment of the process goals. Planning follows the numbered sequence shown in Figure 5.8, and works as follows:

1. Enterprise goals are set by the Leadership Team, based on customer requirements and financial stakeholder expectations.

Figure 5.8 Performance Planned Sequence

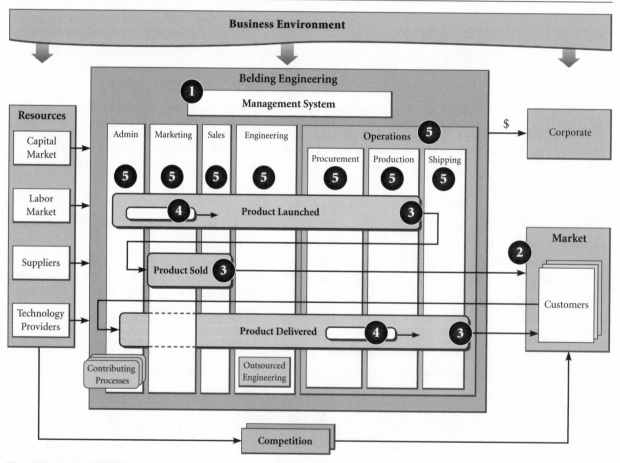

The critical role of Belding management is:

1. The alignment of the organization's goals, strategies and priorities with the reality of the super-system (Management of the **Adaptive System** through strategy formulation)

2. The effective and efficient operation of the internal processing system to meet customer and financial stakeholder needs—that is, manage the work (Management of the **Processing System** through Value Creation Management)

2. Goals for the value creation system and primary processing sub-systems (that is, Launched, Sold, and Delivered) are set to achieve enterprise goals.

3. Process goals are set to support the primary processing sub-system goals.

4. Function goals are set to support individual process and primary processing sub-system goals.

5. Sub-function and individual goals are set to support function and process goals.

Performance Managed Process

The meeting agendas of the Leadership Team have been altered to allow adequate time for reviewing, troubleshooting, and decision making of Belding's VCS rather than having functional updates as the dominant subject. The management of value and resources goes like this:

1. Ask: Are we meeting the value goals?

2. If not, find out why not, troubleshooting down through the layers of process to the contributing resource centers that are performing the value-adding work.

The performance data available to manage the various components of the Belding Value Creation System are summarized in Figure 5.9. These data are made available to appropriate executives and management teams via performance tracking reports.

CEO's Observations

One year after the Value Creation Management System was implemented, CEO Owens commented that the entire set of Value Creation Architecture maps provides some capabilities that he and the Leadership Team did not have before: "These architecture maps are a powerful set of views for the business, but even more, they are analytical and decision-making tools for my executives."

Among the benefits these views provided were that they:

- Enable detailed analysis of proposed changes (for example, strategy, organization restructuring, outsourcing)

- Enable detailed analysis of potential impact of trends in the super-system

  - What changes are required to respond to such trends

  - What-if scenarios

- Aid identification of opportunities to improve processes or groups of processes

- Aid identification of where in our Value Creation System (Launched, Sold, Delivered) we can build in more competitive advantages

- Provide an excellent framework for tracking the various initiatives being carried out in the organization

  Owens added,

> Within the documentation that depicts our Value Creation Architecture, our jumping off point
> for decision making is the Cross-Functional Value Creation map for each product line. For any
> of these businesses, it shows how every function impacts the customer in all three phases of
> the Value Creation System. Any group or management team can troubleshoot any customer
> issue using this map.

Figure 5.9 VCS Performance Data

VP Measures (Old Belding Engineering)		• Admin Budget (Plan/Actual)	• Mktg Budget (Plan/Actual)	• Revenues (Plan/Actual) • Sales Budget (Plan/Actual)	• Engineering Budget (Plan/Actual) • NPD Projects (Plan/Actual)	• Operations Budget (Plan/Actual) • Units Shipped (Plan/Actual) • Cost Per Unit Shipped (Plan/Actual)
Function Indicators for Product Launched	New Product Developed and Launched	• Systems Capability (to Support New Product) Available On-time	• Business Case Accuracy • Research Project Budgets (Plan/Actual) • Research Project Plans (Plan/Actual) • Product Support Effectiveness • Product Support Costs • Product Support On-time • Product Launch Budget (Plan/Actual)	• Sale Rep Product Training Completed On-time	• Product Performance—Failures • Product Performance—Sustaining Eng Costs in 1st Year • % Technology Reuse • % Materials Reuse • % Mfg Process Reuse • Design Costs for New Product • Design Project Plan (Plan/Actual) • Spec Pkge Accuracy	
	Product Portfolio Managed		• Product Analysis Quality • Product Support Costs (existing products) • Product Support Effectiveness (existing products)	• % Install Base Transitioned	• Sustaining Eng Costs • Design Project Plan (Plan/Actual) • Materials Cost Reductions Realized • Mfg Cost Reductions Realized	
Function Indicators for Product Sold	Demand Generated		• Lead Quality (% qualified, % closed) • # Leads by Source • Cost Per Lead • Rev Value of Qualified Leads			
	Customer Committed			• Orders—Revenue (Plan/Actual) • Orders—Units (Plan/Actual) • Cost Per Sale • Close Ratio • Proposals Submitted • COS Accuracy—Rework Due to COS Errors and Omissions		
	Customer Relationship Managed			• Additional Sales • Referrals • Account Plans (Plan/Actual)		
Function Indicators for Product Delivered	Job Designed				• Design meets Spec • Rework due to Design • Failures due to Design • Jobs Designed On-time • Design Costs • Job Costs	
	Job Produced					
	Order Shipped and Invoiced	• Invoice Timeliness • Invoice Accuracy • CT Invoice to Cash • Late Payments Due to Errors				
	Product Supported and Serviced	• CT to Issue Resolution			• Customer Service Costs • Warranty Costs • CT to Issue Resolution	• On-time Service

			L, S, D Measures	VCS Measures
• Procurement Budget (Plan/Actual) • Materials Costs Per Unit Shipped (Plan/Actual)	• Production Budget (Plan/Actual) • Production Cost Per Unit Shipped (Plan/Actual)	• Shipping Budget (Plan/Actual) • Shipping Cost Per Unit Shipped (Plan/Actual)		
• Prototype Materials Available On-time	• Prototypes Production On-time • Prototype 1st Pass Yield • Prototype Labor Costs • Mfg Process Design Available On-time • Mfg Capacity Available On-time • Service Capacity Available On-time • Mfg Cost Reductions Realized		• Market Share (Projections/Actual) • Product Performance • Failures • Warranties • Margins • Sustaining Costs • Product Developed and Launched On-time and CT • Product Developed and Launched Costs (Plan/Actual)	• Customer Satisfaction • Product Met Spec • Returns for Specs not Met • Rework for Specs not Met • Complaints for Specs not Met • On-time Delivery • On-time Service • Product Failures • Invoice Errors • Rev—Product Shipped and Invoiced • # Units—Products Shipped and Invoiced
			• COS Errors • Product Meets Customer Needs • Returns for Wrong Product Specified • Orders—Revenue • Orders—Units • Cost of Sales	• Product Margin • Market Share
• Materials Available On-time • Inventory	• Product Meets Spec • Rework Due to Production • Failures Due to Production • 1st Pass Yield • Jobs Produced On-time • Production Costs • Job Costs	• Jobs Shipped On-time • Shipping Costs	• Production Errors • Failures Due to Production • Failures Due to Design • Invoice Errors • Products Shipped On-time • COS to Ship CT • On-time Service/Replacement • CT to Completed Service/Replacement • CT to Issue Resolution • Job Costs • Warranty Costs • Service Costs • Customer Service Costs	
• Service Costs—Materials	• Service Costs—Labor • On-time Service or Replacement • CT to Completed Service or Replacement			

And with these maps, every proposed change to organization structure, policy or process can be quickly assessed as to impact on customers, suppliers, or partners; what will be impacted internally (people, processes, functions); and who needs to be involved in assessing, designing and implementing the changes.

Features of the Value Creation Management System

In summary, these are some of the major highlights of the management system adapted at Belding:

- Collaboration is no longer an option.

- The job of process management is fully integrated into the roles of executives and managers at every level of the organization.

- The Value Creation Architecture documents are used by executives and managers to plan, analyze, and make decisions about the organization's strategies, direction, structure, work processes, and performance.

- The Value Creation Management System incorporates a formal mechanism for the selection, initiation, and management of all change efforts, thereby focusing scarce resources on those change activities that matter most.

- Various staff resources, each with their own agendas and methods, are integrated into one group, empowered by the Belding Leadership Team and accountable for the maintenance of the Value Creation System at all levels.

CLOSING POINTS

For those who design and implement process management systems (or would like a better way to do this), these are some of the implications of the approach we have outlined in this chapter:

1. We have described here the evolution of a management system.

   - Stage 1: Enterprise-wide management of resources only

   - Stage 2: Value and resource management for a single but significant cross-functional process (that is, Belding's first iteration)

   - Stage 3: Enterprise-wide integrated management of resources and value (that is, Belding's current management system)

The reason for this evolutionary approach is practicality. Nearly every organization we know of and have worked with to install process management has done so after gaining some practical experience in applying process improvement methodology and then building the beginnings of a process management system on top of that redesigned process.

In organizations in which the decision from the outset has been to install a companywide management system of the sort we have described here, success was still possible but harder to attain. In part, that is because without some experience in process improvement first, the organization has not really learned the language or benefits of a process approach to business. Tackling process management first keeps the concept of process in the theoretical realm, where it's harder for people to understand why they are creating this new approach to management. But with a process improvement project already conducted that has yielded tangible results, it is much easier to convince people that the process approach is of great potential value.

2. There is no need for a process governance system.

This approach integrates management of process into management of the business. This approach is the exact reverse of efforts we have seen in companies that get into process improvement and then attempt to install "process governance" because they recognize the need for some kind of control over the wildly growing demands for process projects and that, once designed, a business process doesn't manage itself. Those efforts in all cases result in a "bolt-on" addition to management rather than integration of process management into business management.

We have found this approach to process management effective because it produces a gradual but lasting transformation to a process-managed organization.

PART TWO

Designing or Improving the Value Machine

CHAPTER SIX

A Framework and Methodology for VCS Design

Historically, process work has focused on the design, redesign, or improvement of individual processes and sub-processes at Levels 4 and 5 of the Value Creation Hierarchy (VCH) (Figure 6.1). But when we view process in the context of value creation, the future becomes the effectiveness of the value creation system from Level 2 through Level 5 of any organization's VCH. This means addressing any and all performance aspects of the Value Creation Architecture (VCA). This is the "new world" of process improvement. It's a tall order and requires a considerable discipline, starting with a robust process design/improvement methodology.

In this chapter and the three following it, we present:

- The Effective Process Framework (EPF), a guiding model for improvement work
- The Rummler Process Methodology (RPM) and critical success factors
- A detailed project walk-through
- Applications of RPM to different process improvement challenges
- RPM and current BPM practices

Figure 6.1 The Past and Future of Process Improvement

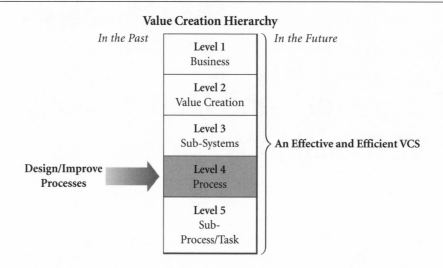

MAJOR REQUIREMENT: A METHODOLOGY FOR THE VALUE CREATION SYSTEM

The design or improvement of the Value Creation System is serious stuff with serious consequences if it is done badly. Messing with the Value Creation System requires a serious process methodology. We are talking about the systematic application of a comprehensive, documented, and proven approach and set of procedures for analyzing, designing, and improving any business process. Such a methodology will:

- Guide the correct definition and scope of a process in the context of a business's total Value Creation Hierarchy
- Address those variables identified in the Effective Process Framework as critical to process performance

Without such a methodology, there is no chance of "process" realizing its potential for improving business results. It appears to us, however, that a great deal of the work currently done in the field of BPM/process is off target and not getting the job done. Some of the problems we've noticed include:

- There is little systematic work to link process performance to organization results.
- There is a ritualistic application of tools and techniques sans any comprehensive methodology or framework.
- There is more interest in BPM software application packages than in the underlying processes.

- There is an assumption that automating a process means it has been improved.

- There is the borrowing of a few models and thoughts from a variety of sources and slamming them together into a PowerPoint deck and calling it a methodology.

We present a *real* methodology here, one that covers all of the required phases—definition, analysis, design, and implementation—and the design of process management teams. We call it the Rummler Process Methodology (RPM).

EVOLUTION OF THE METHODOLOGY

The Rummler Process Methodology is the culmination of twenty-plus years of process work by the PDL partners and their clients. It evolved as follows.

Based on his industrial engineering background of the 1950s, his performance analysis and improvement work during the 1960s and 1970s and the concept of "organizations as systems," Geary Rummler conceived of a process modeling (including the now widely used "swimlane" format) and improvement methodology, which was applied in the early 1980s in such organizations as GTE, Douglas Aircraft, and Motorola.

Alan Ramias, an internal consultant at Motorola, became the co-architect of this fledgling "process methodology" as it was applied to a wide variety of critical businesses at Motorola that "changed the way the company does business worldwide, helped us save more than $950 million in the last few years and played a leading role in Motorola's winning the Malcolm Baldrige National Quality Award."[1]

This same methodology became the basis of the Rummler-Brache process improvement methodology described in 1990 in *Improving Performance: How to Manage the White Space on the Organization Chart* by Geary Rummler and Alan Brache.[2]

The methodology was extended to include designing and improving processing *systems*, development of process metrics, and design of process management systems. This version of methodology was applied worldwide through affiliates in a dozen countries. Hundreds of process improvement facilitators were trained in the approach. Eventually, the methodology was adopted as the global process methodology of such companies as HP, Dow Chemical, Citibank, 3M, and ABB.

In 2005, Geary Rummler, Rick Rummler, Cherie Wilkins, and Alan Ramias joined forces to pool their knowledge and experience to respond to new opportunities for "process." The result is a new process improvement platform that includes the simultaneous analysis and design of a business process, related information technology, process management, and change management. This new platform is based on two old values:

1. Process work should be done in the context of organizations as systems.

2. Business results are the number 1 goal.

THE EFFECTIVE PROCESS FRAMEWORK (EPF)

The Value Creation System is a network of processes, described in greater and greater levels of detail as depicted in the tools of the Value Creation Architecture (see Chapter Four). To design new processes or improve existing ones, one must understand what makes a process effective and efficient. We have identified the eight major variables that determine the effectiveness and efficiency of any work process:

1. Desired process outputs/results
2. Process design
3. Underlying models
4. Resources
5. Inputs/triggers
6. Jobs/roles
7. Technology
8. Process Performance Management System

These variables comprise the Effective Process Framework (EPF) and are depicted in Figure 6.2 and described in Table 6.1.

Given that "process" is the fundamental building block for the Value Creation Hierarchy and is thereby scalable, from sub-process all the way up to business unit, the EPF is also scalable, as illustrated in Figure 6.3. The problem is that in the vast majority of process improvement efforts, only two or three of these variables are ever systematically addressed. Therein lies the explanation for many of the failures of work processes.

The EPF model can be easily operationalized as a template for troubleshooting poor process performance or as a process design checklist by asking the following questions:

1. Are the desired process outputs/results requirements:
   - Linked to organization and customer requirements?
   - Clear?
   - Communicated?
2. Is the *process* designed to meet output requirements?
3. Are the *underlying models* appropriate?
4. Are necessary *resources* available?
5. Do the required *inputs/triggers* meet input standards?
6. Are *jobs/roles* properly aligned and executed (including organization structure)?
7. Is the required *technology* aligned and executing?

Figure 6.2 The Effective Process Framework

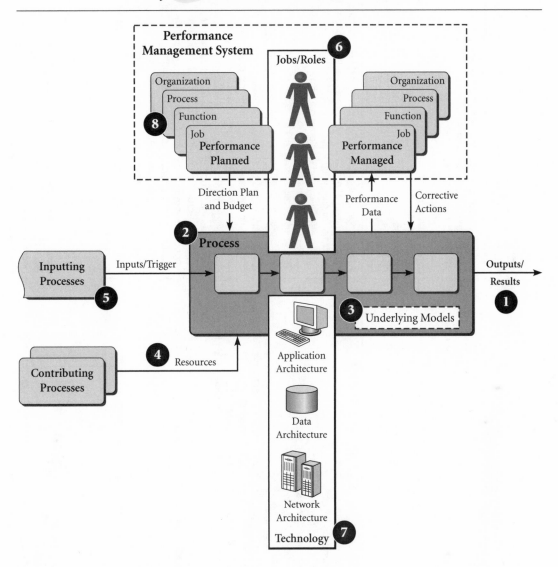

8. Is an appropriate *Process Performance Management System* in place?

- Aligned?
- Executing?

Note: We are no longer talking about "process design," but rather process *performance* design, so we address all eight of the variables, not just the design or redesign of the work process. The Effective Process Framework is an antidote to all the single-point solutions to process performance problems that have failed. The major insight and implication of the EPF is that process performance design must address all eight of these variables—no exceptions. If the

Table 6.1 Process Performance Variables

	Key Variables Affecting Process Performance	Description/Explanation	Discussion
1	Desired Process Outputs/Results	*The requirements for process outputs/results must be* Linked to organization and customer requirements (as pointed out by the Value Creation Hierarchy) Clear Communicated to all parties designing, improving, performing, and/or managing the process. Failure to meet these requirements is the greatest single contributor to process performance failure. This variable is the starting point for any process performance design or improvement effort.	The desired process outputs/results (and their requirements) are derived through a hierarchy of business Value Milestones, starting at Level 2 of the Value Creation Hierarchy. The establishment of process output/results is a key output of the "Should" Process Design Specification step of the RPM. The requirements of a process output/result fall into these dimensions or general categories: Quality Timeliness Economics Volume
2	Process Design	*The process must be designed to meet output requirements.* Common process design disconnects include: "Batch" versus continuous flow Serial process flow versus parallel flow Unnecessary (non-value-added) steps Redundant (non-value-added) steps Bottleneck operation	When designing/improving a work process, keep in mind the RPM definition of *process*: a construct or artifice for articulating and organizing work so that it Can be effectively and efficiently performed (to achieve a business valued milestone) Can be effectively managed (Where practicable) provides a competitive advantage
3	Underlying Models	*The underlying models of a process must be appropriate for the desired process outputs/results and resulting process design.* Examples of "underlying models" in a process include: Staffing load model for a call center, retail store, restaurant, or similar service business The inventory reordering model for a retail organization or production function It is critical that the algorithms basic to these models match the requirements of the process	We call attention to this variable because: Occasionally the cause of poor process performance is misdiagnosed as being "process design" when, in fact, the overall design of the process flow is appropriate but the root cause is an inappropriate underlying model such as the "inventory reorder" point. (If a vendor supply time has lengthened, it may require ordering more parts, sooner, in order to avert a part shortage and line shut-down.) When designing or redesigning a process, you must align the critical underlying models possibly buried in each process step.
4	Resources	*Resources necessary to perform the process must be available.* These include: Equipment Material/supplies Staffing	Resources are the output of some contributing or supplying processes.
5	Inputs/Triggers	*Inputs/triggers must meet input standards.* Processes are triggered by: Events (a customer inquiry, an order, an invoice, and so on) Time (process is performed on the first day of each month)	Inputting events may be the output of some internal process or external source. If the source is an internal process, there may be an opportunity to clarify, reestablish, or negotiate input standards to achieve desired process results.

#	Variable	Description	Commentary
		In the case of an event, there are requirements or specifications for the input that is to be transformed by the process. The process is designed to produce the desired output given that input. A cause of a process failing to produce desired outputs can be the inputs not meeting standards or requirements. The standards for an input can include: Size Timing Quality dimension Volume	However, if the source is external to the organization, reestablishing or negotiating input standards may not be possible, in which case either process output requirement or process design criteria will have to be altered. The establishment of process input/trigger standards (or expectations) is a key output of the "Should" Process Design Specification of the RPM.
6	Jobs/Roles	*Jobs/roles must be properly aligned and executed.* There are two elements that must be aligned: 1. The jobs/roles must be aligned with the process. The job/role outputs and requirements must be aligned with the process and relevant process step outputs and requirements. The job/role must be appropriately designed to perform the required process step. The job/role must have access to the necessary resources, tools, and technology to produce the desired outputs. All the above conditions apply to the hierarchy of jobs relevant to the performance of the process. Are the support and management jobs aligned with the job interacting directly with the process? 2. The individual performing the job/role (at any level in the job/role hierarchy) must: Know and accept the desired job outcomes and requirements Have the knowledge/skills necessary to perform as desired Have the capacity (physical, mental, emotional) to perform as desired Receive the feedback necessary to determine if they are performing as desired Experience a balance of positive and negative consequences that supports the desired performance	Design and execution of this variable in process performance is frequently the most overlooked and inadequately designed. Failure to address this variable adequately will assure continual poor process performance and disastrous process improvement implementation. Certain disciplines and approaches to "process improvement" (note: not process *performance* improvement)—most notably IT and Six Sigma—are notorious for ignoring this variable.
7	Technology	*Technology is properly aligned and executing.* Technology is an increasingly relevant variable to process performance. Technology and humans, together and separately, constitute the two performers of all process steps.	To date, IT is probably the greatest ignorer of the other seven variables of the EPF.
8	Process Performance Management System	*Process Performance Management System (PPMS) must be in place, aligned, and executing.* Figure 6.2 displays a hierarchy of Performance Planned and Performance Managed systems that must be in place, aligned, and executing at the Job, Function, Process, and Organization levels. The basic component at each level is the same: The Performance Planned function sets direction and assures the necessary capability to achieve stated goals. The Performance Managed function monitors performance, assesses and closes gaps between planned and actual performance.	One of the common pitfalls in attempting to build and implement a Process Performance Management System is to build it in a vacuum, not linked to Organization, Function and Job Management. Such a PPMS will fail.

Figure 6.3 The VCH and Key Variables Requirements

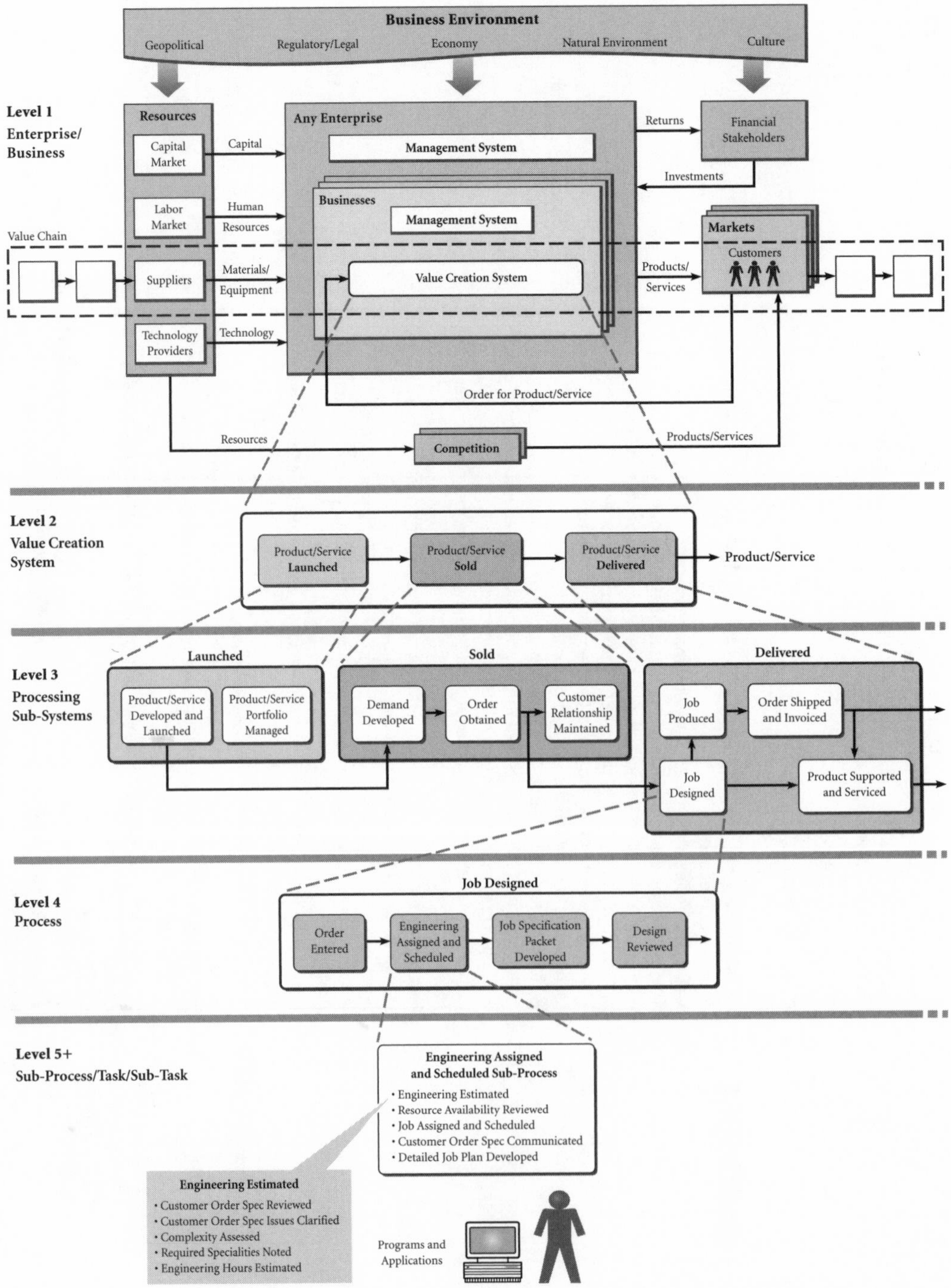

Business Environment

Geopolitical   Regulatory/Legal   Economy   Natural Environment   Culture

Level 1
Enterprise/
Business

Resources
- Capital Market — Capital
- Labor Market — Human Resources
- Suppliers — Materials/Equipment
- Technology Providers — Technology

Any Enterprise
- Management System
- Businesses
  - Management System
  - Value Creation System

Returns — Financial Stakeholders — Investments

Markets — Customers — Products/Services

Value Chain

Order for Product/Service

Resources — Competition — Products/Services

Level 2
Value Creation
System

Product/Service Launched → Product/Service Sold → Product/Service Delivered → Product/Service

Level 3
Processing
Sub-Systems

Launched
- Product/Service Developed and Launched
- Product/Service Portfolio Managed

Sold
- Demand Developed → Order Obtained → Customer Relationship Maintained

Delivered
- Job Produced → Order Shipped and Invoiced
- Job Designed → Product Supported and Serviced

Level 4
Process

Job Designed
- Order Entered → Engineering Assigned and Scheduled → Job Specification Packet Developed → Design Reviewed

Level 5+
Sub-Process/Task/Sub-Task

Engineering Assigned and Scheduled Sub-Process
- Engineering Estimated
- Resource Availability Reviewed
- Job Assigned and Scheduled
- Customer Order Spec Communicated
- Detailed Job Plan Developed

Engineering Estimated
- Customer Order Spec Reviewed
- Customer Order Spec Issues Clarified
- Complexity Assessed
- Required Specialities Noted
- Engineering Hours Estimated

Programs and Applications

Figure 6.3 *(Continued)*

	Effective Process Framework Variables							
	Desired process outputs/results requirements: • Linked to organization and customer requirements • Clear • Communicated **1**	Process is designed to meet output requirements **2**	Appropriate underlying models **3**	Resources are available **4**	Inputs/triggers meet input standards **5**	Jobs/roles are properly aligned and executed (includes management jobs/roles) **6**	Technology is properly aligned and executed **7**	Process Performance Management System (PPMS) • In place • Aligned • Executed **8**
Belding Engineering								
Value Creation System								
"Delivered" Sub-System								
"Job Designed" Process								
"Engineering Assigned and Scheduled" Sub-Process								

goal is improved *process performance*, you cannot improve or operate on any one of these variables in a vacuum. The ultimate value of process is as the *integrator* of the variables necessary for value creation and organization improvement.

The Effective Process Framework has implications for those many disciplines that attempt to improve process performance from their special but limited view of the process "elephant." The IT function focuses almost exclusively on the technology variable, frequently ignoring the output requirements of the process, the design of the process, and the relationship of technology to job/role requirements. Six Sigma focuses on defect fixing but often without a view of the impact of that solution on the other variables. Lean focuses on process design but frequently ignores the job and role requirements and the Process Management System. Human Resources designs systems to evaluate the performance of humans (for example, competency-based appraisal systems) but that ignore altogether any connection to job and process performance and the variables that affect them. Finally, managers in general frequently have no concept of the variables that must be aligned to get process performance. Therefore they do not engage in any systematic troubleshooting of poor process performance and exacerbate the problem by demanding attention to just one of the more visible variables (for example, some form of technology or training).

In short, if you are messing with process performance, you have the obligation to understand the whole system:

1. Where you are in the Value Creation Hierarchy
2. The variables that affect process performance

   The eight variables included in the Effective Process Framework have major implications for

- Process performance system design
- Process performance system improvement
- Process change implementation (particularly IT)
- Process management design/improvement (The process management system must be able to manage the performance of the remaining seven variables that impact process performance)

As you might suspect, those variables must be addressed in any process performance design/improvement methodology; we do that in this book. The EPF model is the foundation of the Rummler Process Methodology.

A Note on Human and Technology Performance Tools

Supporting the Effective Process Framework is a set of analysis tools that can help the process practitioner understand and diagnose two of the most important EPF variables: the human performer and technology.

The Human Performance System

Our tool for understanding, analyzing, designing, and improving human performance is the *Human Performance System* (HPS), a model that describes the variables influencing the behavior of a person in a work system.[3] The model is based on several important tenets:

- Every organization is a complex system designed to transform inputs into valued outputs for customers.

- Every performer, from CEO to line worker, inside any organization is also part of a unique personal performance system.

- When an individual fails to produce a desired outcome in an organization, it is due to the failure of one or more components of that person's HPS.

The components of any HPS are illustrated in Figure 6.4. The performer (1) is expected to produce some set of outputs (2). For each output there is a set of inputs (3). For every output produced (as well as for the action it took to make the output), there is a resulting set of consequences (4)—something that happens to the performer, which in turn is interpreted by the performer as either positive or negative. This interpretation is the key to understanding the performer's future behavior, because the HPS is governed by the behavioral law that people's behavior is affected by consequences, meaning people are likely to repeat behaviors that bring them positive consequences and also likely to avoid behaviors whose payoff is negative. The final element of the HPS is feedback (5) to the performer about the output.

This template of human performance can be used to diagnose any performance problem, and perhaps even more important, it can be used to design better jobs. Figure 6.5 presents the ideal HPS, with descriptions of each component in its ideal state.

In its usage over many years, some patterns of performance have become apparent. For example, 90% of the time, performance deficiencies that might appear to be caused by a

Figure 6.4 The Human Performance System

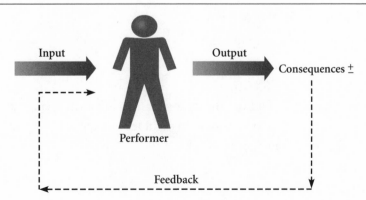

Figure 6.5 The Ideal HPS

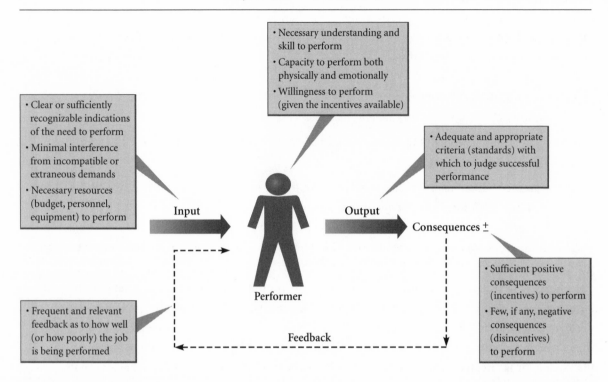

human performer, or a class of performers all doing a given job, are the result of other things that are wrong in the HPS:

- Missing materials
- No clear direction or expected output
- Interference while trying to do their work
- Lack of any meaningful feedback
- Strong negative consequences for trying to do the job
- No positive consequences for succeeding
- Broken, unavailable, obsolete equipment
- Lack of training or other preparation

It is sometimes stunning to find out the circumstances in which average performers keep on grinding away in their duties in spite of a dreadful lack of support. HPS analysis can help bring this kind of situation dramatically to light.

The Technology Performance System

In many of today's organizations, technology has become so pervasive that it functions as a frequent enabler of human performance as well as, in many cases, a performer itself. Can the HPS concept be useful here as well? Absolutely. Technology can fail to support a process or its human performance because the circumstances in which it exists don't support its effective utilization. What we call the *Technology Performance System* (TPS) can suffer from missing or poor inputs (bad data, bad data entry); unclear goals or outputs (meaning the technology may be designed to produce outputs different than what is actually desired); a bad surrounding performance environment (interface problems, software issues).

Even consequences play a role in the effective performance of a TPS, in that a system, database, or application can be misused or abused so that it does not do the job it was designed to do. Witness the jerry-rigging of legacy systems to perform tasks they were not originally made for, eventually leading to a crash-and-burn. Even machines don't necessarily just suffer silently. There is feedback, as in the HPS model, but it is received and interpreted by the maintaining function. The final element of the TPS is user impact. In the cases where IT and a human performer must produce the output together, the system performance is also influenced by the user. And of course the user's performance is equally influenced by the system. This is our connection back to the HPS. We have all seen the impact on a technology system when the users do not have the appropriate knowledge and skill to use the system. Likewise, we know that a user is likely to avoid, if possible, using a system or technology that they perceive as punishing to use—too many screens to click through, repeated entry of the same data, and so on.

Figure 6.6 depicts the components of the TPS.

RUMMLER PROCESS METHODOLOGY OVERVIEW

The Rummler Process Methodology (RPM) is summarized in the project structure shown in Figure 6.7. As represented on the horizontal axis, the RPM follows this sequence of seven phases:

1. Align

This phase identifies the business reason for doing the project, the process and its boundaries, the goals and timetable, and the project supporters and participants.

2. Analysis

This phase produces a view of the condition of the existing "is" process and determines causes of poor process performance.

Figure 6.6 The Technology Performance System

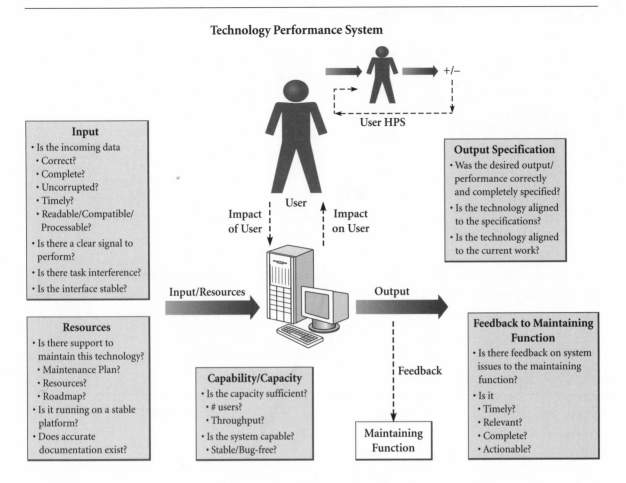

Figure 6.7 RPM Project Structure

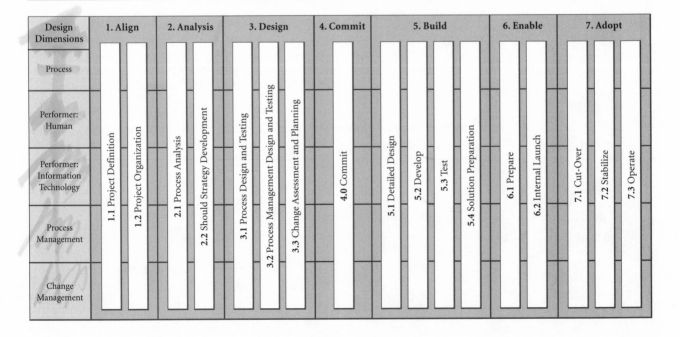

3. Design

This phase creates a process design that achieves the project goals and eliminates process deficiencies.

4. Commit

This phase prepares the organization to support the detailed design, development and implementation of the "should" process.

5. Build

This phase produces a detailed design of all the components of the "should" process and any supporting changes in policy, technology, tools, and so on.

6. Enable

This phase readies the performers (that is, users, operators, supporters, and managers) of the "should" process to undertake their roles.

7. Adopt

This phase puts the "should" process in place while adjusting the design to ensure it meets process and project objectives.

DESIGN DIMENSIONS

At each phase of a project, the Rummler Process Methodology systematically addresses five process performance design dimensions, as shown on the vertical axis in Figure 6.7. The dimensions are:

1. Process
2. Performer: Human
3. Performer: Information Technology
4. Process Management
5. Change Management

The dimension of *process design* is the organization of work to accomplish a Business Value Milestone. The criteria for judging the degree to which a process is well organized is whether the work can be performed effectively and efficiently, can be managed, and has the potential for providing competitive advantage. Process design work may include modification of:

- Process outputs/standards/requirements
- What work is done

- How work is done
- Who does the work
- Sequence of work
- Resources required
- Underlying models/algorithms
- Inputs to be processed

The dimension of *Performer: Human* addresses the specification of human contributions required to perform the designed or improved process. This may include modification of the following for a single job or role, for a hierarchy of jobs/roles, or a team of jobs/roles (including management):

- Job/role outputs or requirements
- Job/role design
- Job/role resources
- Human Performance System variables of Consequences, Feedback, and Knowledge/ Skills
- Organization structure and policies to accomplish or support the above

The dimension of *Performer: Technology* addresses the specification of technology required to perform the designed or improved process. This may include modification of:

- Data flow
- Application functionality
- User interfaces
- System interfaces
- IT strategy and systems architecture
- Technology Performance System variables of Downstream Consequences, System Feedback, and Capability/Capacity

The dimension of *Process Management* addresses the design or redesign of the Performance Planned and Managed System required for the process to perform as designed.

The dimension of *Change Management* addresses the specification and development of strategies and actions required to successfully implement the "should" process and management system.

Design Dimensions and the Effective Process Framework

Four of these dimensions address the eight variables of the Effective Process Framework (EPF), thus ensuring that the EPF is thoroughly employed in developing a comprehensive "should" process design, as shown in Table 6.2.

In addition, there is the critical dimension of "change": those practices required to ensure readiness for change and to effectively implement the changes associated with the variables listed in Table 6.2. Obviously, change management is critical during implementation (Phases 5–7). But our experience is that assessing potential barriers to change begins with Phase 1 (Align). The issues and challenges of change management and successful implementation need to be "front of mind" at the outset of a project and assessed continuously throughout all phases of the project.

Details about the RPM project phases are shown in Table 6.3.

RPM ASSUMPTIONS

Key assumptions about the application of the Rummler Process Methodology to a process design or improvement effort include:

- The ultimate objective of any such effort is the improvement of the performance of a process—the closing of some measurable gap in process results. The assumption here is that the process being designed or improved is not one of the sub-sub-sub-processes to which the methodology is frequently misapplied.
- Ideally, all phases of the project involve a cross-functional project team, numbering six to twelve members. Team members in most cases are individuals who ultimately will be involved in the performance, support, or management of the process.

Table 6.2 RPM Design Dimensions Versus EPF Variables

RPM Design Dimensions		EPF Variables	
1	Process	1	Desired process outputs/results requirements are linked, clear. and communicated
		2	Process is designed to meet output requirements
		3	Underlying models are appropriate
		4	Resources are available
		5	Inputs/triggers meet input standards
2	Performer: Human	6	Jobs/roles are properly aligned and executed
3	Performer: Technology	7	Technology is properly aligned and executing
4	Process Management	8	Process Performance Management System is in place, aligned, and executed

Table 6.3 RPM Detail Overview

Phase	Phase Objectives	Sub-Phase	Outputs/Deliverables
1.0 Align	Agreement on project objectives Agreement on scope Assignment of and commitment to appropriate and adequate resources Development of a plan with milestones and deliverables to allow for effective project management	1.1 Project Definition 1.2 Project Organization	Critical Business Issue (CBI) Critical Process Issue (CPI) Project Goals Team Structure Project Plan
2.0 Analysis	Agreement by project participants and stakeholders on: Boundaries of the process or processes affected Extent of process performance issues and effort required to improve performance Agreement on the specifications, assumptions, constraints, and development strategy for a successful "should" design	2.1 Process Analysis 2.2 "Should" Strategy Development	"Is" process documentation "Is" performance data "Is" disconnects "Is" assumptions "Is" management system documentation "Is" management system performance data "Is" management system disconnects "Should" strategy "Should" design specifications "Should" innovation ideas "Should" macro process map Updated project plan
3.0 Design	Development of change requirements which define the "should" design and supporting management system Assessment of the organization's readiness to implement the required changes Identification of an appropriate change strategy and development of a macro project and related budget	3.1 Process Design and Testing 3.2 Process Management Design and Testing 3.3 Change Assessment and Planning	"Should" process design "Should" roles/responsibilities "Should" details document "Should" change requirements "Is" to "Should" summary "Should" measures chain "Should" management calendar "Should" management roles/responsibilities "Should" performance trackers Change assessment data Change strategyMacro implementation plan/budget
4.0 Commit	Development of detailed plans for all implementation change requirements Development plans which include change management activities to manage resistance and ensure adoption of "should" design		Implementation team structure Team implementation plans Integrated implementation plan
5.0 Build	All components of "should" design developed and ready for implementation	5.1 Detailed Design 5.2 Develop 5.3 Test 5.4 Solution Preparation	"Should" components Test plans/results
6.0 Enable	Prepare users, operators, supporters, and managers of the "should" design	6.1 Prepare 6.2 Internal Launch	Training plans Training materials
7.0 Adopt	Implement the "should" process performance system Monitor performance of "should" process and implementation progress Evaluate results against business case	7.1 Cut-Over 7.2 Stabilize 7.3 Operate	"Should" process/components in place, debugged and operating

- The project is guided by a trained Process Consultant, either internal or external to the organization. The Process Consultant knows the RPM project framework, understands what must be accomplished in each phase and how to achieve the desired results.

RPM ROLES

Key client roles always include:

- Project Sponsor
- Project Team (guided by the Process Consultant)
- Project Team Leader

Depending on project scope, a project structure might also involve:

- A Steering Team consisting of senior managers or executives who represent the functions or organizations involved in performance of the process in question. The Project Sponsor functions as the Chair of this Steering Team.

The exact application of the RPM project structure varies with the scope and objective of a particular engagement. The variety of scope and objectives are reflected in Table 6.4. Each cell in the matrix represents a variation on application of the RPM, captured in an appropriate engagement model.

Table 6.4 Process Engagement Grid

Value Creation Hierarchy	Engagement Models					
	Primary Variables					
	Process Scope		Activity/Scope			
			Definition/ Documentation	Process Design	Process Redesign/ Improvement	Process Management System Design
Enterprise/Business model	Whole business					
Value Creation System	All of Value Creation System (Launched/Sold/Delivered)					
Processing Sub-System	Multiple Processes	Primary				
		Contributing				
Process	Single Process	Primary	×		×	×
		Contributing				
Sub-Process/ Task/Sub-Task	Sub-Process	Primary				
		Contributing				

RPM CRITICAL SUCCESS FACTORS

Built into RPM are several factors critical to success of any process design or improvement project. These factors are shown in Figure 6.8 and are listed following.

1. Design Dimensions

Every project (unless it is of very narrow scope, such as a sub-process) needs to address all five design dimensions, in some cases repeatedly.

2. Critical Business Issue (CBI) Identification and Process/Project Scoping

To be successful, every project must be driven by an issue important to the business, and that CBI should be the main determinant of the process and project scope.

3. Clear End-to-End Project Accountability

First steps in ensuring project success include establishing a structure appropriate to the size and complexity of the process and identifying appropriate roles and responsibilities, and then ensuring throughout the project that project management responsibilities are carried out effectively.

4. "Is" Analysis Discipline

Some process practitioners attempt to save time by skipping the analysis phase, thinking the problems are already well understood, but it is never the case that problems are understood by everyone the same way. A lack of analysis causes endless rehashing and even cancellations of projects.

5. Visual Modeling

We have a large variety of tools in RPM for creating depictions of the situation, the causes, the potential solutions, and the performance. All these devices aid the project participants in their understanding and agreement as they proceed through the phases.

6. "Is" to "Should" Strategy

The juncture between "is" and "should" can be mishandled in a number of ways, which can cause participants to leave or stall, so a structured approach to this critical passage is highly recommended.

7. Performer Integration: Technology and Human

Both analysis and design must reach the performer level or there is a risk that the analysis will be inaccurate and the solutions unfeasible.

8. Process Management System Design

The manageability of a process is as important as its effectiveness and efficiency; manageability must be included in the project analysis and design work.

Figure 6.8 RPM Critical Success Factors

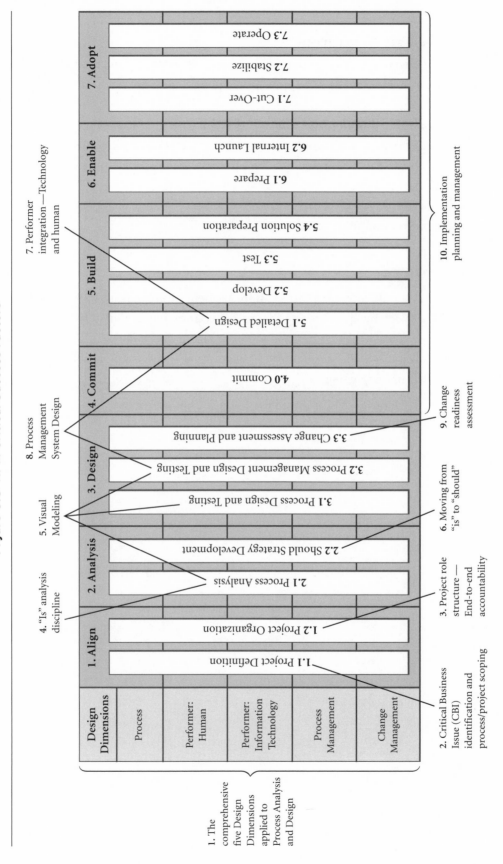

9. Change Readiness Assessment

A good process design can fail if the receiving organizations are unprepared or unwilling. Gauging their readiness and making the appropriate preparations are critical to success.

10. Implementation Planning and Management

The Achilles' heel of many process improvement projects is poor implementation, and very often this is traceable to bad planning or a failure to reassess the original project plan in light of the process design.

Each of these critical success factors is further discussed in Chapters Seven and Eight, in the context of a project walk-through.

CLOSING POINTS

In Chapter Seven, we walk through a process improvement project at the single-process level using RPM. The project involves defining the process, improving it, and addressing relevant components of the management system, so we have placed checkmarks in the appropriate cells of Table 6.4 to indicate the scope of the project. We also give examples of several other engagement models in Chapter Nine.

RPM Project Walk-Through: Align, Analysis, Design

In Chapter Six we presented the elements of the Rummler Process Methodology (RPM). Now we walk through a typical project so you can see how these elements are adapted to particular project variables. But before we do that, we need to situate this project in some context.

As stated in the previous chapter, the Rummler Process Methodology can accomplish a number of activities (for example, process design, process improvement) for various levels of process. Table 6.4 shows a grid that summarizes the various applications of the RPM. Every application of RPM is a unique engagement in response to these key variables:

- Process Scope (in general, the levels of process shown in the Value Creation Hierarchy):
  - A sub-process
  - A single process (primary or contributing)
  - Multiple processes (primary or contributing)
  - Value Creation System
  - Business
- Project Scope, including:
  - Process definition and documentation
  - Process Design
  - Process Redesign/improvement:
    - Improved effectiveness and efficiency of a process

- Reduced operating cost of a process
- Merging two or more processes
- Designing a Process Management System
  - Various technology focused projects, which are discussed in Chapter 11

The combination of these variables determines which steps in RPM are included in a project design and the degree of rigor of their execution. The results of these determinations are an Engagement Model—that is, the basic Project Framework applied to a unique set of project variables results in a specific Engagement Model.

We now illustrate the adaptation of RPM to the following situation:

- Process Scope: Single process
- Project Objective: Process Improvement

In this chapter, we walk through the first three phases: Align, Analysis, and Design. Chapter Eight describes the final four phases: Commit, Build, Enable, and Adopt.

STERLING PUBLISHING

Situation

Sterling Publishing is a subsidiary of Corporate, Inc.; it designs, sells, and produces packaged training materials for the performance improvement industry. Figure 7.1 shows the Sterling Publishing organization chart.

On January 15, Janice Wilson, the Sterling Director of Finance, contacts the Corporate Performance Support Group, whose function is to provide performance improvement expertise and resources to Corporate's many diverse subsidiaries. Wilson requests assistance in improving the Sterling Order Entry process.

Sara Harmon is the Performance Consultant assigned to follow up on the Sterling request. Sara has been with Corporate for five years, but this is her first assignment with Sterling. Sara is a certified RPM Process Consultant, with several years' experience at Corporate. As such, she understands:

- The Rummler Process Methodology.
- That organizations are adaptive and processing systems and that businesses are virtual Value Machines.
- The value of the Value Creation Hierarchy for properly locating and defining processes.
- That any process she might be asked to address is part of a business process architecture (or Value Creation Architecture), which represents the Value Dimension of the business. She also understands that she must work within this VCA, whether it has been formally documented or not.

This is the story of how Sara applied the RPM project structure to respond to the Sterling request for assistance. She follows the phases and sub-phases of the RPM as detailed in Table 6.3. We describe activities as she accomplishes each major event within the sub-phases. During her work, she applies the Critical Success Factors we listed

Figure 7.1 Sterling Publishing Organization Chart

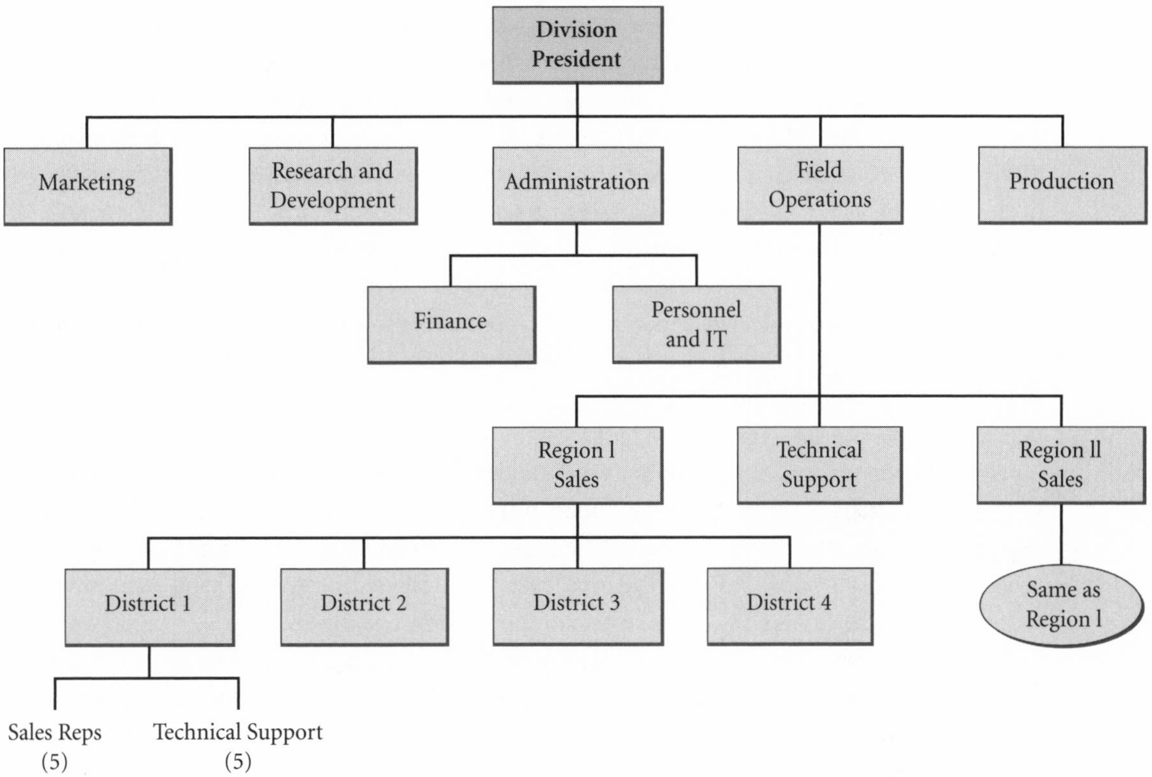

in Chapter Six. These ten practices are critical to the success of a process design/improvement project *and*, by and large, unique to the Rummler Process Methodology.

The project flow is discussed on two levels. First, we walk through the sequence Sara followed, referencing each Critical Success Factor when and where relevant. Second, following the project walk-through, we discuss in detail the relevant Critical Success Factors.

Phase 1.0 Align

Phase	Sub-Phase
1.0 Align	**1.1 Project Definition**
	1.2 Project Organization

January 15

Sara begins the Project Definition Sub-Phase of the RPM immediately.

Since this is Sara's first assignment within Sterling, she gathers some background information on the business after she returns the call of the Director of Finance. She checks Sterling's history, products and markets, financials and organization chart. She checks to see if the Corporate Performance Support Group has already developed a Business

Process Framework (BPF) for Sterling—but no such luck. She also tracks down several employees who had worked in Sterling Publishing for years before transferring to Corporate. From those people, she is able to get a lot of information and develop several insights about the history and operations of Sterling.

Sara mentally reviews what she knows about the process structure of any business, including Sterling. Sara understands that within the Value Creation Hierarchy, an Order Entry "process" is really a sub-process (Level 5 of the VCH) or front end of an Order Fulfillment process or Order to Cash process (Level 4 of the VCH), which is in turn part of the Sterling Product Delivered Processing System (Level 3 of the VCH). The VCH framework allows Sara to quickly put the Order Entry "process" in context.

Given the VCH context of the Order Entry sub-process, Sara realizes the performance requirements of the Order Entry sub-process will come from the performance requirements (customer driven and business driven) of the entire Order to Cash process. And to a considerable degree, the Order to Cash customer and business requirements are driven by the requirements placed on the Products Delivered Processing Sub-System. Improving the Order Entry sub-process alone will have very little impact on customer satisfaction if the remainder of the Order to Cash process remains unchanged. Further, the performance of the Order Entry sub-process is affected by "upstream" components of the VCH, characteristics of the products developed in "Launched" and order taking procedures currently practiced in "Sold." Therefore, attempting to improve the performance of the Order Entry sub-process in isolation from the total Order to Cash process, and ignorant of the inputting requirements of "Launched" and "Sold," is likely to be a waste of Sterling time and money.

Even though there is no Business Process Framework for Sterling, Sara begins to form a picture in her mind of the process structure of the Value Creation System of the company. (See Figure 7.2.) Based on her experience with the RPM, Sara notes several things she needs to accomplish as part of Phase 1.0. The most critical are to:

- Establish the business case for improving the process in question. She needs to determine a Critical Process Issue that can be linked to Critical Business Issue.

- Expand the process scope beyond Order Entry, which is a sub-process within a single organizational function (Engineering) to the end-to-end Order to Cash process.

If the process scope can be expanded, it will be easier to establish and measure performance goals for the full Order to Cash process, which in turn can be linked to Critical Business Issue goals and measures. And even more important, this would avoid the wasted effort of improving the Order Entry sub-process when the poor performance of other downstream sub-processes in the Order to Cash process prevents the customer from experiencing any improvements. And Sara knows from past experience that working on a minor portion of a process and expecting big results only casts doubt on the value of process improvement work.

Finally, if Sara can get the process scope expanded, she will be able to define the project as improving a *cross-functional process*, requiring the involvement of key personnel and management from all functions that have significant involvement in and impact on the Order to Cash process.

January 16

Sara speaks via phone with Sterling Finance Director Wilson. Based on their conversation, Sara concludes:

Figure 7.2 Sterling Publishing "Is" Value Creation System

Sterling Publishing "Is" Value Creation System

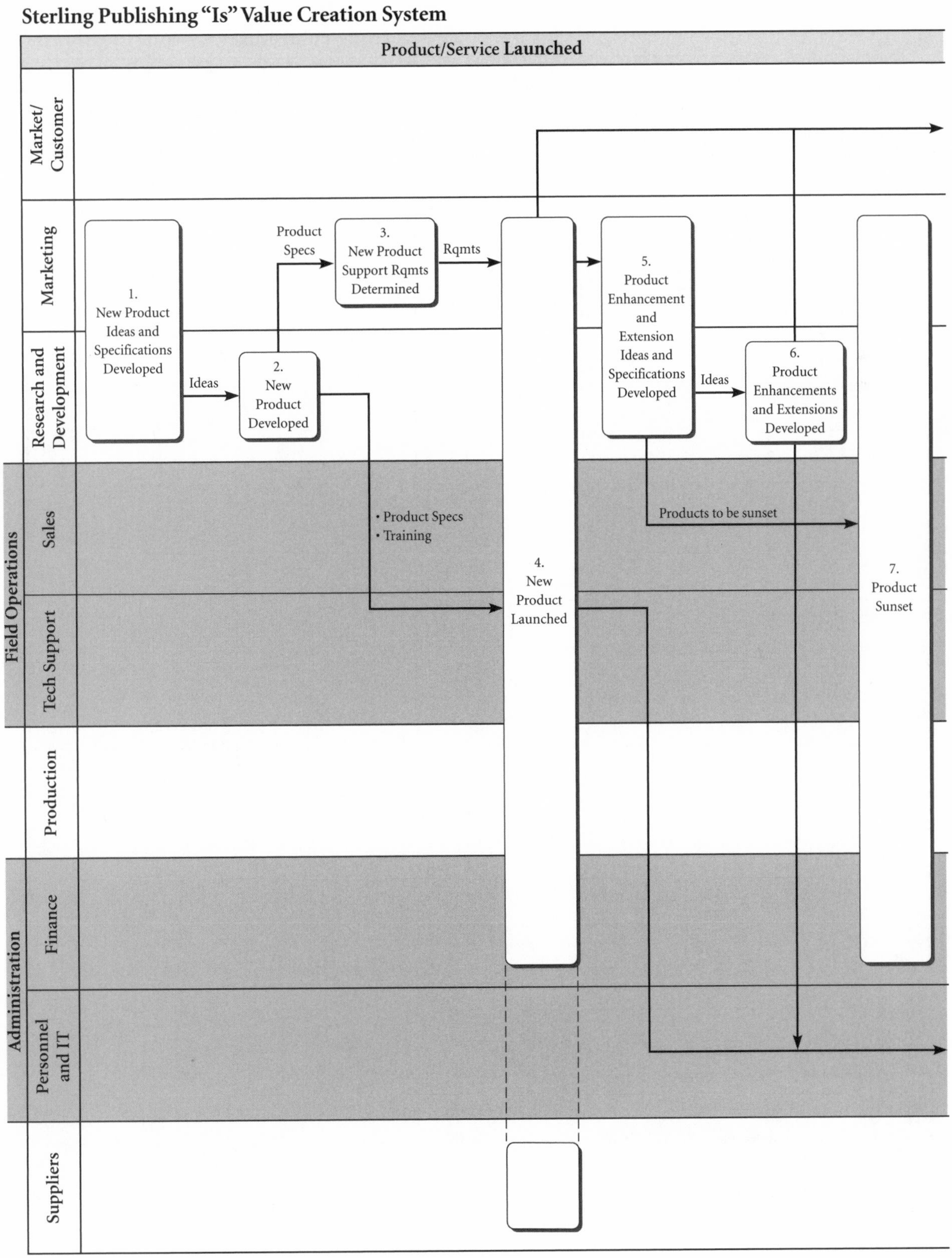

Figure 7.2 (*Continued*)

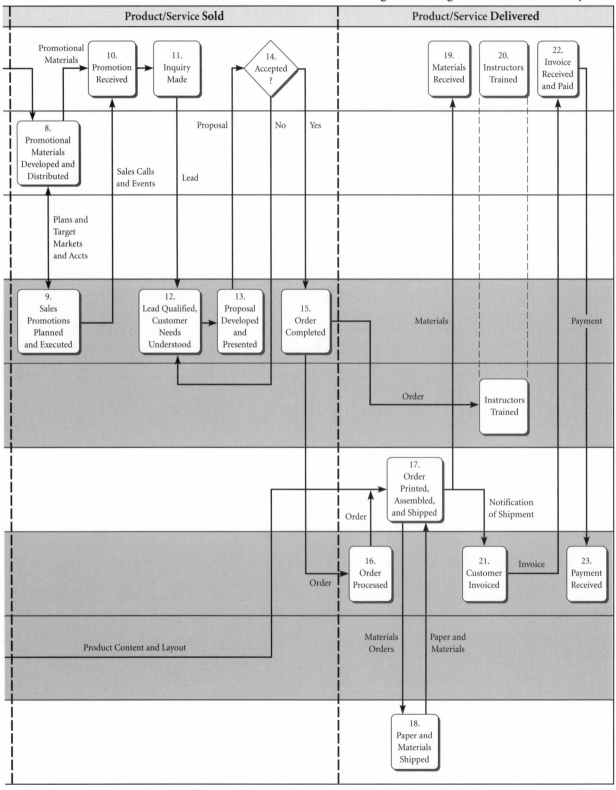

Sterling Publishing "Is" Value Creation System

- There are data suggesting a significant Critical Process Issue at the Order to Cash process level.

- There is probably a critical mass of senior managers who think the Order to Cash process should be improved at this time.

- She must engage Sterling management in Phase 1.0 of the RPM. If the objectives of Phase 1.0 cannot be met, then the effort can be aborted or restructured.

Phase	Sub-Phase
1.0 Align	1.1 Project Definition
	1.2 Project Organization

January 21

Sara arrives at Sterling Headquarters to continue her data gathering and begin the Project Organization and Planning work. Per column 3 of the RPM overview in Table 6.3 Sara's objectives for the Align Phase are

- Agreement on the project objectives

- Agreement on process scope—including any constraints

- Assignment of and commitment to appropriate and adequate resources

- Development of a plan with milestones and deliverables to allow for effective project management

Sara meets with Director Wilson and establishes a plan for completing the Align Phase. Next, Sara meets with executives and managers who are affected by the Order Entry and the Order to Cash process to validate the need to improve and gain agreement to the scope and approach. After Sara's presentation on project objectives, scope, constraints, and other key objectives of this phase, the group agrees to proceed with the project. They also select an Executive Sponsor (VP of Administration), identify the Steering Team (VPs of Sales, Administration, and Production and Director of Finance) and agree to meet again in two days to review the final project charter, plan, and budget.

January 22

Sara meets one on one for an hour with each Steering Team member in order to learn more about how the process operates and his or her views on the issues and barriers to improvement.

Sara assembles several visual models of the organization. One depicts the functions that participate in the Order to Cash process and their interactions, another shows all of the processes that touch the Order to Cash process. This is in essence a sub-set of the full Sterling Business Process Framework (BPF) that Sara hoped had been developed previously. She uses the same basic framework for this sub-set that she would use to organize the full BPF (that is, Management, Value Creation, and Contributing processes with Value Creation processes further categorized into "Launched," "Sold," and "Delivered").

These models are the most effective way of describing and getting agreement about the context of the work and changes that will be in (or out) of scope.

Working with the Executive Sponsor (VP of Administration), Sara completes a project business case and definitions document—a repository for all the important agreements and decisions that Sara knows are critical to make before beginning the project. She knows that getting this kind of alignment from the Steering Team and key players will dramatically increase her probability of success for this project. The agreements include the Critical Process and Business Issues, Project Goals, Project Scope (and what is out of scope), Project Constraints (on the solution and the

Table 7.1 Align Phase Pitfalls/Success Factors Matrix

Potential Pitfalls/Risks During This Phase	What Sara Did to Mitigate Risks	RPM Critical Success Factors Addressed
Wrong process or project scope; scope has been predetermined	Sought evidence that larger scope (all of Order to Cash process instead of Order Entry sub-process) would have greater impact on results Looked for support of key executives for redesign of Order to Cash	2: Process scope 3: Ownership and roles
Lack of a clear picture of existing processes (no defined BPF)	Created her own version of portion of BPF and validated with Project Sponsor	5: Visual modeling
Lack of clarity about the business issue or need for improvement	Developed a business case with critical business issue and critical process issue identified	2: Critical business issue

work/resources to get to the solution), Project roles, resources and support, and plan and budget. Pitfalls and success factors for the Align Phase are presented in Table 7.1.

January 23

The Sponsor brings Sara to a meeting with the Steering Team for several hours. The agenda is

- Review and approve the project as described
- Review and agree to the project plan and subsequent Steering Team meetings throughout the project
- Identify Project Team members
- Choose a Project Team Leader

Align Phase Summary

Phase deliverables:

1. Approval of:
   - Project Rationale
   - Project Scope
   - Project Goals
   - Project Profile
   - Project Constraints and Assumptions
   - Stakeholder Analysis and Plan
   - Project Roles
   - Project Support Requirements

- Project Plan
- Phase 2 Resource Plan

2. Business Case
   - Time: Three days (January 21–23)

Phase 2.0 Analysis

Phase	Sub-Phase
2.0 Analysis	2.1 Process Analysis
	2.2 "Should" Strategy Development

February 11

Sara arrives at Sterling Publication's headquarters to begin the Analysis Phase (Phase 2) of her project. Per the RPM project framework (Table 6.3), Sara's objectives for this phase are

- Agreement by project participants and stakeholders on:
  - Boundaries of the process or processes affected
  - Extent of Process issues/opportunities ("Disconnects") and effort required to improve process performance
- Agreement on the specifications, assumptions, constraints, and development strategy for a successful "should" design

Sara and the Executive Sponsor meet with the Project Team members for a half-day kick-off briefing. This event enables Sara to meet the Project Team Leader and engage him in development of a data-gathering plan. They decide that Brian Robeson, the Team Leader should schedule an interview with each Project Team member to learn about his or her role in the process as well as to gauge his or her level of enthusiasm and readiness for this project.

The next objective (Critical Success Factor 1) is to gather data on the "is" process (what it is and how it is performing); on "is" process management (what it is and how it is performing); and on "is" process technology support (what it is and how it is performing).

A major activity in this data gathering is to document the "is" process so that there will be something explicit and concrete to examine. The format shown in Figure 7.3 (Sterling "Is" Cross-Functional Process Map) is effective for accomplishing this objective. The functions or entities that participate in the process are shown on the left-hand, vertical axis. The "customer" is at the top of this list, since they are the focus of the process. The functions that perform the process are listed next, usually in the order that they first participate in the process. Thus, in the Order to Cash process, the customer is followed by the Sales sub-function of the Field Operations function. The Cross-Functional Process Map displays the major steps required to perform the process, shows which steps are performed by which functions, and makes the necessary "hand-offs" between functions clear.

February 12–14

During the next three days, Sara interviews Project Team members (and other identified subject matter experts) to understand how their jobs and functions interact with the Order to Cash Process. She quizzes them on the "disconnects" in the process that negatively affect their effectiveness or efficiency.

Figure 7.3 Sterling "Is" Cross-Functional Process Map

Sterling Publishing As Is Customer Order Process

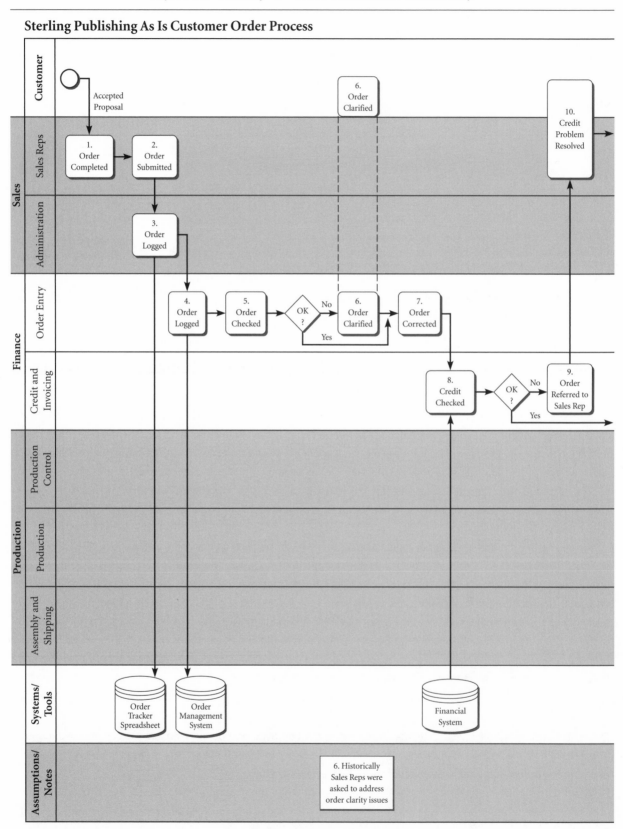

Figure 7.3 (*Continued*)

Sterling Publishing As Is Customer Order Process

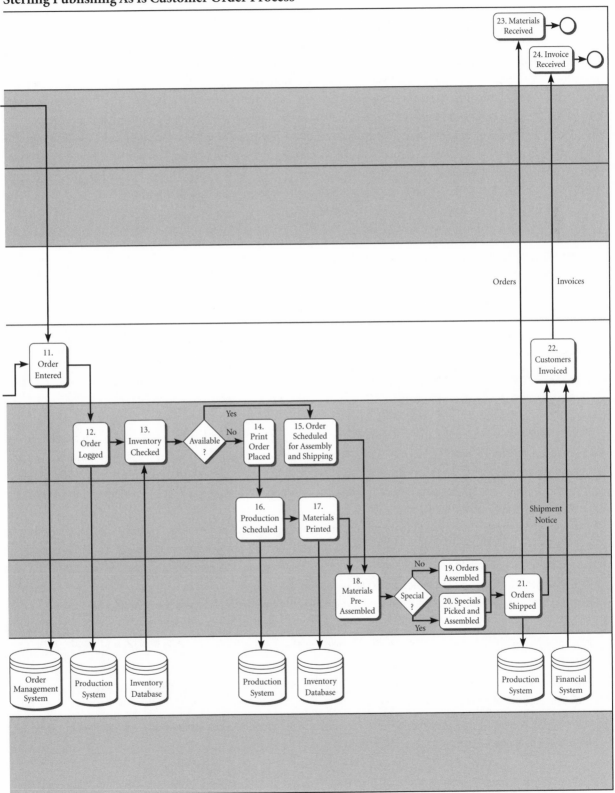

Simultaneously, Sara and Brian begin to convert the descriptions of the process into a cross-functional map like that shown in Figure 7.3. She also compiles a list of process disconnects mentioned by Project Team members.

February 18–21
Once the interviews are done, Brian and Sara finalize the draft "is" map they have constructed. Their objective is not to have a perfect "is" map (which is impossible), but to have a map that is 70%–80% complete. This will be enough to guide the Project Team through the process validation and disconnect identification step, which is next. They also have mapped the current management process for Order to Cash in the form of an "is" management calendar. Brian develops and prints large wall charts of the "is" process maps. They are not unaware of high-tech substitutions for "Big Paper" such as projecting the map, but have rejected them in favor of the low-tech approach because it is difficult to validate a map while scrolling through the visible portion on the screen. Sara wants to add to and draw on the map to visually guide the conversation. Ultimately she and Brian want the team to feel ownership of the map (this should be their map, not hers), which is easier to achieve with a tangible artifact on the wall.

February 25
Brian and Sara arrive at the reserved conference room early and prepare for the two-day "is" session. The objectives for this session are

- Validate the accuracy of the "is" map
- Identify disconnects in the process (and other elements of the Effective Process Framework) that are causing the Critical Process Issue (that is, cycle time and product/service quality)
- Group and prioritize the disconnects according to impact on the Critical Process Issue and therefore the Critical Business Issue

On the wall are some ground rules, including one that says "No Should Ideas." When the project team arrives, Sara—backed by Brian—explains this rule. They know that the team members need to fully understand the "is" process before they can begin to identify "should" solutions, or they will be at risk of creating a lot of workarounds or "balloon-squeezing" solutions that tend not to add up in the end. The team can talk "should" when they begin the Should Strategy Development Sub-Phase.

Project team members arrive and are amazed at the "is" map. This is the first time they have seen it all together, its complexity, the number of hand-offs in the course of filling an order. Sara and Brian use a very disciplined approach to having the team validate the map. During the validation, they capture the disconnects and their impact on the CPI. Later they prioritize the disconnects according to impact on the CPI.

Brian is pleased with the progress for the day. The Project Team is exactly where they need to be:

- They are all agreed that the Order to Cash process is seriously (even dangerously) broken and needs to be fixed ASAP.
- They all recognize that no function is exempt from having contributed to the ineffectiveness and inefficiency of the process. No "blame-game" going on.
- They are all "pumped" about the opportunity to make a significant difference that will benefit Sterling and make their collective jobs easier.

February 26

Brian and Sara manage the validation of the management process for Order to Cash in much the same manner as the "is" work process. They capture disconnects and underlying assumptions of the "is" management system. Key conclusions included:

- Planning activities are siloed. There is very little cross-correlation of underlying plan assumptions used in the silos.
- The primary goals of the functions are often at direct odds with one another (for example, speed versus risk, cost versus quality).
- Few of the goals are connected to what the customer wants.
- Corrective actions taken in one silo often have a negative impact downstream.

Reviewing the list of process and management system disconnects, the Project Team concluded the following about the impact of information technology on the process and management system:

- There are multiple legacy systems that do not talk to or feed each other data, causing redundant data entry.
- Information in one system that could be beneficial to other departments is not accessible to those departments.
- Data updates are often run in batch mode.
- There is newer technology available that Sterling is not taking advantage of.

The Project Team summarized what they thought the major "change management" challenges were going to be as the project moved toward implementation.

Phase	Sub-Phase
2.0 Analysis	2.1 Process Analysis
	2.2 "Should" Strategy Development

February 27

With completion of the Process Analysis sub-phase, it was time to begin preparing for "should" design. The transition from "is" to "should" is traditionally very difficult. Many well-intended efforts can be derailed at this critical point. Some teams get stuck in endless analysis because they can't make the transition. Others resort to "fixing up" the "is" map.

The RPM methodology is systematic in its approach that both encourages breakthrough thinking and provides a discipline to follow. Brian and Sara have planned to achieve the following in the next two days:

- Development of a set of specifications or blueprint for the "should" design
- Finalization of process/project goals
- Development of innovation ideas for the process
- Development of "should" assumptions for the process
- Development of the Macro Process: a high-level view of the new process

Figure 7.4 "Should" Design Specifications

Inputs →   **Order to Cash Process**   → Outputs

Inputs

Input(s)	Critical Dimension(s)	Target
Standard Order	Quality—accuracy	100% accurate
	Quality—completeness	100% complete—required fields
	Time—Timely submission	Within 4 hours of capture
Custom Order	Quality—accuracy	100% accurate
	Quality—completeness	100% complete—required fields
	Quality—compliance to customization standards	100% compliance
	Time—Timely submission	Within 4 hours of capture
Sales Forecast	Quality—accuracy	Within +/- 10% by product

Order to Cash Process

Category	Should Design Characteristics
Roles	• Minimal functional hand-offs • Sales Reps maintain accountability for orders • Parallel processing wherever possible
Technology	• Real-time order entry • Order information is immediately visible to all upon entry • Real-time order status is transparent
Compliance/ Sustainability	• Hazards identified and safety practices defined • Emissions within Sterling standard
Adaptive	• Capable of handling a 50% increase in throughput and transition to electronic delivery in next 3 years • Mechanisms in place to recognize and adapt to changes in internal and external requirements
Management	• Functional goals tied to process goals • Clear accountability for performance

Outputs

Output(s)	Critical Dimension(s)	Target
Order	Time—Cycle Time	10-day cycle time
	Quality—accuracy (meet customer spec)	100% accurate
Invoice	Economics— Handling cost/order	$11 Per Unit
	Quality—accuracy	100% accurate
	Time—on time	Received same timeframe as order
Process Performance Data	Accuracy	100% accurate

The team reconvenes in the morning fairly excited because they know that today they are allowed to start talking about the "should" process. The old ground rule is gone. The "is" map and the flip chart pages of disconnects are still hanging in the room—but they have been moved to the side walls.

Brian opens the meeting, explaining that this process cannot achieve the desired performance goals simply by fixing the many disconnects that they found. The Project Team needs to consider breakthrough designs in order to meet the goal. To do that, the team rethinks the process from the highest level down. They start by rethinking it as a single box—create a set of "should" design specifications. Together the team specifies what the inputs, outputs, and characteristics of the new process need to be, and they set standards and performance specifications. The team is specifying the process—creating a blueprint that can guide the design. Their work is shown in Figure 7.4.

With specs completed, the Project Team next works on the "should" assumptions. They refer to the list of "is" assumptions developed earlier in the week. They challenge each assumption to determine if it is true for the "should." They then record any new assumptions that will govern the "should" process. Sara knows that some of the greatest breakthrough designs can come as a result of challenging the old "is" assumptions and that this is an often-overlooked step in many process improvement projects. (See Figure 7.5.)

With these basics in hand, it is time to get creative. Sara explains the objective of the innovation brainstorming exercise. She tells them that if they only have one idea, it will be their best idea and their worst idea. Using a time-limited structured brainstorming technique, the team develops upward of thirty potential innovations for the process. They will refer to these as they begin the next levels of redesign. They end the day on this high note.

February 28

With all of the ideas generated and their blueprinting work, the team realizes that they can exceed the original project goal, so they go ahead and set a more aggressive goal, shaving additional cycle time off order fulfillment.

Now Brian and Sara facilitate the Macro Process design. This is a repeat of the output, input, and characteristics specifications for each of the sub-processes. But Brian challenges them to not be satisfied with the way the process is currently "chunked" into sub-processes. For instance, for the order entry sub-process (which started this whole effort), he challenges the end point of "order entered" and asks what a better milestone would be—one that has value to the organization and customers. They realize that what they are really after is an actionable order that is available to everyone who needs to take action. So they redefine the first sub-process accordingly. They continue until they arrive at the new macro process—with all inputs and outputs, critical dimensions, goals/standards, and characteristics defined. (See Figure 7.6.)

Already the team can see a very different process with very different performance emerging, even with only this level of detail. The team decides what artifacts and information they are going to share at the upcoming Steering Team meeting and dismiss for the week, very upbeat.

Figure 7.5 "Is" Versus "Should" Assumptions

"Is" Assumption	Valid for "Should"	Not Valid for "Should"	"Should" Assumption
There will continue to be a market for paper-based products	X		
30 days order-to-ship cycle time will satisfy most customers		X	Customer expectations for delivery cycle time will continue to decrease
Standard order size of 20 will meet most customer needs		X	Customers will want mix of product in their order

Figure 7.6 "Should" Macro Process Design

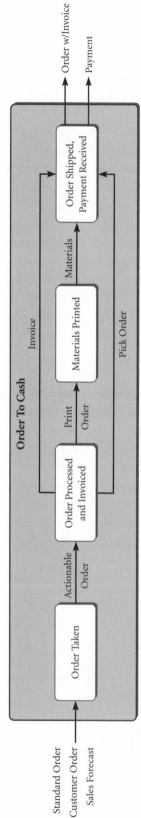

Should Characteristics
- All functions get orders real-time
- Sales Reps maintain accountability for order
- Immediate order visibility
- Real-time order status
- Credit check on new customers at time of order
- Web-based order system

Should Characteristics
- All functions get orders real-time
- Real-time inventory is visible
- Invoice viewable in system as print preview

Should Characteristics
- Capable of 50% volume increase over next 3 years
- Safety standards met
- Environmental standards met
- Assembly in modules
- Print to forecast for standard orders

Should Characteristics
- Capable of 50% volume increase over next 3 years
- Invoice printable at loading dock
- Inventory in modules

Order To Cash

Standard Order
Customer Order
Sales Forecast → Order Taken → Actionable Order → Order Processed and Invoiced → Print Order → Materials Printed → Materials → Order Shipped, Payment Received → Order w/Invoice / Payment

Invoice · Pick Order

Input	Critical Dimension	Goal/Standard
Standard Order	Quality-Accuracy	Matches customer needs
Customer Order	Quality	Matches customer needs
		100% compliant with customization standards
Sales Forecast	Quality-Accuracy	Within +/-10% byproduct

Output	Critical Dimension	Goal/Standard
Actionable Order	Quality-Accuracy	100% accurate
	Quality-Complete	100% complete
	Timeliness	Within 4 hrs of capture

Output	Critical Dimension	Goal/Standard
Print Order	Quality-Accuracy	100% accurate
	Timeliness	Cycle time of <2 hours
Pick Order	Quality-Accuracy	100% accurate
		100% available in inventory
	Timeliness	Cycle time of <2 hours
Invoice	Quality-Accuracy	100% accurate
	Timeliness	Available to print with cycle time of <1 day

Output	Critical Dimension	Goal/Standard
Materials	Quality-Accuracy	99% error free
	Timeliness	Cycle time of <2 days
	Cost	Unit cost of $10

Output	Critical Dimension	Goal/Standard
Order w/Invoice	Quality-Accuracy	99% error free
	Timeliness	Cycle time of <3 days
	Cost	Unit cost of $20
Order w/Invoice	Timeliness	Late payments due to our error <3%

March 4

The day of the Steering Team meeting, Brian and Sara come in early to make sure that all of the copies of the presentation and artifacts are ready. They hang some of the wall charts (the "is" map and a large version of the macro process) on the walls of the conference room.

As the Steering Team members arrive, they study the "is" map and ask what the numbers above some of the boxes are referring to. Brian explains that those numbers refer to the disconnects found in the process, some of which they will review in the meeting. One Steering team member remarks at the vast number of disconnects.

Once they get started, Brian kicks off with the following agenda:

1. Review of "is" findings
2. Review the "should" specifications and design direction
3. Review the Phase 3.0 project plan
4. Gain Steering Team approval or address concerns

The meeting goes smoothly. Most of the presentation and discussion is led by the Project Team. Sara supports them when Steering Team members have questions about the approach or methodology. The pitfalls and success factors of the Analysis Phase are presented in Table 7.2.

Analysis Phase Summary

Phase deliverables:

1. Disconnect Analysis Findings
2. Validated "Is" Work Process
3. Validated "Is" Management System for the Work Process
4. "Should" Specifications

Table 7.2 Analysis Phase Pitfalls/Success Factors Matrix

Potential Pitfalls/Risks During This Phase	What Sara Did to Mitigate Risks	RPM Critical Success Factors Addressed
Lack of understanding of the "is" process or current performance	Created a detailed "is" process map and walked the Design Team through the map Collected process performance data and disconnects during interviews and the Design Team "is" review meeting	1: Process design 4: "Is" analysis discipline 5: Visual modeling
Dwelling too long on mapping or "is" analysis	Developed an aggressive project schedule and stuck to it Guided "is" analysis session with ground rules	3: Project management 4: "Is" analysis discipline
Blaming each other for process disconnects	Managed a controlled discovery of disconnects and documented them with the Design Team	4: "Is" analysis discipline
Unable to advance from "is" analysis to "should" thinking	Provided structure and tools to guide the Design Team Had the Design Team challenge the project goals	6: "Is" to "should" strategy
Lack of support from management for the analysis or the next phase	Held a formal Steering Team meeting and engineered support	3: Project accountability
No clear direction after analysis	Provided a detailed plan for Phase 3 (Design) and gained Steering Team agreement for the plan	6: "Is" to "should" strategy

5. "Should" Assumptions

6. "Should" Macro Design

Time: 23 days (February 11–March 4)

Phase 3.0: Design

Phase	Sub-Phase
3.0 Design	**3.1 Process Design and Testing**
	3.2 Process Management Design and Testing
	3.3 Change Assessment and Planning

March 5

Following the successful Steering Team meeting, Brian and Sara get to work the next day on preparations for the Design Phase. The objectives for this phase are

- Development of change requirements that define the "should" design and supporting management system

- An assessment of the organization's readiness to accept the required changes

- The identification of an appropriate change strategy and development of a macro project and related budget

The plan is to hold five weeks of "should" sessions that will last four days each. The bulk of the work will be done with the same Project Team that has been engaged in the project so far. However, Brian plans to augment the team during the "should" session that focuses on the design of the management system with some of the managers who currently manage portions of the process. But this management system work can't begin until they have the basic "should" process design—the focus of the first two weeks of "should" sessions.

Brian has arranged for the same conference room to be their exclusive work space for the next two months so that the team can leave all of their work in progress hanging on the walls and not spend time packing it up at the end of each session. This will also serve as the project "war room"—a place where other stakeholders can come and engage in reviews of the designs in progress in order to provide feedback and prepare for the changes that are coming.

March 10–13

Once the Project Team arrives, Brian reorients them to the "should" macro design, with all of its input specifications, output specifications, and characteristics they wanted to build into the process. He also reminds them of their inno-vation ideas, which are hanging around the room, that they will consider as they design the process. Then Sara explains that they are going to continue designing in a top-down manner in sub-teams. The teams are eager to get started, but Sara has a few rules for them. She points to a flipchart that says, "First what, then how, and last who." She tells the team this is still a linear process flow—at this level of design they should only focus on what gets accomplished—not how or who. Those will come later.

The team breaks into two sub-teams to begin the work. Brian and Sara float back and forth between the two groups to keep them on track and following the "what only" rule. Then the two groups present their designs to one another. After some back and forth to clarify, the team settles on the front half of Group 1's design but prefers the back half of Group 2.

The teams continue in this manner during the rest of the day until all of the sub-processes have been addressed and the teams have a linear flow for the whole process.

The next morning, Brian explains that they will do one more level of linear design before moving to cross-functional—finally addressing the "who." For this level of design, the teams can begin to think about how each step of the process takes place, in addition to what gets accomplished. As the teams begin their work, Sara encourages them to capture the details that they discuss and agree upon—otherwise they will need to recreate the conversations later. Getting to the next level of design takes the team the rest of the day and into the next day until lunch time.

After lunch, Brian has put the linear map high up on the wall; below it is a long length of blank paper. Sara explains that they are going to now move the design to a cross-functional format. The teams will create the "swimlanes" as they determine who will perform each step of the process. They can add more detail to the process as they go. Sara goes to the first step in the linear map and asks who will perform this step, who receives the input. The first response is the Sales function. Sara suggests that rather than use the names of the current functions they instead use a descriptive role—names that describe the role being played (for example, Producer, Receiver, Advocate, and so on). So they settle on Customer Advocate as the performers in the first swimlane. As they continue assigning steps to swimlanes, they also create a system swimlane, assigning to that swimlane all of the steps that they want performed in an automated way. They also add system accomplishments to that lane for any steps that a human performer and a system will accomplish together. Every time the team thinks it is time to hand off to another swimlane, Brian makes the following challenge: "Is there a way to avoid a hand-off here by having the other performer enable this first performer to do that step themselves?" By considering this challenge, the team avoided a hand-off to the Finance Department. Instead they enabled the Customer Advocate role to perform the credit check itself with information provided by Finance.

Brian and Sara challenge anything they see that is counter to good process design principles, like:

- Batch versus continuous flow
- Serial process flow versus parallel
- Unnecessary (non-value added) steps
- Redundant (non-value added) steps
- Bottleneck operation
- Push versus pull

The team focuses on the design of the Order to Cash process for standard orders first. Then they circle back and add a few alternative flows for custom orders. Before they declare themselves finished the next afternoon, Sara has them test the design by using the disconnect list that they generated during analysis. They determine that 60% of the disconnects have been eliminated completely. Sara assures them that they will continue to work the rest of the disconnects as a part of their work in next week's session. The team is dismissed.

Figure 7.7 "Should" Role-Responsibility Matrix (excerpt)

Function Process Steps	Sales	Credit and Invoicing	System	Production Control
Order Received	Order reviewed and clarified with customer. Orders not meeting minimum requirement addressed with customer			
Credit Checked Via On-line Service	If *new* customer: Customer information submitted on-line to Credit Check service. Credit verification received		Credit check service available through web portal	
Credit Checked via Customer Database	If *existing* customer: Look-up customer on database Check that credit status is OK	Customer credit data maintained in database	Credit status displayed	
Order Entered and Submitted	Complete order template Order submitted		Order and status available Order queues updated	Order queue viewed
Order Processed				New Orders viewed Inventory verified If fillable from inventory, pick ticket generated

March 17–20

The next week the team continues with "should" design by determining the detailed roles and responsibilities for the process (Figure 7.7). Sara has them identify which steps in the process have been radically changed or are new steps. Brian chooses several team members to draft a detailed document for those steps (Figure 7.8). By completing this work, the team will think through the task-level details, rules, roles, exceptions, triggers, performance support requirements, and (in the case of human performers) the Human Performance System (HPS) for the new or changed steps. The Design Details Document accomplishes the following:

- Drives the design down to the performer level at which the change will be implemented
- Considers the Human Performance System impact
- Describes technology interfaces
- Creates the detailed process documentation that is necessary to support implementation

Again, Sara asks the team to check the designs against the disconnects list. They determine that they have now addressed 70% of the disconnects.

Figure 7.8 "Should" Details Document

Process Name:	Sterling Publishing Order to Cash Process		Design Details Document ID:	AJA COP 41

Is to Should Change Summary Description				
Is to Should Change Summary #:	#2 – Credit Checks Real Time		**Should Process Step #(s):**	#4 – Credit Checked Online #5 – Credit Checked via the Sterling Customer Database

Is	Should	Benefits (if available)
Disconnects: • Credit checks performed on every order, even for existing customers, causing bottlenecks • Credit checks are performed days after the order has been taken from the customer **Description:** • *Finance Credit and Invoicing Associates* check credit with credit bureau for all orders, regardless of customer's history with Sterling	**Description:** • *Sales Reps* check credit of existing customers using the Sterling database prior to submitting order • *Sales Reps* check credit on-line with credit bureau for new customers only • *Sales Reps* involve *Credit and Invoicing* for problems they can't solve or to release credit "hold"	• Time – Reduction in cycle time to process orders • Cost – Reduction of labor in Finance Credit and Invoicing • Time / Cost – Sales Reps have the leverage to resolve credit issues on the spot and can do it faster.

Step Action(s):					
	New Step(s) / #	X	Modified Step(s) / #4		Unchanged Step(s) / #

For Modified Step(s) – check all that apply:					
X	Input		Output	X	Procedure
X	Technology	X	Role		Other:

2. Project Information

Project(s):	Customer Focus		
Project Team Leader	B. Robeson	**BPF Process Name and Number**	Order to Cash VCD-11

3. Should Description

Should Step / Group of Steps Objective:	Minimize the outstanding Accounts Receivable with minimal negative impact on order fulfillment cycle time.		
Should Step / Group of Steps—Critical Dimensions and Goals:			
Should Step / Group of Steps' Output:	**Critical Dimensions:**	**Goals:**	**Receiving Step(s) and Performer:**
Credit approval or rejection	Volume	100% of customers are checked on line or via database	Sales Rep
	Quality	100% complete 100% accurate	
	Time	100% checked daily, before orders are entered	
Should Steps Trigger:	• Sales Rep receives an order or is completing an order		
Should Step(s) Input:	• Completed order form • Order information	**Source Step(s) and Performer:**	• From Customers

Figure 7.8 *(Continued)*

Main Flow of Activities Events in Should

Sub-Steps Involving Both Human and / or System Performers:			
Sub-Step:	**Who:**	**What:**	**Business Rules / Policies:**
#4	Sales Reps	1. Log into Quasar Credit Bureau	Read-only access
		2. Enter customer data – EIN, name, address, phone	
		3. Submit credit request	
	System	4. Verifies completeness of customer data; highlights any errors or omissions	
		5. Returns credit score	
	Sales Reps	6. Monitor credit software	
		7. Receive, reviews credit score and records score, approval / rejection on order form.	If Sales Reps choose to skip credit check, they risk termination if a customer doesn't pay.
		8. Log off system	
#5	Sales Reps	1. Log into Finance Customer Credit database	Read-only access
		2. Enter customer data—Sterling customer number, name, address, phone	
	System	3. Verifies completeness of customer data; highlights any errors or omissions	
		4. Returns credit approval or rejection; if rejection, includes reason why	
	Sales Reps	5. Receive, review credit score and record score, approval / rejection on order form.	Rejection data is confidential; to be used with customer to solve issues so the order can proceed without financial exposure to Sterling
		6. Log off system	

Additional Should Elements

Definitions/ Glossary:	• New customers' approval = credit score of 700 or better • Current / former customers' approval = no outstanding payments of 60 days or more; no credit hold indicators from Finance

Process Assumptions:	• Quasar's modifications for our needs will be completed by 4/15
	• Sales Reps:
	  ○ Have software connecting them to Quasar and to Finance's Customer Credit database
	  ○ Are completing an order on laptop at customer location
	  ○ Are completing an order with a customer via phone on laptop at home office or Sales office
	  ○ Are reviewing a completed order received from a customer in home office or Sales office on desktop computer
	• There is no "fail-safe" system for customer credit checks. Sales Reps have to consciously check that they did the credit check step or not; are essentially "signing" that they did it.

Security/ Access Requirements:	• Sales Reps need a (Quasar) code to access Quasar's system and STERLING PUBLISHING code to access Finance' Customer Credit database.
Exceptions/ Alternate Flows:	• Sales Reps will check credit via Quasar for every international customer order.

Figure 7.8 *(Continued)*

Process Inter-dependencies:	• The success of the Sales Reps checking credit is contingent on the commission change being implemented. (In Should, Sales Reps will be commissioned upon payment by the customer instead of when the order is entered.) • With rejected credit, Sales Reps are to attempt to solve the problem with the customer. Only Credit Department can authorize the release of an order if Quasar or Customer Credit Check database signaled rejection.

Alternative Process Options Considered:	Reasons Options Not Chosen as a Solution:
Considered having Credit and Invoicing handle credit checks with automated systems.	• Still creates time delays for all orders and significant "back and forth" exchanges between Credit and Invoicing and Sales Reps if there are issues. • Sales Reps are there or talking on phone with the customer and can handle issues instantly. • Keeps Sales Reps closer to the customer.

Performance Considerations

Step/Group of Steps' Consequences:		
	Positive Consequences:	Negative Consequences:
Desired Should Performance: Check customer's credit	• Sales Reps have greater control over the process • Faster identification / solution of credit issues means fewer delays in commissions	• Checking credit takes a little time • Potential perception by Sales Reps that this is "admin" work
Undesired Performance: Not checking customers' credit	• Finish a sale faster	• Order form indicates that credit status hasn't been entered • Sales Reps don't receive commission or commission is delayed • Skipping credit check can result in termination if a non-checked customer doesn't pay

4. Document Information and Revision History

File Name:	DDD201.3 Order Processing Reductions			
Original Author(s):	P. Cunningham		Date:	3/15
Current Revision Author(s):	P. Cunningham			
Document History Log:				
Rev #:	Date:	Revision Reason:	Author:	Signature:
1	3/20	Update policies	P. Cunningham	

Late in the week, Brian brought in some subject matter experts who work in a portion of the process, manage a portion of the process, or receive outputs from the process. The Project Team performed a conference room test of the process by walking the SMEs through the process, using all of the documentation they had created thus far. They answered questions and recorded any concerns the SMEs had about the new design. The Project Team then took the information and added clarifying detail to the process or made other changes to address the concerns of the SMEs.

Phase	Sub-Phase
3.0 Design	3.1 Process Design and Testing
	3.2 Process Management Design and Testing
	3.3 Change Assessment and Planning

March 24–27

Finally it was time to work on the redesign of the Management System for the Order to Cash process. Several managers from the functions that participate in the process join the project team for the week. So the better part of the first day is spent getting the new team members up to speed on the new process design. The Project Team must accomplish the following this week:

- Determine the important variables that need to be managed for this process

- Determine the management roles needed for managing and planning

- Design the "should" management calendar (that is, the timing and sequencing of management activities across the roles)

- Develop the first draft of the management trackers (that is, the data sets and displays that the managers will use to monitor process performance)

The next day, they begin with the "should" macro process that hangs on the wall. Using the input, output, and sub-process information from this artifact, they construct a measures chain. Working backward from the end-of-process outputs and associated customer and company requirements, the team identifies the sub-process outputs and variables that affect the results they need. They determine the relevant critical dimensions and a good measure or set of measures that will provide insight into the performance of the process. By working in this manner, they create a troubleshooting logic and a set of leading indicators. (See Figure 7.9.) The invited managers use their organizational knowledge, and Sara uses her background in performance measurement and management to help the team avoid "bad" metrics. Sara coaches them to be sure that the measures are specific, measurable, relevant to the performer, time based, and achievable.

With the measures chain completed, the next task is to identify the management roles for the process: For each identified management position, the team determines what value the role adds to the process. Then, for each role, they identify the assigned tasks for planning, monitoring, and taking corrective action. They assign the measures developed from the measures chain to the management positions—who is looking at what measures. (See Figure 7.10.)

Figure 7.9 "Should" Measures Chain

Input Metrics	Sub-Process Metrics Order Taken	Sub-Process Metrics Order Processed and Invoiced	Sub-Process Metrics Materials Printed	Sub-Process Metrics Order Shipped, Payment Received	Internal End of Process Metrics	External End of Process Metrics	Related Enterprise Metrics
Inputs	Sub-Process Outputs	Sub-Process Outputs	Sub-Process Outputs	Sub-Process Outputs	Process Outputs		
Standard Order Custom Order Sales Forecast	Actionable Order	Pick Order Print Order Invoice Ready for Print/Send	Standard Materials Modules available in Inventory Custom Materials Modules	Customer Materials Invoice Payment	Customer Materials Invoice Payment		
Timeliness Metrics							
Sale Forecast Accuracy Customer order compliant with customization standards		Cycle time order processed	Cycle time print—Standard Modules Cycle time print—Standard Modules % filled from inventory	Cycle time assembly to ship (by custom/standard) Backlog Late Payments	Cycle time order to ship	Late Orders (by Custom/ Standard)	Customer satisfaction Market share Cost of Goods Sold
Quality Metrics							
Order matches customer need	Order entry errors	Pick/Print order errors Invoice errors	Print errors	Assembly errors Ship errors	Rework by reason	Incorrect orders shipped Errors by type Invoice errors	Customer satisfaction Market share
Economic Metrics							
		Handling cost/unit	Units printed Print cost/unit Inventory	Assembly cost/unit Ship cost/unit	# units ship # orders ship Cost per unit		Revenue Cost of Goods Sold

Figure 7.10 "Should" Management Domain Matrix (excerpt)

Position	Mission/Value Add	Performance Planned	Performance Monitored	Looking for . . .	Corrective Actions
VP Production	Build/Maintain capacity and functional excellence in production, assembly and shipping Accountable for Product Delivered performance as a member of the Process Mgmt Team Accountable for Product Available performance as a member of the Process Mgmt Team Manage development plan milestones of the Production Management Team members	Production operating plan and expense budget Product Delivered (including Customer Order) Process Improvement Plan (as a member of the Process Mgmt Team) Development plans for production mgmt staff	Product Delivered and Customer Order Process performance Plan to Actual Product Available Process performance Plan to Actual Development Projects plan to actual (milestones and budget) Production Function performance plan to actual (Production Control, Printing, Assembly and Shipping) Improvement projects plan to actual Relevant Super-system trends	Trends across jobs/orders that indicate that the Product Delivered process is not capable of meeting goals (Customer Materials Orders and Training Delivery trends) Trends across development projects—Indications that the "is" process is not capable of meeting the goals Function execution issues, resource issues, HPS issues Orders/Jobs in jeopardy due to production issues	Reallocate/change resources across jobs, functional areas Initiate process improvements Initiate function improvements Accelerate staff development Staff changes HPS changes/improvements
Production Controller	Ensure the prompt scheduling of all jobs/orders Optimize schedule/ performance across all jobs/orders Ensure that jobs are on track—identify roadblocks	Production Schedule	Jobs in Process # Units shipped % Units shipped on time % Units printed on time % Units assembled on time Rework Inventory Inventory trends Cycle time for printing, assembly, and shipping	Trends across jobs that indicate the need to adjust schedule or adjust scheduling model Trends across orders that indicate the need to adjust inventory or inventory model	Adjust schedule Adjust scheduling model Adjust inventory Adjust inventory model

In the afternoon, Brian divides the team into two groups. Half of the team works on completing the management calendar. Sara reminds this team to remember to follow the planning sequence:

1. Organization
2. Process

   then

3. Function
4. Job

She also brings out the "is" management calendar as reference for the management meetings that already take place. Brian encourages the team to utilize existing management forums and meetings wherever possible and simply change participation and agendas to better serve the process. He and Sara know that the better integrated these are into the existing management system, the higher the likelihood of success.

The other half of the team works on the details of the management trackers (Figure 7.11a and b). The managers who have been working with the Project Team are enthusiastic about the new data they will have to manage with in the future, but they have some doubts about the willingness of upper management to change their expectations to match this new process management view. Sara assures them that this will be addressed with the Steering Team.

March 31–April 3

The following week is a flurry of activity aimed mostly at packaging up the design in order to communicate it effectively to the Steering Team and then to the Implementation Teams that will carry the change forward.

The Project Team identifies all the process changes and for each change develops the following information:

- Summary description of the change
- Benefits: all dimensions of benefit of the change
- Expected results: quantified results (minimum, best guess, and maximum)
- Expected costs: (minimum, best guess, and maximum) (Some team members are assigned to get supporting data from IT and others)
- Risks: What could go wrong, likelihood, and signals
- Disconnects/Issues addressed: which disconnects this change addresses
- Stakeholders affected: who is affected by the change
- Key milestones for Implementation

  (See Figure 7.12.)

Figure 7.11a Process Management Tracking

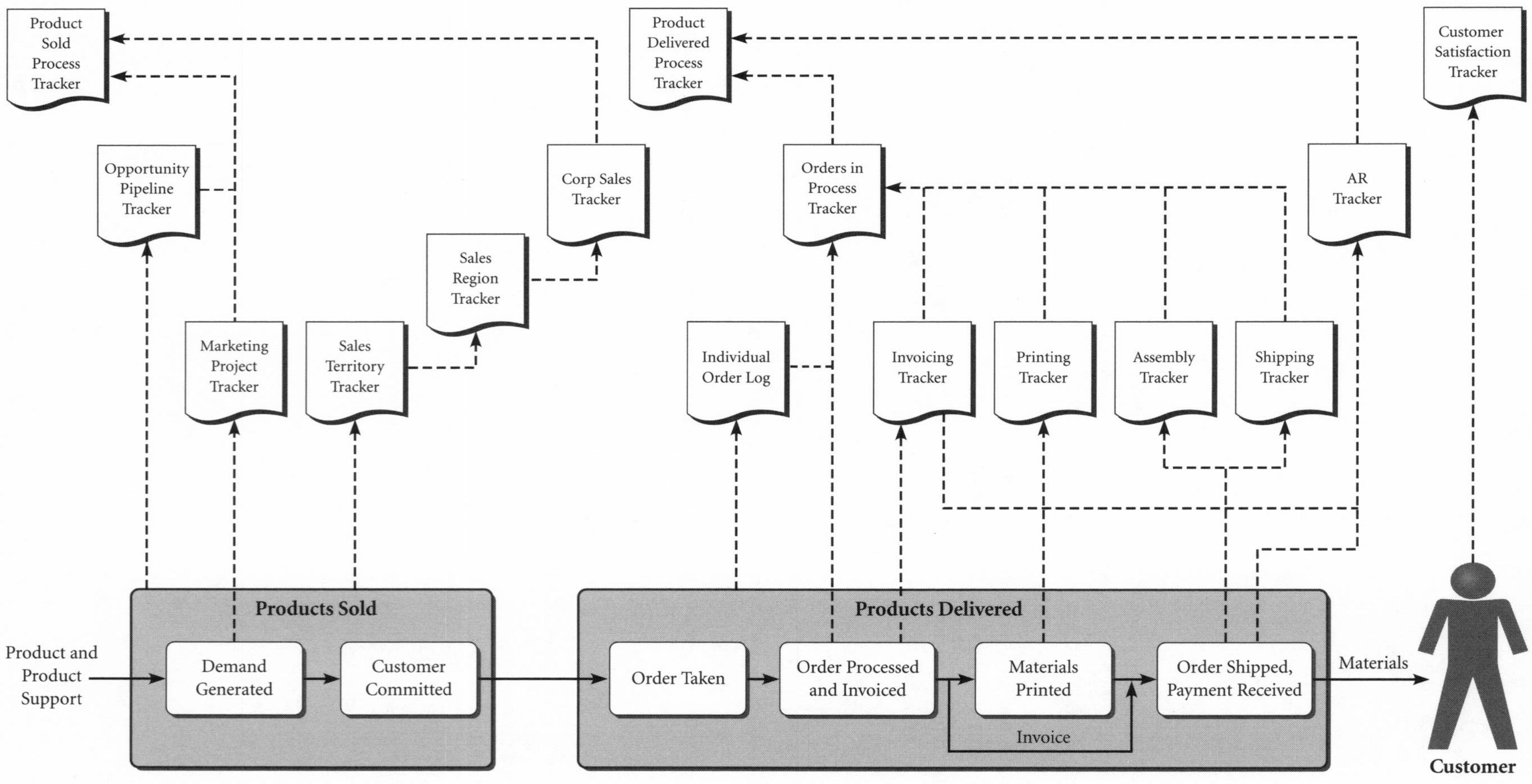

Figure 7.11b Process Management Tracking

Critical Dimension	Measure		Week 1	Week 2	Week 3	Week 4	Week 5	Month to Date
$/Volume	# Units Shipped	Actual	4150	4375	4029			12554
		Plan	4500	4500	4200			13200
	# Order Shipped	Actual	40	42	39			121
		Plan	43	43	43			129
	Cost Per Unit	Actual	$82	$72	$69			$73
		Plan	$70	$70	$70			$70
	Inventory	Actual	9500	10050	9430			9430
		Plan	9000	9000	9000			9000
Quality	Incorrect Orders Shipped		3	10	8			21
	Errors		5	12	10			27
	Wrong Product		2	3	1			6
	Poor Print Quality		1	1	3			5
	Assembly Error		2	3	3			8
	Wrong Ship To		0	0	0			0
	Invoice Errors		0	6	3			9
Cycle Time	Cycle Time Order To Ship	Actual	10	11	9			10
		Plan	10	10	10			10
	% Filled From Inventory		92	75	92			89

Figure 7.12 "Should" Change Requirements Document

STERLING PUBLISHING Order to Cash Process

Requirement Number 10

- **Summary description:**

> Revise the incentive compensation system for Sales Representatives to pay commission when the order is shipped rather than when it is submitted.

- **Benefits:**

> - Holds Sales Rep accountable for providing complete and accurate information, so that the order can be processed quickly and without error.
> - Reduces cycle time by avoiding order clarification steps
> - Avoids commission on cancelled orders and orders stopped for credit issues

- **Expected results:**

	Min.	Best Estimate	Max.
Time saved:	3 days	6 days	10 days
❑ Faster to customer			
❑ On-time delivery (customer satisfaction)	95%	98%	100%
❑ Invoiced sooner (10% of sales)	$70,000 / mo.	$78,000 / mo.	$83,000 / mo.

- **Expected costs:**

	Min.	Best Estimate	Max.
❑ Design new system	$3,000	$5,000	$7,000
❑ Implement new system (0.5 hour briefing per Sales Rep)	$1,300	$1,500	$2,000

5. Risks:

What Could Go Wrong?	Likelihood	Effect	Signal
Sales Reps resist and form union	Medium in view of recent off-site organizing meeting	Reduced flexibility; higher costs	Second organizing meeting
Sales Reps resist and quit	Low; We pay well and the economy is slow	Increased costs to hire and train new Reps	Turnover rate

6. Disconnects/issues addressed:

> Disconnect #7: Orders from Sales Reps are incomplete and inaccurate and must be clarified with the customer by Order Entry, causing further delays and increasing costs.
>
> Disconnect #9: Sales Reps receive commission at the time of order, even though the order may never ship (cancelled by customer, stopped for credit). Commissions are paid for non-revenue orders and Sales Reps are not held accountable for the quality of the orders

7. Stakeholders affected:

Stakeholder	Impact
Sales Rep	Must provide complete/accurate order data. Commission delayed and paid only on completed orders.
Customer	Will receive order faster.
Finance	Will pay commission when they receive order shipped notice.

8. Key milestones for Implementation:

> - Communicate new commission plan to Sales Reps
> - Complete system changes that will send shipped notification to Finance
> - Change Finance Accounting system to meet new requirements
> - Cut Over to new plan
> - Monitor for compliance

Once the descriptions are completed, the team reviews the sets of changes against the following:

- Should specifications: Have all the specifications been met?

- Disconnects: Have all the disconnects been addressed?

- Effective Process Framework: Have they addressed all of the components of process effectiveness?

- Project goals: Will the "should" design meet the project goals?

The final task of the week is to create a "should" design enablers worksheet (Figure 7.13) by reviewing the System swimlane on the "should" process map. For each technology change they identify, they describe the change and characteristics and then determine:

1. Current status of each item
   - New, does not exist
   - In development

Figure 7.13 "Should" Enablers Chart

Change	Desired Characteristics	Related Design Details Documents	Human Performance System— Status and Impact	Technology Performance System— Status and Impact	Estimated Cost/Time to Implement
Electronic On-Line Submission System (includes Triage Rules Engine)	Can receive submissions from a variety of sources (e.g., Sales Reps, Customers, Field Offices) Extensive business rules validate completeness of submissions	2.2.1 *Process Receipt of RFP* 2.2.2 *Order Change Request*	No precedent for accepting orders from anyone other than company Sales Reps Requires a significant change in role understanding and review of incentive system design	Technology does not exist in the organization today, but does exist in market and is a mature technology Requires creation of new Service Module Requires additional infrastructure	6–9 mos $$$
Order Routing System	Connects to workflow software Receives input from Submission System Database records all proposal activity with appropriate retention Include interface to production scheduling and inventory systems	2.2.3 *Proposal Routing*	No implications	Currently in development but will need enhancement	6 weeks to code enhancements $

- In development but requires enhancement

- Exists today

2. Requirements for each technology item derived from Design Details Documents and Measures/Trackers documentation

3. Specific design documents related to each item

The worksheet is a summary of all of the technology requirements for the process and management system. The Project Team then turns to the human performer swimlanes on the map. They look for new positions or departments, new required skill sets for existing performers, structure changes, compensation impacts, capacity changes, and other impacts. Those are documented on the worksheet along with status, requirements, and related documentation.

Phase	Sub-Phase
3.0 Design	3.1 Process Design and Testing
	3.2 Process Management Design and Testing
	3.3 Change Assessment and Planning

April 7–10

This will be the final week of "should" sessions. Sara opens the session with a declaration that the design is complete and packaged. She explains to the Project Team that their attention now turns to implementation of the design. They need to assess the readiness of the various parts of the organization to make the required changes for the "should" design and understand the complexity of putting the changes in place. With that understanding, they can recommend an appropriate implementation strategy—with timing and phasing that is feasible and emphasis on the appropriate level of change management activity.

Sara has some proven tools to help in this assessment. The team determines where they can move swiftly in implementation and decide where they may need a phased or go-slow approach. They group the improvement requirements into sets of changes that can be implemented together and carefully stage the changes to achieve impact and match the appropriate implementation strategy. All of this is documented in a macro implementation plan (Figure 7.14). The team identifies the resources needed for the Commit Phase planning sessions and for implementation.

They spend the week reaching out to stakeholders to complete the assessments and develop a stakeholder management plan. The final day is spent rehearsing for the upcoming Steering Team meeting.

April 14: Steering Team Meeting

On the day of the Steering Team meeting, the Project Team presents its information—with Brian leading and Sara supporting as needed (for example, on the kick-off, transition between subjects, approval of the overall design). They follow this agenda:

1. Review of "is" work process and management system documentation and validation efforts, previously presented in detail (5 minutes)

Figure 7.14 Macro Implementation Plan

Improvement Requirements Bundle	Dimension	Period					
		1st Quarter			2nd Quarter	3rd Quarter	4th Quarter
		Month 1	Month 2	Month 3			
A—Accurate and Timely Orders: 3—Sales Reps submit proposals to all new customers 7—Sales orders capture software will require orders to be complete before submission 8—Sales orders are submitted daily or at time of order 10—Commission on the sales is not paid until the order has shipped 24—Standard proposals will be available on-line for sales reps	*Activity*	Standard Proposals Developed Laptops issued Reps submit orders daily via fax	Reps begin to submit proposals Commission change in effect		Web development	Proposals On-line Sales Order Software in use via web	
	Cost	$100,000			$80,000	$40,000	
	Impact		Payroll reduction $25,000 Increase in order accuracy and completeness			Payroll reduction $50,000 Cycle time reduction of 7 days	Payroll reduction $50,000

Table 7.3 Design Phase Pitfalls/Success Factors Matrix

Potential Pitfalls/Risks During This Phase	What Sara Did to Mitigate Risks	RPM Critical Success Factors Addressed
Lack of creativity	Led the team in developing innovation ideas, which helped assess their ability to come up with creative design ideas	#6: "Is" to "should" strategy
Too much or too little detail in the "should" design	Applied a macro-to-micro design approach, which helped the team add more and more detail until they reached task level	#5: Visual modeling
Neglecting management of the process	Had an augmented Project Team develop the process management system for the process	#8: Process management system design
Dragging out the Design Phase with too many short TQM-style meetings	Proceeded according to a project plan that required spaced multiday sessions that produced large amounts of work	#3: Project management accountability
Not addressing elements of the Effective Process Framework against process design	Methodically reviewing the design against the EPF and building in more changes as required	#1: Design dimensions
Failing to consider alternatives to the overall design or to various disconnects	Used innovation ideas to create multiple options Led the Project Team several times in reviewing the design against the disconnects list and creating more solutions where necessary	#6: "Is" to "should" strategy
Not getting the design down to the performer level	Checked the designs against the Human Performance System and Technology Performance System Captured and detailed all of the changes related to human and technology performance in the enablers chart	#7: Performer integration
Providing too little detail about the "should" changes implied in the "should" process	Project Team developed full descriptions of all the major changes built into the "should" process	
Not testing the feasibility of the "should" design	Conducted a tabletop feasibility test with selected SME team	
Not assessing organizational readiness for the "should" design	Formally conducted assessment of organizational readiness	#9: Change readiness assessment

2. Review of disconnect analysis findings, previously presented in detail (10 minutes)

3. Review of "should" specifications, assumptions, and macro design, highlighting any updates since last presented (15–30 minutes)

4. High-level introduction to the "should" work process and process management system (30–60 minutes)

5. Presentation of work process and process Management System Testing (10 minutes)

6. "Is" to "should" change summary (20 minutes)

7. Presentation of "should" process technology requirements (5–20 minutes)

8. Presentation of improvement requirements (60–90 minutes)

9. Presentation of macro implementation plan (30 minutes)

10. Presentation of stakeholder management plan (30 minutes)

11. Request for approval of "should" design

The Steering Team approved the design with no hesitation, much to the delight of the Project Team.

Design Phase Summary

Phase deliverables:

1. Tested "Should" Work Process

2. "Should" Process Technology Requirements

3. Tested "Should" Work Process Management System

4. Improvement Requirements

5. "Is" to "Should" Change Summary

6. Macro Implementation Plan

7. Stakeholder Management Plan

Time: 41 days (March 5–April 14)

CLOSING POINTS

We have walked through the first three phases of a typical process improvement using the Rummler Process Methodology. We have seen the Process Consultant, Sara Harmon, start the project by enlarging the project scope so that it addresses an entire process. Then, with considerable help from the Project Team Leader, she conducts a thorough analysis of the "is" process and leads the project team in designing a "should" process that addresses all major deficiencies and meets the project goals.

In the next chapter, the Sterling project example continues, as Sara and the Project Team advance into the phases of Commit, Build, Enable and Adopt. We will again pay close attention to how Sara, the process practitioner, and Brian, the Project Team Leader, guide the project according to RPM critical success factors.

CHAPTER EIGHT

RPM Project Walk-Through: Commit, Build, Enable, Adopt

As tracked in Chapter Seven, the Sterling Publishing Project Team has successfully navigated the Align, Analysis, and Design phases of the Rummler Process Methodology. Now Sara and Brian have logistics to prepare for the Commit Phase implementation planning sessions. This is where many more project participants come on board, in order that they learn all of the work of implementation but also to broaden their buy-in and engagement with the "should" design.

Once the Steering Team has approved the "should" design and authorized its implementation in the Commit phase, the detailed work of the Build phase takes place, which involves the participation of many experts to produce all of the components of the design. In parallel, the organizations where implementation takes place are trained and prepared during the Enable phase, and the design is rolled out during Adopt.

Phase 4.0: Commit

Phase	*Sub-Phase*
4.0 Commit	

April 15–18

The objectives of the Commit phase are

1. To put detailed plans in place for the implementation of all change requirements so that an informed approval of the next phases can be made and so that the project is predictable and manageable

2. To broaden the change effort to include many more participants required to complete the work of implementation and to expand support and buy-in for the changes

3. To develop plans that include change management activities for managing resistance and ensuring institutionalization; otherwise, the organization will continue to do things the old way

4. To develop plans that include end-state conditions for all of the changes so that performance can be evaluated

Sara knows what it takes for successful implementation and that many projects run into serious troubles at this point. She and the team have already addressed many of the issues that plague implementation: lack of a clear vision of why the change is necessary, a compelling Critical Business Issue and Critical Process Issue, leadership commitment, a sound implementation strategy appropriate to complexity of process and organization. Now she knows it is time to address some of the other potential "gotchas" of implementation efforts. She knows that they must have a detailed plan that includes:

- Adequate steps to manage resistance
- Implementation infrastructure in place
- Roles and responsibilities clarified
- Right people on the implementation teams
- Clear accountabilities established

Originally the Project Team got some pushback from the Steering Team as to why these plans couldn't be developed by individual workgroups, without the need for a big event that all the participants would attend. The Steering Team even suggested that the Project Team could develop the plan. Sara explained to them the risks of doing so: that those doing the planning would not know all the work needed to implement the various changes, as they are not the experts on the "should" design. They would be committing resources to tasks and timelines that may in fact not be doable. And at the end of it all, the Project Team is as yet the only group that believes in the vision of the "should"; that is too small a number of employees to drive the change forward in a big organization like Sterling Publishing. Even if they took the approach of having the implementation teams work separately on the plan and then integrate, Sara knows that this would take much longer and the plan would be of lesser quality. (She knows, because she has tried this before.) And they would get none of the benefits of having the big Commit event, namely:

- Integrated implementation plan creation in a relatively short period of time (three days or less), the most efficient and effective way to do this
- The energy factor of getting the larger team together. Also a strong kick-off (lots of momentum) for the next phases
- High-visibility reward for the Project Team's effort
- High-visibility demonstration of sponsorship
- Making the time and cost commitment sends a big message to the organization and the newly formed implementation teams

Brian has planned for the session to be off-site at a local business hotel in order to accommodate all of the meeting participants and to minimize distractions. He has reserved the main ballroom and several rooms to be used for breakout planning sessions. The Steering Team will be present for the kick-off. All of the Project Team members have a role in the kick-off. A set of project documents has been created for each implementation team member to use as reference during the planning sessions.

There are seven Implementation Teams for the Order to Cash process, based on the seven groupings of improvement requirements identified by the Project Team. The Implementation Teams included expertise from each area that would be required to work on the detailed design as well as representatives of the groups that would be receiving the changes. A team leader for each team has been selected. Five of the team leaders are Project Team members, who will now pick up this new role for implementation. There is at least one Project Team member on each team in order to keep continuity.

April 21–23

The day begins with the kick-off in the big ballroom. They followed the agenda presented in Table 8.1.

The Project Team members were eager to present the "should" design to this larger audience. They felt good about the level of excitement that it seemed to generate. Once the kick-off had concluded, the individual Implementation Teams went to their assigned breakout rooms per Sara's Instructions.

The task was to develop and sequence the tasks required to build, enable, and adopt the change requirements (one change requirement at a time). The plans were built on big paper on the wall, much like a process map—each task on a sticky note. The implementation leaders directed the teams to start first by sequencing the milestones up on the wall. (These were given to them in the change requirements documentation.) Then the teams filled in the tasks required to get from milestone to milestone, according to the experts in the room. Along the way they identified and recorded on flip charts any interdependencies with other teams or the organization (from and to), along with the expected date of that interdependency. All tasks were assigned to resources, assigned start and end dates, an estimate of the days needed for each task, and any support that would be required. If they had to confirm availability of a resource not in the room, they made calls or sent e-mails to get confirmation. Sara had told them that this needed to be a realistic, achievable plan—which meant no "wishful" resourcing or timelines.

Table 8.1 Implementation Planning Agenda

Agenda Item	Objective	Presenter
Project CBI, CPI, current level of performance and major disconnects	Reason we launched this effort Build the case for change	Sponsor and Director of Finance
Process and Implementation methodology overview (RPM)	Build confidence in the approach Build confidence that this will get implemented Orient audience to the big picture of the task for the duration of the project	Sara
"Should" design	Walk through the process Create a clear vision of the changes, features, and benefits Answer questions	Project Team members
The immediate task of implementation planning	Describe and give instructions	Sara

It took all the way to the end of the third day for all of the teams to finish. When they were all done, each team had a plan that addressed:

- Detailed design that remains to be completed
- Development
- Testing
- Piloting where necessary
- Packaging
- Preparing the receiving organizations: expectation setting, communication, and training
- Disabling the old way of doing things
- Cut-over to the new way
- Stabilizing
- Operating and verifying the results

April 24–25
Sara met with the Implementation Team Leaders the following morning. Then they began the work of integrating the plans into one plan. Along the way they reviewed each interdependency and negotiated and adjusted dates. They identified key milestones for project tracking purposes. The integration took the full two days. In the end, one of the Team Leaders commented that in his history with Sterling, he had never seen such a detailed and thoughtful plan for the implementation of any change—big or small. Another team leader retorted that may be why they failed to implement most projects.

April 30
Back to the Steering Team again, though this time the meeting was only one and a half hours. They reviewed the plan milestones and took a look at the resources required to implement. The Steering Team was impressed with the level of detail in the plan and the amount of insight they would have into how the plan is progressing during these next phases of the project. Then Brian reinforced the role of the Steering Team going forward into implementation. During these phases of Build, Enable, and Adopt, the Steering Team was expected to provide continued active stakeholder management, continued champion role, continued help to remove barriers to required resources, and participation in end-of-phase reviews. Commit phase pitfalls and success factors are shown in Table 8.2. The Steering Team approved the plan and budget.

Commit Phase Summary
Phase deliverables:

1. Change Requirements Package Summary
2. Detailed Implementation Plan
3. Implementation Definition Document
4. Implementation Budget
5. Phase 4 Approval Presentation

   Time: 15 days (April 15–April 30)

Table 8.2 Commit Phase Pitfalls/Success Factors Matrix

Potential Pitfalls/Risks During This Phase	What Sara Did to Mitigate Risks	RPM Critical Success Factors Addressed
Unwillingness (Steering Team or others) to spend sufficient time in implementation planning	Provided sound arguments for the benefits of the planning activity	#10 – Implementation planning and management
Loss of Project Team member continuity	Recruited some Project Team members as Implementation Team Leaders	#10 – Implementation planning and management
Implementation plans that don't integrate well into one solid plan	Had Implementation Team Leaders consolidate their plans into one agreed-upon plan	#10 – Implementation planning and management

Phase 5.0: Build and Phase 6.0: Enable

Phase	Sub-Phase
5.0 Build	5.1 Detailed Design
	5.2 Develop
	5.3 Test
	5.4 Solution Preparation

Phase	Sub-Phase
6.0 Enable	6.1 Prepare
	6.2 Internal Launch

March–Mid-May

Now a flurry of activities—all according to the plan—begins and continues for the next several months. Both the Build phase and the Enable phase are kicked off in parallel. What Sara knows about these phases and the next phase, Adopt, is that they must be closely managed. Much individual expert work must be done in order to build and implement the process changes—work like application development or policy development. The natural tendency of the experts who have been assigned to this work is to go off in their silos to do the work and emerge only when they have the final product. Sara knows that this could be very bad for the project. This is why she has set up regular meetings and reviews with the implementation team leaders. This is also why the testing plans include the integration and testing of components from across the silos.

The other thing that Sara understands about implementation is that these phases are usually the longest in duration, and the organization can lose the sense of urgency and focus that it has had on this effort to date. It is important to manage expectations about the timing and impact of the changes as they are rolled out. The teams had built in Stakeholder management activities into their implementation plans—but Sara and the Implementation Leaders will also be working on an overall communication plan and adding any additional stakeholder interventions as needed.

Last, Sara also knows one other important fact about implementation. The first part of Build is Detailed Design. The design was intentionally left incomplete at this level so that the broader organization would now be involved in completing the design, which helps build a broader base of buy-in for the changes. It is entirely possible that during detailed design, others may come up with new enhancements to the process or that the organization will place new demands on the process. But it is imperative that these not derail the existing effort. For this reason, they have put in place a formal process for submission and review of design change requests.

During the detailed design sub-phase, detailed functional and technical specifications are developed. The design is driven down to performer and task level for all of the changes. One of the Implementation Teams works on the details to support the management of the process. Test plans are developed for all of the changes.

Phase	Sub-Phase
5.0 Build	5.1 Detailed Design
	5.2 Develop
	5.3 Test
	5.4 Solution Preparation

May–November

Once the detailed designs were completed, it was time to begin the development, construction, or acquisition of all components that needed to be put in place. Teams at Sterling were busy building the new order database, the new credit checking policies and practices, the new sales compensation changes. Training and training plans were developed. Contingency plans for implementation were also a part of this phase.

Many of these components were brought together and tested in an integrated fashion, in order to ensure that they worked as a total system. Training materials on tracking orders were tested together with the new database and policies on order standards.

Phase	Sub-Phase
5.0 Build	5.1 Detailed Design
	5.2 Develop
	5.3 Test
	5.4 Solution Preparation

Phase	Sub-Phase
6.0 Enable	6.1 Prepare
	6.2 Internal Launch

November–December

With all of the changes built and successfully tested, the last several weeks of the year were spent packaging the components and changes in such a way as to be most helpful for the users, operators, or supporters of the process, to increase their perception of value and to minimize their frustration during implementation. Then all of the physical elements, information elements, and instructions were transferred to the receiving teams at all of the implementation sites. Implementers were prepared as a part of the internal launch of the process. Build Phase pitfalls and success factors are presented in Table 8.3; Enable Phase pitfalls and success factors in Table 8.4.

Table 8.3 Build Phase Pitfalls/Success Factors Matrix

Potential Pitfalls/Risks During This Phase	How Sara Addressed These Factors	RPM Critical Success Factors Addressed
Performer level not adequately understood or addressed	Build teams were established to build both technology and human performance capabilities into the process	#7 – Performer integration—technology and human
Uncoordinated implementation efforts	Sara held a formal implementation planning session and followed up with implementation team leaders to produce an integrated plan	#10 – Implementation planning and management
Potential drifting away from the original design by implementation teams	Regular meetings of team leaders Formalized design change process	#10 – Implementation planning and management

Table 8.4 Enable Phase Pitfalls/Success Factors Matrix

Potential Pitfalls/Risks During This Phase	What Sara Did to Mitigate Risks	RPM Critical Success Factors Addressed
Unpleasant surprises when end users try to perform as the "should" design requires	Testing for every Build component Formalized integration of every component (policies, documents, tools, technology) into the "should" process at performer level Involvement of receiving organizations on the implementation teams from planning forward	#10 – Implementation planning and management #7 – Performer integration — technology and human #9 – Change readiness assessment

Build Phase Summary

Phase deliverables:

1. Functional Designs

2. Technical Designs

3. Performer Job/Role/Organization Design

4. Management Role Design

5. Requirements Detailed Design/Development/Test/Sign-offs

6. Should Design Components Deliverables Summary and Delivery Plan

   Time: 8 months (May 1–December 3)

Enable Phase Summary

Phase deliverables:

Validated Implementation Plan (with detailed tasks for Cut Over, Stabilize, and Operate)

   Time: 8 months (May 1–Dec 31) running in parallel with Build Phase

Phase 7.0: Adopt

Phase	Sub-Phase
7.0 Adopt	7.1 Cut over
	7.2 Stabilize
	7.3 Operate

January 5–March

At last, cut-over day had arrived for the Order to Cash process. The new process became effective on Monday morning. In order to ensure that process performers did not revert back to old habits, Sara and the implementation teams made sure that some of the old process was also "disabled." For example, fax machines in the Sales admin office were moved so that orders could no longer be faxed in.

After a short period of stabilization, with rapid response to any issues, the process did indeed produce the results that Sara and the team set out to achieve. The Process Management Team for the Order to Cash process began to plan for continued improvements in the process in order to stay competitive.

Adopt Phase Summary

Phase deliverables:

1. Stabilized process changes

2. Process Performance Data

   Time: 2 months (January 1–March 1)

Table 8.5 Adopt Phase Pitfalls/Success Factors Matrix

Potential Pitfalls/Risks During This Phase	What Sara Did to Mitigate Risks	RPM Critical Success Factors Addressed
New process doesn't "take"—old practices continue	Formal cut-off Old tools, practices made impossible, or at least inconvenient	#6 – "Is" to "should" strategy
Problems after implementation are not dealt with	Period of debugging was built into the schedule	#10 – Implementation planning and management

Table 8.6 Project Timetable

Phase	Elapsed Time	Calendar
Align	3 days	January 21–23
Analysis	23 days	Feb. 11–Mar. 4
Design	41 days	Mar. 5–Apr. 14
Commit	15 days	Apr. 15–Apr. 30
Build & Enable	8 mo.	May–December
Adopt	2 mo.	Jan.–March

Project Summary and Timetable

From start to finish, Sara's project involved dozens of Sterling employees and hundreds of hours and took a little over a year. A timeline is presented as Table 8.6.

CLOSING POINTS

In recounting Sara's experience, our intention was to give you a close-up look at the Rummler Process Methodology in action, with enough detail and "color commentary" that you could get a better sense of how to apply the process and tools than you would from just looking at a set of filled-in diagrams and charts. From the challenges you saw thrown in Sara's way throughout the project, you know that this work is not at all easy or by-the-numbers, despite the structure the RPM affords. For more on who should do this kind of work, see Chapter Ten. Meanwhile, we examine various applications of the RPM approach to different situations in Chapter Nine.

CHAPTER NINE

Other RPM Applications

Our example of Sterling in Chapters Seven and Eight illustrated the use of the Rummler Performance Methodology for a single cross-functional process, but RPM is applicable to any level of the Value Creation System, from a sub-process to a complete process all the way up to an entire line of business (as in Figure 7.2). In this chapter, we illustrate the range of possible applications of the methodology with a series of examples drawn from different situations in different industries. We conclude with a comparison of RPM with other prominent tools and methods used today in process improvement work.

Example 1: Whole Business Redesign/Multiple Processes

Organization
Insurance company that wanted to double in size within five years

CBI
Operations hampered by legacy systems that caused work processes to be highly complex, liable to errors, noncompetitive, and an obstacle to growth or change in business approach

CPIs
Varied by process, but most were too slow compared to competition and prone to human error because of system and process complexities

Approach
- Executive Team analyzed its current super-system and business model, then developed possible future-state scenarios and identified the capabilities (process/technology/people/management/ general infrastructure) required to succeed in the future.

- Project Team (composed of process excellence specialists, IT representatives, and middle managers):
  - Updated an "is" Value Creation Architecture down to Level 3 (they already had an "is" Business Process Framework and existing Level 3 "is" process maps)
  - Distributed the required capabilities along the VCA, which revealed capability gaps
  - Developed high-level (whole business) alternative designs and discovered that the future business would require not one, but three different L-S-D Launched, Sold, and Delivered designs (that is, high tech, high touch and large corporate customers)
- The Project Team then was divided into three sub-teams, each of which developed a full VCA down to Level 5, following the standard RPM methodology (from design phase on) but with three designs in parallel and applied to multiple processes within each VCA.
- Each design included models of all the future-state processes showing both human and technology performers in detail and their Human Performance System/Technology Performance System requirements.
- The three VCAs were presented to management for approval and funding.
- The three VCAs were implemented together into the existing business, as they were not three different lines of business but three ways to deliver the company's products and services.

Key Points About This Case

- Scope was not predetermined: Project started with a super-ordinate business goal (that is, growth) and CBI, then led to a gap analysis between current state and future business scenarios showed that the entire business had to be in project scope and potentially redesigned.
- Executive team engagement in first stage of work ensured their ongoing support and active interest in the result of the project.
- RPM methodology is scalable to multiple processes and even entire lines of business.
- Technologists were key members of each design sub-team, providing design ideas and guidance about the practicality of technology usage in the processes, and watching over alignment of the designs with the company's Enterprise Architecture vision.
- Once the three sub-teams were formed, they met frequently to review progress and share their designs. The sub-teams were encouraged to borrow process and technology designs from each other, which helped to minimize the total cost of the proposed "should" VCAs. (For example, the Large Corporate Customer sub-team largely adopted a mix of processes from the High Tech and High Touch sub-teams and created few of their own.)
- The "alternative designs" technique is scalable: such designs can address any aspect of the Effective Process Framework for a process, the entire process architecture, or even an entire business (which happened in this case).
- Despite the large scale and scope of work, the project was completed in just twelve weeks, because the Project Team members devoted at least three days per week to the project for its duration, and they were supported by the executives who gave the project the highest priority.
- The speed of the project was also helped by the fact that the team had earlier developed something of an "is" Business Process Framework and had Level 3 process maps, so the Analysis Phase was relatively brief.

Example 2: Business Process Framework Definition and Utilization

Organization

Global cement, aggregates, concrete, and other building products company

CBI

A key component of the organization's strategy was growth through acquisition. The speed and quality of assimilation was insufficient and greatly affected the ROI of each acquisition.

CPIs

The assimilation efforts suffered endless and expensive stabilization phases because of the narrow focus on the IT systems integration without understanding and addressing the work processes. The organization leadership had made a decision to take a process approach to this work but lacked a common framework for making critical decisions regarding the scope and phases of ERP and process practices migration.

Approach

- Existing process lists, business line definitions, and process domain views that already existed were gathered and synthesized into a single draft Business Process Framework (BPF).

- A group of Processes & IT representatives with significant business understanding were assembled to validate and adjust the Business Process Framework (BPF) in a series of sessions.

- Teams of Processes & IT staff were assigned to create profiles of each Value Creation, Management System, and Contributing System process identified in the BPF. The profiles included:

  ◦ Process mission statement

  ◦ Process scope (inputs, outputs, and sub-processes)

  ◦ Key performance indicators

  ◦ Operating functions involved in executing the process

  ◦ Related ERP and other IT systems and applications that supported the process globally

  ◦ Global process variations

  ◦ Standardized and harmonized process components

- The process profiles were shared across teams and cross-referenced to minimize potential for process overlap and gaps.

- The BPF and supporting process profiles were reviewed and endorsed by senior Processes & IT managers.

- The BPF was used as a framework for ERP migration planning by creating customized views highlighting those processes that were directly and indirectly supported by each ERP module and the desired staging of the module migration in acquired operations.

- The BPF was used a framework for identifying standardized and harmonized process components to be migrated into acquired operations. Interim process actions for processes supported by ERP modules that would not be migrated immediately were identified.

Key Points About This Case

- Mature global organizations operate a platform of standardized processes and information technology. These platforms are interdependent but unique. Both present opportunities for optimizing the cost and effectiveness of doing business globally.

- Without a view of the work system (the business processes and IT systems) and its relationship to the value created for customers, the organization had no valid criteria for making tradeoffs between desired requirements/functionalities and potential performance efficiencies. This created great debates among all stakeholders (the acquired operations, business management and the Processes & IT Department) that tended to center around the responsiveness of Processes & IT instead of the impact on organization performance. This was a no-win situation for Processes & IT, which typically defaulted to accepting an "order taker" position. The resulting organization impact was complex systems that accommodated every requirement/functionality but were expensive to maintain and costly and slow to evolve.

- The BPF effort was one of four key components of their process approach. It was supported by the other three components: Process Improvement Methodology, a process-oriented Project Portfolio Management System, and common tools, conventions, and repository for capturing process documentation.

Example 3: Contributing Process

Organization
Financial services company/Human Resources Recruiting Department

CBI
Insufficient qualified new talent, affecting bottom-line results

CPI
Line department managers considered the "is" recruiting process inefficient, bureaucratic and overcontrolled by HR

Approach

- Project cosponsors from HR and line organizations established a Steering Team and Project Team.

- While project target was the Recruiting Process, scope included downstream processes that were affected by slow recruiting (that is, department on-boarding, training).

- Standard RPM Analysis Phase was conducted.

- Analysis revealed that some key disconnects (slowness in finding qualified technical candidates) was caused by poor or nonexistent relationships with local and state sources such as universities as well as failure of line managers to get their recruiting needs into the recruiting pipeline on time.

- Project Team conducted fact-finding visits with selected universities to explore options for campus recruiting (for example, fairs, job postings, and so on).

- "Should" design incorporated several possible new sources and techniques for finding candidates.

- Project Team recommended piloting of campus fair concept as well as tightening up of recruiting process to minimize wait times between interviews.

- Steering Team reviewed and endorsed the "Should" design and authorized the pilot.

Key Points About This Case

- Even though a small contributing process, the recruiting process was cross-functional so its improvement required a full project team.

- HR was viewed as the process owner (and the cause of all the problems), but the project demonstrated the need for cross-functional accountability and revealed that some problems were not being caused by HR.

Example 4: Support Function and Contributing Processes Redesign/Multiple Processes

Organization

The library of a government research lab

CBI

The research lab and library had suffered from years of funding cuts, but the area of research had recently received renewed mandate to advance the field. The research lab recognized that leading researchers would require strong library services to access past research and monitor the field, and the lab considered investing in a major upgrade to the library to support their new mandate. However, after decades of making due with less, library personnel had difficulty conceiving of the services, processes, and facilities required to support a "library of the future."

CPIs

Varied by process, some were more time sensitive than others, but the primary driver was value: the library services had to meet real needs with the right level of service and at a reasonable and competitive cost.

Approach

- A team of Library Representatives analyzed its current super-system and identified the lab's value creation processes, then identified the points in value creation at which customers/users could benefit from library services.

- The Library Team then defined the services of the "Library of the Future":

  - Reviewed and challenged the value of existing services

  - Brainstormed new services and service extensions, including the possibility of teaming with internal and external service partners; in some cases these were already existing services but had to be translated so that the customers could understand the value (for example "Bibliographic and Citation Verification" to "Publishing Assistance")

  - Defined or redefined all services using customer-oriented terms

  The Library Team then developed draft profiles for each service, including service description, value proposition, delivery assumptions and options, customer requirements, key performance indicators, funding assumptions, and facilities requirements.

  Focus groups were conducted with different cross-sections of customers, users, and other stakeholders to get feedback on the value of each service, alternative services, and service requirements.

- The service profiles were adjusted based on the feedback, and the baseline list of Library of the Future services established.

- With this input, the Library of the Future Business Process Framework (BPF) was developed. They developed a framework that could deliver all of the services and still leverage the fewest number of unique processes.

(The library's Value Creation Processes would rightfully be depicted as a Contributing processing system on the research lab's VCA.)

- The Library Team successfully presented the vision, services, and supporting facilities to lab management and the architects supporting the transformation of the lab.

Key Points About This Case

- In most cases, a support function's value creation processes would appear as contributing processes on the greater organization's BPF. The support function's VCA would also include management and contributing processes. The management processes identified were consciously aligned with the greater organization's management process (for example, planning and budgeting sequencing aligned). The contributing processes were a combination of unique-to-the-library contributions and greater organization contributions from other support functions (for example, human capital inputs from Human Resources).

- The work was cast as "process improvement," and that was clearly the desired end point. However, processes cannot be designed in a vacuum, so the focus became "what" value was to be provided by the library (the processes would define "how" the value would be delivered).

- Using a services-based approach to reviewing support functions was an effective way of understanding the value contribution of a support function. However, it was critical that these contributions be linked in a tangible way to the greater organization's BPF to establish credibility and establish the value of each service to the greater organization.

- Development of the support function's BPF started with the "Products/Services Delivered" portion of the Value Creation processes, since these processes link directly to the service profiles (the services being delivered). At this point, a key element of organization strategy comes into play by asking two questions: "What are the unique service delivery characteristics that we need to be careful not to lose or compromise?" and "What are the desired and required synergies between the service delivery processes?" In this case, the eleven Library of the Future services were organized into four service delivery sets and processes.

- After defining the "Delivered" portion of the BPF, the focus shifted upstream to the processes for creating awareness and getting commitments to utilize the services ("Sold"), and the processes for refreshing, adapting, creating, and launching services ("Launched"). In each portion of the BPF unique process characteristics and process synergies were identified, and the resulting process strategy was different in "Sold" than it was in "Delivered," and different again in "Launched."

RPM AND OTHER PRACTICES

We presume that many of the readers of this book work in organizations that have already adopted various tools or methods from the vast and probably indefinable field of "improvement" and want to understand how the Rummler Performance Methodology compares to those other approaches. Some readers, we are certain, will be interested in whether RPM could replace their current practices, augment them, or be integrated with them. So allow us to comment on some of the more prominent tools and methods from our RPM vantage point.

What We Mean by Methodology

We think that a sound process improvement methodology should be:

- Teachable

- Repeatable

- Yield the desired results every time the methodology is followed, as long as it is followed as prescribed

What distinguishes a good methodology from an inferior one is that a good one:

- Is guided by principles

- Is highly structured into a logical, coherent, phase-by-phase, step-by-step flow

- Contains a logical sequence of guiding principles, roles, steps, tools, techniques, examples, and alternatives

- Is reasonably scalable (so that it can be applied to different-sized projects)

- Is addresses all dimensions of business process improvement (as described in the Effective Process Framework in Chapter Six)

- Is adaptable to specific business, process, and project needs and characteristics within the boundaries defined by the guiding principles

In other words, a methodology should itself be a well-designed process, as illustrated in Figure 9.1.

When a methodology is so designed, there are benefits to companies that adopt it. Among those benefits:

- Improvement can be planned. (When a methodology is so well laid out that you can see the participants and the time and effort required of them, the precise timetable, the step-by-step activities, you can develop adequate project plans. Methodologies that lack such details, by contrast, usually play havoc with schedules and expectations.)

- Large numbers of people can participate in improving processes. (A methodology that is widely teachable and applicable to many situations means you can engage many people in learning and applying the techniques, which not only makes possible more widespread application, but greater numbers of people truly understand the methodology, become committed to it, and come to appreciate the positive effects of improvement.)

- Results can be predicted. (A sound methodology yields the results for which it was designed; those less well designed are far less predictable in their ultimate outputs.)

- Costs can be controlled. (A well-designed methodology tends to reduce the likelihood of unexpected extra steps or detours, or a surprising need for additional resources.)

Figure 9.1 A Well-Designed Process

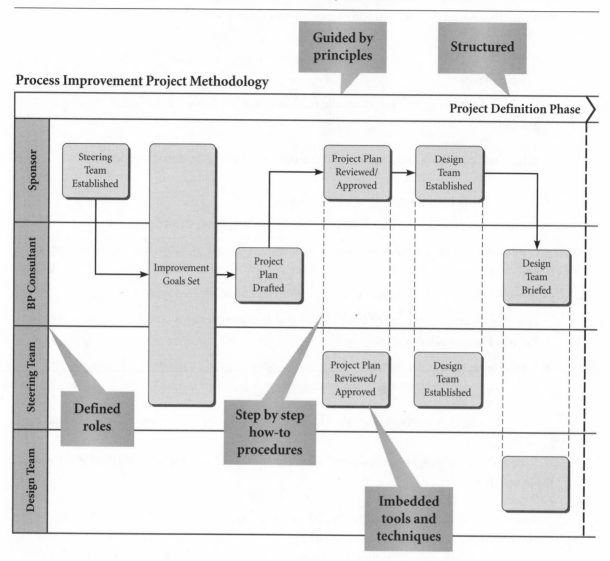

Contrary to the misperceptions of some who prefer to create approaches that are unique to each and every project, a good methodology enables flexibility (not limits it) by allowing practitioners to focus on defining appropriate strategies and tactics to meet the few truly unique requirements.

"Non-Methodologies"

One of the toughest challenges in finding and selecting a suitable improvement methodology is that many things that aren't true methodologies are often mistaken for such. Sometimes this confusion is accidental, based on appearances mostly; but there are also deliberate attempts to peddle some tools, techniques, models, and so on, as methodologies when they most certainly are not. Things masquerading as methodologies include:

- Philosophies
- Aphorisms and exhortations
- Principles
- Models
- Tools and techniques
- Best practices
- Schools of practice

Several of these items are in fact helpful and necessary ingredients for sound methodologies, but they shouldn't be mistaken as methodologies in and of themselves. Table 9.1 defines each of these items along with an example or two from the improvement field.

Table 9.1 Components of Methodology

	What It Is	Its Value in Process Improvement Efforts	What It Does Not Necessarily Provide	Examples
Philosophy	Belief that something is important or true	Explains WHY something should be pursued	How to do that something	Kaizen
Aphorisms and Exhortations	Sometimes witty sayings designed to inspire or provide insight	Entertaining but questionable in a methodology	Anything practical	"Reengineering means industrial-strength change"[1]
Principle	Heuristic—high-level rule of thumb	Guides the specific application of tools and techniques	Some guidance but lack of specific step-by-step application	Single source of truth Data-driven decision making
Model	Depiction of relationships between elements or parts	Describes the components of a methodology; depicts the landscape	How to apply the model	Value Creation Hierarchy
Tool or Technique	Specific item for executing a task	Methodologies are made up of tools & techniques	Linkages between tools, techniques	Control chart Process modeling/ mapping software Mistake-proofing
Best Practices	Specific applications of tools, techniques, methods inside companies; collections of these practices	How a tool or technique could look as a finished product	How it can be used successfully in a given situation	AQPC products
Program (often associated with Philosophies and Schools of Practice)	A set of organized activities with high-level steps and functional participation requirements, usually supported by a program office	Engages line managers; promotes activity; creates career development opportunities	A focus on sustainable performance improvement	"Innovation process" "Quality process"
School of Practice	A loose (not necessarily official) collection of people in a field that may or may not be well defined	Practitioners both share practices and compete, enriching the practice but potentially causing confusion	A consistent methodology	Six Sigma

Table 9.2 Some RPM "Methodologies"

Example	Focus	Type	Our Critique	Relationship to RPM
Defect Reduction				
Six Sigma	Quality improvement Error reduction Statistical process control	School of practice	Because Six Sigma focuses on a single metric and root causes of defects, is best applied to a sub-process or task (Level 5 of the VCA) Best employed for small continuous improvement projects after a redesigned process has been implemented To bring the process back into control To increase process capability	Strong toolkit for analysis that can readily be used primarily during RPM Analysis phase
Lean	Waste reduction Improvement of flow across process steps	Methodology, philosophy	Philosophy ("Waste is bad") is highly compatible with RPM principles	Lots of tools and techniques for streamlining processes that can be used during Design Phase of RPM
Reference Models				
SCOR V-COR ITIL	Process definition Performance measurement/benchmarking	Model	SCOR does have a step by step approach but is known more as a process architecture model Limited (for example, SCOR focuses on supply chain, ITIL on IT processes) Promotes comparability across companies and industries at the expense of gaining insight into the value of adopting a process perspective	Could be useful as a starting point for building a Business Process Framework, but dangerous to rely on a reference model below Level 2 (every organization is different) Could be used as a test for comprehensiveness of an existing Business Process Framework. Starting with a generic model and adapting it will result in faster agreement on a list of processes, but it fails to develop an understanding of process definition option strengths and weaknesses and linkage to business strategy which is an essential component of a process culture.
Maturity Models				
CMMI	Evaluation of an organization's processes against an ideal	Model	Mostly focused on defining "maturity" and whether an organization has all the bureaucracy in place to meet the model's ideal definition No principles, tools or methodology	Little use in RPM
Technology Development Methodologies				
RUP SDLC	Method and tools for developing systems/software	Methodology	RUP and SDLC are not process improvement methodologies although they are sometimes described as such; they are high level frameworks specifically focused on systems/software development and lack specific steps and tools	RUP and SDLC provide useful frameworks for Commit Phase planning of implementation and detailed Build Phase planning when a "Should" Design has identified business requirements for technology to support specific parts of the work process

Process Notation				
BPMN/ BPEL UML	Tools for process mapping & documentation	Tools	UML tools are primarily useful to technology developers; some (that is, activity diagrams) are promoted as process capture tools but are too low-level	BPMN are entirely compatible tools for capturing "is" processes during the Analysis Phase and for developing "should" designs during the Design Phase
Process-Centered Organization				
Programs, concepts taught by Michael Hammer	Process ownership Process-centered organizations	Primarily philosophy, aphorisms and exhortations, and best practices	Primarily provided a public forum for success stories. Courses were principle-based. While some of Hammer's principles were sound, the general tone of his work was feel-good exhortation rather than how-to methodology. Encouraged challenging or "throwing out" current practices and striving for process excellence without any design methodology or transition roadmap. Encouraged process governance but provided little guidance on sustaining the additional management roles	No real methodology No relationship to RPM
Process Measurement				
Balanced Scorecard	Balanced set of organization-level metrics	Model	Primarily a dashboard approach to developing a set of performance metrics. Often incorporated into improvement efforts but not a methodology in itself. Unless anchored in an organization's Business Process Architecture, Balanced Scorecard designs tend to end up unused	Could be used in developing the "should" metrics for a process management system if the metrics are integrated into the whole management hierarchy
Process Culture				
Process-Centered Organization System Thinking	Viewing the objective of process work as installing a type of organizational "culture" or a "way of thinking"	Philosophy, behaviors	While it is true that organizations that succeed in changing their organizations through process redesign, the effective focus has always been on the business, not the resulting culture. Every attempt at "cultural transformation" we've ever seen has failed	Organizations become "process-centered" by applying methodologies like RPM, but becoming "process-centered" is not an end in itself
Process Governance				
Process managers, owners	Establishing a formal role or even a department as being in charge of process	Philosophy	The only way that process management works is when it is entirely integrated into the business management system of an organization. Process management teams can be effective in overcoming "white space" issues but they need to be populated by line managers who already have accountability for the processes in question	RPM includes the design of process management (i.e., roles, metrics, planning, monitoring, controlling) into the redesign of work processes. RPM also aims at integrating process management into the organization's existing management system. Process governance of the value creation system is the subject of our forthcoming book for managers and executives

The final category (that is, "school of practice") is our own made-up designation for those cases in which there may indeed be a methodology (that is, DMAIC, which is the classic Six Sigma methodology), but actual practice varies so much from one place to another (and from one provider to another) that it is impossible to claim that a single methodology exists. For us, the sign that a school of practice (many people practicing a large number of variations of a particular approach, tool, method, and so on) exists is that when we walk into a company that labels itself as, for example, a "Six Sigma" place, we cannot predict with confidence what will be going on in there. And in fact, we have walked into so-called Six Sigma companies, and sometimes we will see that practices amount to using a few easy, nonstatistical tools like histograms and check sheets; then we go somewhere else and the place is bristling with Black Belts, multiple project teams, and control charts. In other cases the Six Sigma "program" is little more than a device for nominating projects and certifying staff. So who knows what "Six Sigma" means anymore?

Available "Methodologies"

With those caveats, let's go to some of the "methodologies" (that is, real ones and seeming ones) and compare them with RPM for compatibility. (See Table 9.2.) In some cases, there are multiple approaches that fall under a given type (for example, reference models).

CLOSING POINTS

In this chapter we illustrated how the Rummler Process Methodology can be applied to a wide range of improvement projects, from single processes to entire businesses, and including contributing processes and functions. We also compared RPM to existing methodologies for those readers who may contemplate integrating their current practices with the RPM approach.

Up until now we have assumed there are people capable and available to do the kinds of process work we've described in this book. In the next chapter we will directly address the issue of capability—what kinds of infrastructure, processes and people does it take?

CHAPTER TEN

Designing Improvement Capability

Given the walkthrough of the Rummler Process Methodology in Chapters Six and Seven and the examples of different applications of RPM in Chapter Nine, you are probably asking how this approach can be institutionalized in an organization and applied to multiple projects. Who should do this kind of work and how the improvement efforts are managed are important questions. It is one thing to execute a single improvement project, as Sara and Brian did, but far more challenging to install an ongoing system for conducting such work across a large organization.

So in this chapter, we address how does one implement the Value Creation System desired, and once it is in place, keep it operating effectively in light of continual changes and challenges from within and from outside?

One starts with the recognition that improvement is not an event but an essential organizational capability: to effectively adjust or improve organization performance in response to changing business and customer requirements. In addition, establishing and maintaining this capability requires process and infrastructure that needs to be planned and managed.

Let's begin by looking at how Belding Engineering approached the need for a more permanent infrastructure and process to execute and manage change efforts.

THE BELDING ENGINEERING CASE: STAGE 3 PROCESS MANAGEMENT

For Stage 3 of its process evolution, Belding Engineering recognized that it had two needs:

1. Belding needed a mechanism for organizing, prioritizing, and funding RPM initiatives. This required a mechanism that was enterprise-wide in scope—it needed to account for all change initiatives in Belding regardless where the idea originated and who would be involved. Any change effort was seen as an opportunity to optimize or sub-optimize Belding's VCA using Belding resources.

2. Belding saw that managing a VCA change process, maintaining VCA documentation, ongoing VCA education, and conducting RPM projects were capabilities essential to their success. They established their own group, called the VCA Support Team, which was modeled after the Corporate Performance Support Group and reported to a director. At the heart of the VCA Support Team was a new role within Belding, the Performance Architect.

Let's first talk about the infrastructure and then about the process implemented to manage improvement at Belding.

Figure 10.1 Infrastructure to Support the Change Process

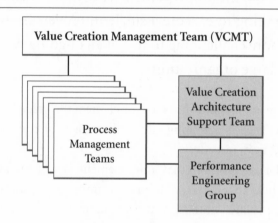

INFRASTRUCTURE TO SUPPORT CHANGE

To establish and sustain an ongoing improvement approach, an infrastructure is required. (See Figure 10.1.) The roles of the Leadership Team and Process Management Teams were introduced in Chapter Five and, as the names imply, are focused on planning and managing changes to processes and the Value Creation System. The addition to the infrastructure is a permanent group to support the management, maintenance, and ongoing improvement of the Belding VCA. This team is called the VCA Support Team. Headed by a director, the team is directly accountable to the Belding Leadership Team.

The VCA Support Team's major operational role is the care and feeding of the Belding Change Control Process. The Belding Change Control Process came about as Belding recognized that the value creation system that delivers value to customers had to be managed. Seen in the context of value creation, there was an unending stream of unmanaged initiatives underway that were unprioritized, potentially redundant, insufficiently important, consuming incalculable amounts of staff time and energy, potentially counterproductive to one another, and most important of all, likely to sub-optimize the performance of the total value creation system. These initiatives ranged from introducing Balanced Scorecards in Engineering to a Six Sigma project in Production to implementing a new CRM application in Sales through the IT organization.

CEO Owens decided that Belding would develop a single Change Control Process that would be managed by the Belding Leadership Team, since they were accountable for the performance of the value creation system and all these proposed changes ultimately affected the performance of the value creation system, positively or negatively. The objectives were to avoid inadvertent sub-optimization; properly prioritize needed changes; and manage the execution of change efforts. This meant that any change effort, at any level in the organization, that required more than a defined number of hours of staff time and/or funding, must pass through the Change Control Process.

Core team members of the VCA Support Team are made up of people transferred in from Engineering, IT, Production, and HR. The team also has access to key resources from Marketing, Sales, and Operations.

Major responsibilities of the VCA Support Team include:

- The Improvement Process (which we describe in some detail later in the chapter)
- Maintenance of the Management Bridge room, which includes:
  - Updating documentation on display in the room
  - Facilitating team meetings as required
- Maintenance and management of performance reporting
- Investigation/analysis of issues raised by the Belding Leadership Team. This is accomplished through the Performance Engineering Group, which reports to the VCA Support Team and has skills in the areas of performance analysis, process improvement and design, Six Sigma, metrics, and OD.

How the Change Control Process Works

The governing policy is that performance improvement initiatives can happen in only one of two ways:

1. As part of the annual planning process
2. With approval of the Belding Leadership Team

All performance improvement initiatives, including IT projects, follow this process:

1. Every proposed performance improvement initiative is summarized in a one-page Initiative Profile.
2. If the initiative is input to the annual planning process, it is reviewed by the Belding Leadership Team in that context. Otherwise, the proposal is sent to the VCA Support Team, who logs it into the Change Initiative data base and conducts a brief feasibility and VCS Impact check to determine if the initiative:
   - Is redundant
   - Is likely to produce the desired result for the proposed cost

- Is to be carried out at an appropriate point and with the necessary scope to be effective

- Could/should be modified to make it more effective

- Will sub-optimize Value Creation System performance

- Fits with longer-term strategic goals

3. The VCA Support Team develops a preliminary project plan, identifying the resources required (type and dollars) to achieve the desired improvement in performance. (For example, the project might include the resources necessary to survey customers, redesign an internal process, customize an IT application, or impart new skills to a cross-section of Belding personnel via training.)

4. The VCA Support Team forwards the Initiative Profile and a recommendation to the Belding Leadership Team for review at its next monthly meeting.

5. The Belding Leadership Team considers the recommendation and makes its decision.

6. If the initiative is approved, the Belding Leadership Team appoints a member as Sponsor of the project, regardless of size. The VCA Support Team then:

- Finalizes the project plan, selects a Project Leader, and assembles a project team

- Enters the project into the Initiative Inventory and Tracking System

- Adds the project to the Initiative Tracking map in the Management Bridge room, which shows the location of all initiatives on the Business Process Framework Map

- Monitors the progress of all initiatives in the pipeline

7. The progress of all initiatives is reviewed quarterly by the Belding Leadership Team.

Change Control Management System Benefits

The benefits of the change control management system include:

- The reduction of the number of initiatives floating around the organization by about two-thirds

- An almost complete stop to the knee-jerk, quick-fix, "do something" responses to ill-defined symptoms of poor performance

- Prioritization of projects at the value creation system level

- Performance "problems" no longer initiated deep in some functional silo and addressed with some narrow, incomplete, or inappropriate "solution"

- Senior leader visibility into all projects, including those involving IT

- Belding Leadership Team accountability for the ultimate effectiveness of improvement efforts

Details of the Change Process

Let's examine this recommended change process in more detail, phase by phase. Figure 10.2 presents a picture of the process. The following are brief descriptions of each phase and its success factors:

Figure 10.2 Improvement Process Overview

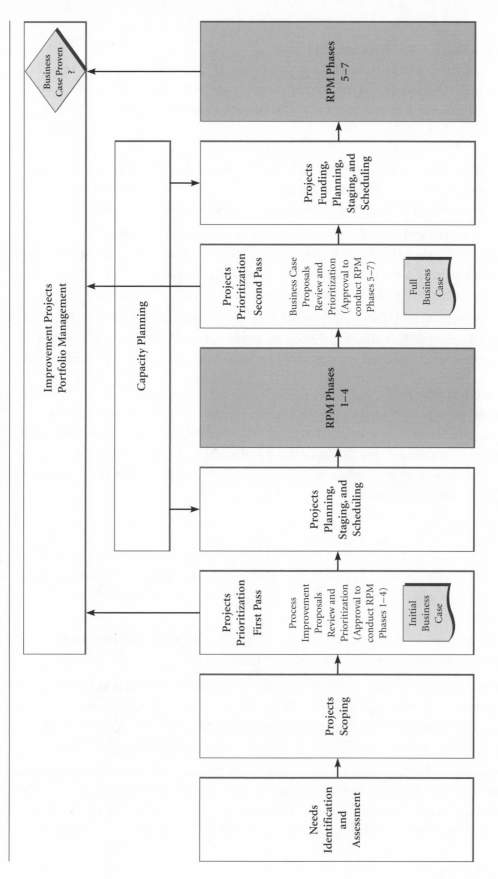

Needs Identification and Assessment Phase

This phase produces a description of the gap or potential gap (if this is a preventive effort) between actual performance and the level of performance required to achieve business and organizational goals and an assessment of the business benefits of closing the gap.

Key Success Factors

- Even in situations where the solution is obvious or externally determined, it is important to define the needs gap and benefits. It is much easier to recognize potential synergies and relationships among needs than it is to see synergies and relationships among solutions.

- Prioritization can and should happen first at the need level based primarily on the business benefits (versus ROI). The intention is not to drop any needs; they may be combined and become a larger need that takes on a higher priority. The value of prioritization is that it aligns stakeholder expectations and the sequence of work in the next phase.

- The assessment should also include analysis of the location of the need in the Value Creation Hierarchy. This allows for objective identification of need synergies that span multiple functional areas that often use different terminology to describe the same need.

Project Scoping Phase

The purpose of this phase is to complete an objective assessment of the scope of the project or projects that would address a need or set of needs. This phase answers the question of what it would take to close the needs gap. *Scope* is defined as the anticipated areas that will be affected by the change as well as the project structure and estimated time, resources, and budget required to execute the change.

Key Success Factors

- The scoping is seen as objective and doesn't produce potential projects with scopes that "somebody wants to hear." Achieving this objective requires that those conducting the scoping are not affiliated with the relevant functional requestor or probable service provider functions.

- Solid understanding of the portions of the Value Creation Hierarchy that relate to the needs gap—processes, systems and functions—to be closed.

- Input from representatives of all of the potential service providers. The people leading the scoping cannot know everything and should not be expected to be experts in all types of change. They should, however, be expert in defining project structures and identifying relevant types of change and coordinating questions and inputs from change specialists.

- Transparency on the status of each need scoped as well as timely and informative feedback to relevant requestors. Even the most expert of service providers must be cognizant of the potential for consternation and dissatisfaction when change requestors are not directly involved in the scoping and don't have reliable, readily available information on status of the effort.

Project Prioritization Phases

These phases produce an objective prioritization or ranking of improvement projects based on the benefits versus cost to the business to guide the allocation of resources and funding. The prioritization happens in two phases:

1. *First Pass Prioritization* (performed prior to RPM Phases 1–4). The project benefits are defined based on the needs that will be addressed by the project or project set. Instead of guessing at the cost of the projects (since analysis and design will follow), the benefit estimate is a relative assessment of the time and complexity to execute a project of this type or projects with similar characteristics. A major benefit of this approach is that it aligns assumptions and expectations among requestors and providers and avoids setting project teams up to fail.

2. *Second Pass Prioritization* (following RPM Phases 1–4). The second pass builds on and updates the assessment given in the first pass. The project benefits can now be objectively rationalized with the knowledge of the specific changes to be executed. In addition, the time estimate can be updated based on the detailed implementation plan, and the complexity assessment can be replaced by the committed project costs. This assessment of priority can be significantly different than the first and can sometimes raise questions about the "wasted effort" of conducting RPM Phases 1–4 if the project is stopped based on this assessment. Nevertheless, the far more expensive phases (5–7) are avoided, and projects in general have a significantly higher potential for success using the two-pass approach.

Key Success Factors

- Periodically, allowing for relative prioritization (prioritization among a group of projects), and situational prioritization, to foster timely decisions of projects that address high-priority needs

- Involvement of senior members of all stakeholder groups (corporate, line, and other functional change requestors as well as service providers)

- Clear and consistent criteria for prioritization

- In addition to continued transparency and feedback to requestors, projects given a low priority include feedback to individual requestors on alternative actions. (One of the greatest myths in most organizations that perform project prioritization is that projects that are not approved and funded centrally don't happen. In fact, they usually do, by going "underground" and consuming the organization's resources in ways that are less visible.)

Project Planning, Staging, and Scheduling Phase

This phase converts the project from a conceptual set of actions and assumptions into a defined project structure, plan, and schedule while also considering its relationship to other projects, organization events, and business cycles. As the name implies, there are three distinct sub-phases:

1. ***Project Planning***. The sponsor and leader roles are named, goals refined, risks identified, structure defined, and execution milestones determined.
2. ***Project Staging***. Optimal timing of projects is determined by factoring in problematic organization and business timing impacts, relationships between projects as well as intended synergies, and the availability of resources to execute the RPM phases that follow.
3. ***Project Schedule***. With the overall sequence and timing of projects established, the milestones for each individual project can now be placed on the calendar.

In the second Planning, Staging, and Scheduling phase (following RPM phases 1-4), the costs can now be estimated with a high degree of certainty for the first time and funding is formally approved.

Key Success Factors

- Project Sponsor and Leader roles defined for the life of the project and include succession plans
- Project Sponsors actively involved in the project planning
- Project staging that uses the Value Creation Hierarchy to "see" project relationships and factors upstream versus downstream change relationships into the sequencing approach

Change Capacity Planning Phase
The resources (internal personnel and external entities) available to conduct change projects are identified, capabilities defined, and assignments and availability tracked.

Key Success Factor

- Resource capability and availability proactively defined and updated to minimize time lost to finding qualified resources and delaying projects

Improvement Projects Portfolio Management Phase
This phase is the ongoing management of the organization's improvement initiatives by senior individuals representing requestors and solution providers.

Key Success Factors

- Senior team monitors the portfolio and makes adjustments to ensure balance among:
  - Short-term impact and long-term impact
  - Problem resolution and opportunity realization
  - Local, product, business, and corporate needs addressed
- Senior team oversees the effectiveness and integrity of improvement efforts by:

- Auditing project impact and analyzing gaps between planned and actual project benefits and costs
- Identifying and analyzing project performance issue trends
- Identifying and sponsoring actions to address change barriers
- Senior team uses Value Creation Hierarchy as framework for monitoring:
  - Linkage between change mix (dollar level and location) and organization and business strategy
  - Linkage/synergies between change projects

THE ROLE OF THE PERFORMANCE ARCHITECT

We have alluded throughout this book to the "process practitioner"—a vague appellation for the collection of people we have found inside organizations who are performing various kinds of "process work." They are documenting processes, archiving and managing process data; they are organizing, conducting, or leading process improvement projects; they are creating models of processes, technologies, and other organizational elements and attempting to use these models to affect business design and decision making; they are analyzing future needs and designing processes and technologies to enable the desired future; they are educating and advising executives, managers, and other key players on the importance of process design and management; they are attempting to collaborate across functional and organizational lines to improve business results. These people are found in many different areas of organizations: inside IT shops, in Process Excellence groups, in HR, OD, Quality, Training, Human Factors Engineering. In some places, they are isolated believers in process, and in other places, they are members of well-defined and funded staff groups.

We certainly see a lot of potential support inside organizations for process work, but if you believe, as we do, that process work is strategic work, we all need to get better organized. The difficulty is that process work requires the skills of many different disciplines—all the ones we listed. There is no term that describes the combined competencies of this work so well as that of "performance architect"—because all of the roles listed have in common their interest in making a positive impact on organizational performance and their use of architectural tools (models and maps) to describe the landscape of their focus. So we suggest that organizations should, like Belding Engineering, consider forming their own cross-disciplinary support teams, like the VCA Support Team, staffed by Performance Architects to aid their organizations in the process work of the twenty-first century.

The current situation in most organizations is that there are pockets of problem-solving expertise scattered among the functional silos of organizations, many of them isolated from each other or, alternatively, vying for the attention of senior management. This results in competitive attitudes that lead to counterproductive sub-optimizing behaviors and inefficient, wasteful projects.

Our suspicion is that the dominant Resource Dimension viewpoint that leads to the optimization of functions (at the expense of the larger Value Creation System) is also the primary driver for sub-optimizing competitiveness among support functions, all of whom must scrabble for their scraps of funding separately and therefore tend to view each other as rivals instead of as allies.

What can be done to overcome this imbedded tendency? We recommend the kind of change control system we have just described, which has a focus on optimization of the enterprise-level Value Creation System. The central figures in developing and implementing this approach are Performance Architects. These are the people we envision doing the kind of process improvement work that we described Sara doing.

Process Architects—whose membership would be drawn from multiple disciplines such as Six Sigma, Human Resources, Quality, Process Excellence, and so on—do the following kinds of work:

- Documentation of the organization's Value Creation Architecture
- Analysis, design, redesign, and improvement of the organization's Value Creation System (all five levels)
- Analysis, design, redesign, and improvement of the organization's Performance Planned and Management System (all management levels)

In short, Performance Architects provide design skills for the two dimensions of the enterprise (both value and resources). They support the organization's leaders.

CLOSING POINTS

To sustain the gains from a VCA definition or improvement effort, organizations need a permanent approach to managing improvement. The key requirements for a successful approach include: a formalized change control process that engages senior executives in identifying, choosing, funding and overseeing the improvements that are most critical to long-term organizational success, and a team of experts who help the executives run this change process.

PART THREE

Implications

CHAPTER ELEVEN

Process and the IT Department

We have already said quite a lot about the importance of technology in the Value Dimension and the importance of IT, the department, in today's organizations. It's hard to make generalizations about IT in business, because so much variation and change are going on.

In some organizations, IT employees function largely as developers of small solutions at Level 5 of the Value Creation Hierarchy, largely taking on projects as they come from functional areas. In other places, however, IT has grown greatly in stature and is seen as helping to define the company's future, providing leadership and expertise to make technology a competitive advantage. This is the "flat world" of Thomas Friedman and others who see technology as an instrument of revolutionary change—indeed the revolution that Michael Hammer espoused. In some organizations, IT leaders have recognized that work processes are what IT is in the business of enabling, and accordingly have become versed in process design and improvement. In other organizations, IT does not comprehend the Value Dimension or confuses BPM the software with BPM the management approach.

But process and IT are now inextricably related, and to deal with process requires that the role of IT be recognized and addressed. In the next pages, we:

- Set the stage by describing the nature of the opportunity for IT in the process world

- Describe the barriers for IT in capitalizing on its opportunity

- Describe a more effective way that change could happen in organizations, with IT as a critical player

- Describe the implications for the work that IT does and how it does that work

- Explore the internal changes IT would need to make in order to realize this vision of operating differently

THE OPPORTUNITY FOR IT IN A PROCESS WORLD

There are several respects in which IT has a singular opportunity to participate in, and even lead, the kind of process work we have been describing. IT is uniquely positioned because of four characteristics of its organizational role: (1) its function as task performer and enabler of human task performance, (2) its span of influence, and its roles as (3) enabler of the Value Creation Management system and (4) strategic advisor on technology.

Technology as Performer

Not long ago, information technology could be described as largely an enabler of process performance. The performers, though, were human beings. Technology was a helpmate to those in a process who were using technology to perform tasks or manage the process. But as we have said elsewhere in this book, these days technology is as much a performer in many processes as it is an enabler of human performers. When systems interface with each other, batching or sending packets of information, retrieving, auto-checking, they are performing parts of the process. Sometimes technology has merely replaced human beings in performing certain tasks, though often faster and more accurately. But just as often, technology can be harnessed to perform tasks that no human performer could do manually.

So now technology often *is* the performer, which can mean the content of a given process is largely technology performing its several tasks. We have worked with many clients on process designs that have only two or three swimlanes: one is for the customer; the second is for an array of systems that the customer is accessing while, for example, ordering a product via the Internet; and the third is for the backend Customer Support organization that may have to get involved if something goes wrong.

What this means for IT is that it is often the designer of entire business processes—or at the very least, always a player and often the chief one. Or it should be.

Span of Influence

IT is one of the relatively few functional departments in most corporations that have a sufficiently broad view to do the kind of Value Dimension design work we have described in this book. IT must be able to see across functional boundaries in order to install corporatewide systems such as ERP.

While other corporate departments also design, install, and maintain corporatewide programs (think of HR's hiring, compensation, employee relations, and diversity programs, for example), these departments are not generally required (though maybe they should be) to develop the deep knowledge of how work is performed and how various employees carry out their duties that IT must have in order to install effective company-spanning systems.

Enabler of the Value Creation Management System

In addition to designing, installing, and maintaining the applications, systems, and interfaces that help the work get performed in organizations, IT provides key resources to management. The management systems in many organizations are still entirely, or largely, manual. However, there are more and more advances in technology that can provide management information at the touch of a button. Business intelligence software is helping to turn management processes that were once labor intensive, lagging, and plagued with inaccuracies into lean, streamlined sources of detailed insight into company operations. IT is the key player in bringing these innovations into corporations—designing them or recommending their purchase to senior management.

Strategic Advisor of Technology

This role has been described in relation to management processes: IT acting as the advisor to management on the potential value of innovations in business intelligence tools. On a larger scale, IT leaders are moving into a crucial strategic advisory role to top management. As technology has advanced from enabler to performer, as its promise of work improvement has come to be realized more and more, some companies have begun to recognize information technology as a potent competitive weapon. And who else is better equipped to provide advice and recommendations on how to wield this weapon than the internal IT department? Helping an organization articulate its Value Creation Architecture is a concrete way for IT to carry out this strategic role.

In our own work as process practitioners, we have partnered with many different internal specialists who shared our interest in organizational improvement. In the 1980s, those partners tended to be inside Training and Development or Organizational Development groups, or in Quality and Industrial Engineering. By the 1990s, we began to find allies in other places such as the Finance Department. Now IT has the opportunity to play the role those earlier pioneers played—of leading the organization into the realm of process design, improvement, and management on a large scale with the ultimate goal of achieving higher business results. But IT has advantages some of those other partners tended to lack: they have technically skilled resources, they are valued for their specialized knowledge, and some have the ear of senior executives. If a given IT department does not have these advantages, it may be that it has squandered some of its capital in ways we describe in the next section of the chapter. But it is not too late to remedy the situation if IT takes seriously its unique position to lead the process movement.

BARRIERS TO SEIZING OPPORTUNITY

There are major barriers to IT seizing the opportunity to realize synergies between Process and Information Technology. The barriers fall into four categories:

1. Business's view of the business

2. The IT organization's view of the business

3. Business's view of the IT organization

4. IT's view of itself

Business View of the Business

Business's view of the business is the most significant and longest standing of the four major barriers. For many reasons, the primary focus of the majority of corporate, line, and other managers is not on optimizing the value created by the organization system as a whole. The focus instead is on the resource dimension and on the requirements for management of resources, which include:

- Individual performance measurement and rewarding
- Doling out of incentives
- Guarding one's boundaries
- Growing one's resources
- Career path management

Over time, such fixation on resources inevitably fosters attitudes and behaviors that hamper any serious attempts at cross-functional collaboration, or transparency about issues, or sharing of information, or sacrificing for the "greater good." Managers are in their own Human Performance System, and if they see themselves as measured on how well they fight to get and keep resources, they naturally focus on that aspect of business to the eventual detriment of other things. In time, nobody (sometimes not even the person at the top) has the ability to align functionally controlled resources to address cross-functional changes, because the functions have taken on a self-perpetuating life of their own. Even those who might not be trapped in the mind-set of hoarding their own resources may be reluctant to venture beyond their functional boundaries for fear of being perceived as treading on the turf of others.

The tendency of individual business managers to make their own functional area their primary focus is logical (it means keeping your sanity and surviving in the corporate storms), but it fundamentally limits the organization's ability to optimize value. This worldview comes about gradually as organizations grow. Entrepreneurs and managers of start-ups and small businesses naturally see and make decisions based on the organization as a whole. But with growth comes complexity, and that original view of the organization as a value-producing entity becomes covered over with functional organization structures. The result is typically a myopic "function" view of the business that taints all business decisions, including the definition of process.

And the view of organizations as buckets of resources is hard to change, even for people who try to bring a process view. Figure 11.1 provides an example of the Rummler toolkit to depict a company's value creation system and its key functional areas. (In other words, this is an attempt at creating the Value-Resource Map that we showed in Figure 4.1.) The good: it shows how processes link and are part of a larger organization system. The bad: all the "processes" have been placed neatly within functional areas. Why bad? Figure 11.1 suggests that each of the processes exists inside a single functional area, even though it is obvious that most of the processes are cross-functional in nature. The processes of "It designed," "It developed,"

Figure 11.1 Example of Functionally Focused Value-Resource Map

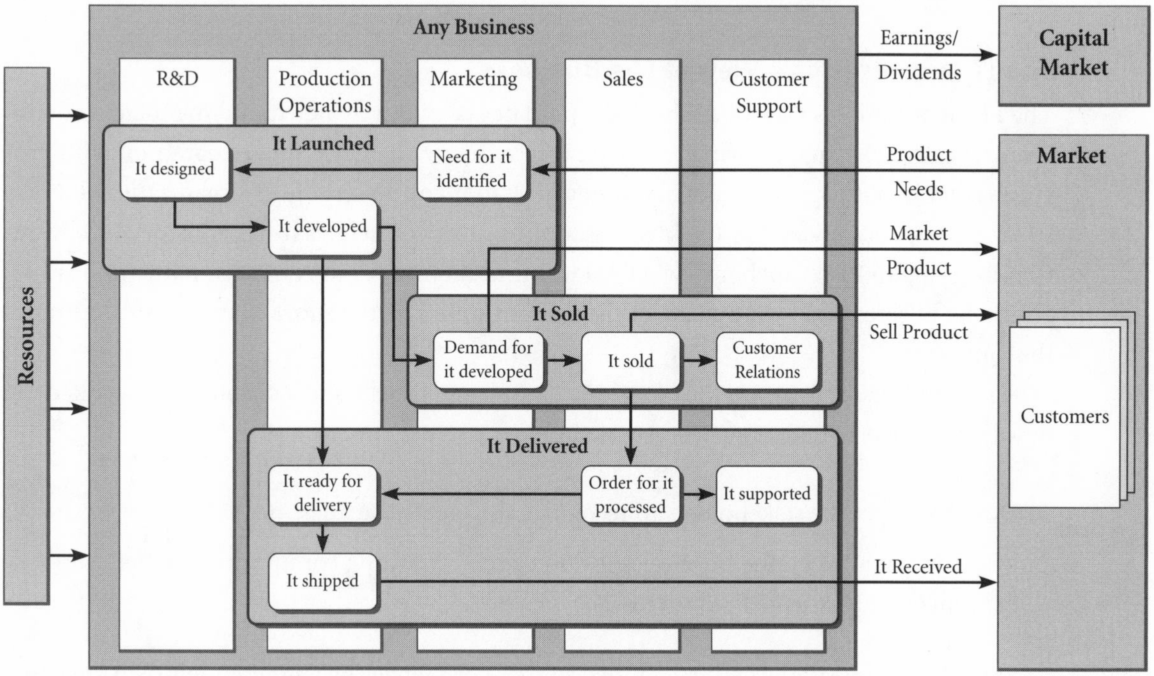

and "It supported" are all very important to the business and all are cross-functional, yet this picture portrays the tendency to see the entire organization as divided into functional silos, with every process having its home in a governing functional area.

This view of process reinforces the assumption that accountability for process performance should be functional. We might think that all we need are functional SLAs to ensure the organization performs effectively as a total system of processes—except that it won't perform effectively because the "total system" is not recognized and managed for value. We lose the primary reason for recognizing, understanding, improving, and managing processes. Processes are the mechanism that link and combine the functional capabilities *across* the organization to create value for the business and customers.

Yet although this view is flawed, many people prefer the processes-within-functions view because it seems easier to get one's arms around it and take action, and it avoids having to involve the entire horizontal organization. However, by placing processes within functions we are doing little more than linking sets of activities within existing functions. Not a lot of added value there.

How does this view, where it exists, serve to hamper the effectiveness of IT? If the IT department's many clients view themselves as largely independent functions who want things from IT regardless of what others may want, IT can end up in the near-hopeless position of trying to engender cross-functional collaboration where nobody wants it, of trying to lead organization-wide initiatives that are bound to be undermined by parochial interests. A thankless role, to say the least.

The IT Organization's View of the Business

The IT organization's view of the business predates its relatively newfound mandate to champion processes. Because information systems have many characteristics in common with processes (that is, both span functional boundaries), in many places, the IT organization does try to take a "corporate view" of the business, but in most companies it has a history of frustration in trying to foster such a view. IT leaders find themselves in continual battle to head off efforts by business leaders to make decisions that optimize the short term and sub-optimize the long term.

Again and again, these are the questions that plague IT when it is dealing with a collection of functionally oriented managers as stakeholders:

1. How do we get the stakeholders to recognize the greater business need?

2. What do we do when the stakeholders don't agree and won't compromise on their individual functionally oriented requirements?

Some IT organizations have responded to these challenges by aligning their own structure and resources to the functional structure of the business. And while being "responsive" to stakeholders is important, accepting a functionally oriented view of the business has many impacts, good and bad:

1. *Good:* It makes it easier to align efforts and resources to the needs of individual functional stakeholders (thus avoiding countless *Dilbert* references to the customer's inability to define requirements by putting people in place that can do it for them).

2. *Bad:* It avoids questions of what's in the best interests of the business and longer-term business impacts and runs the risk of making functional sub-optimization easier.

There are two sides to the so-called IT–Business Gap. The business does not tend to view itself as a system. The value view is not the predominant view—instead, the resource view is. So can we then expect that IT would do anything other than align to that view in its quest to align to the business? If you look inside most IT organizations you will find Business Analysts, Functional Analysts, and Application Support Groups or "Domains" that neatly align to the resource/function view of the organizations they serve. And you would not be surprised to learn that the various IT departments also interact with each other in a generally siloed fashion, because their loyalties tend to lie with their functional clients. This has led to:

- IT Applications are functionally aligned: the Sales System, Finance system, Procurement System, HR system, and so on. (Even SAP modules are aligned this way.)

- IT now has many individual clients to serve—Sales, HR, Finance—and, in desperation, often uses first come/first served as its principle for choosing projects rather than any rationale based on business value.

- IT does not have a client that represents the business, save for the top executive.

- Projects are either funded by IT itself or come out of one of the client's budgets.

As Geary Rummler commented while he listened to example upon example of the fabled "gap" between business and IT: "It sounds like there is no gap at all. The business sees itself as a bunch of functional areas and so that's exactly how IT sees them. Perfect alignment."

To see how this domain approach can impede progress, we look at the example of an insurance organization that was trying to make the transition to a process approach in their IT work. They had spent some significant time reorganizing their business analysts into a set of new domains, which made them responsible for all of the organization's processes. But a close look at this new process/domain architecture made it clear that it was essentially a function/resource view.

An example from this company's own industry showed how a major part of their work (that is, underwriting) was in fact not a process but a collection of activities scattered across the three Value Creation Processing Sub-Systems of "Launched," "Sold," and "Delivered." Adding a domain structure on top would clarify nothing; instead it would further confuse matters.

In many other organizations, the IT–business gap is addressed by "governance" overlays, but instead of fixing or clarifying anything, these layering approaches risk making the gap worse by confusing the relationship between line and staff.

Business's View of the IT Organization

In the same way that the IT organization's view of the business predates its role as process champion, so does the business's view of the IT organization.

The fact that there are many synergies between process and information technology is often lost on stakeholders who habitually contact the IT organization only for hardware and information systems needs. In many cases they have learned that they need to have already defined and analyzed their processes in order to satisfy IT's up-front questions and business case requirements. Asking them to come to IT when they first recognize a need to change or improve a process requires unlearning behaviors that were years in the making.

In some organizations, the view of IT by business leaders amounts to a kind of "magical thinking." Because information technology is so complex and fast moving, it is an area of mystery to many managers. Their reluctance to understand IT is perpetuated by the behavior of some IT practitioners themselves who indulge in arcane language and concepts and clannish behavior. To some senior executives, IT is like Merlin the Magician, an expert in dark arts whose actual practices you don't really want to know. When a manager has a request, he or she travels reluctantly down the hallway to knock on Merlin's closed door, make the request, and stuff money under the door. The manager doesn't want to know what Merlin does, but always wants faster, cheaper, better stuff and lots of it. And given those unrealistic expectations, the manager often ends up disappointed.

IT provides IT solutions. So before knocking on IT's door and asking for help, the business leader must first know that an IT solution to the business problem is needed. All one need do is look at the Effective Process Framework (Figure 11.2) to realize that the successful resolution to a business issue is likely to need more than IT's involvement. But where do you go for the "general contractor" of business solutions?

Figure 11.2 The Effective Process Framework

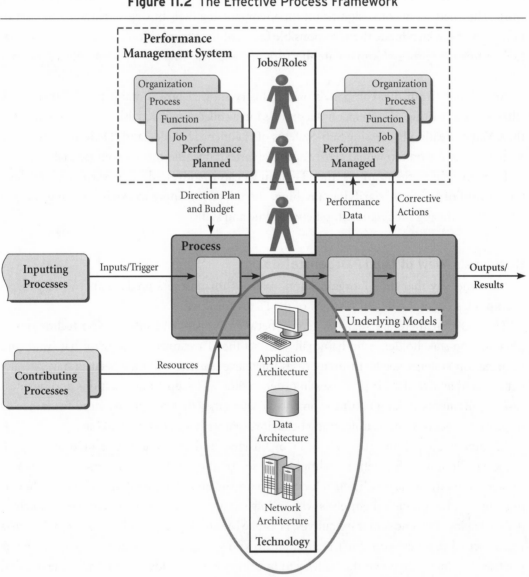

More and more organizations are putting a "process-front end" on making business change. This has the potential to make solutions more process based, but these process shops tend to put the emphasis where they have expertise. If they are housed in IT, their focus is a process front end to IT-oriented change. If they are housed in HR, the focus is a process front end to an OD or training solution.

And when IT implements a systems change that affects process and thereby some other discipline, they can have a difficult time tapping into the required resources—from HR, from the client organization, from finance—if they have had a practice of holding themselves apart from other corporate players.

A fundamental impediment can be the lack of a partnering relationship between the business and the IT organization that a mere willingness to understand and improve processes and assignment of "business partners" will not easily undo. Even IT people talk casually about "business versus IT," revealing the common acceptance that IT is not always seen as a member of "the business," but is somehow set apart and focused on its own preoccupations.

An effective partnering relationship between IT and business would require new roles and behaviors with different skill sets (as described in the discussion about the Performance Architect in Chapter Ten) in the IT organization to enable it go beyond its current state and to bring new perspectives and performance improvement and management concepts to the business. And just as important, it requires a new behavior of business leaders to engage with IT with realistic expectations and a willingness to manage the relationship. If this relationship is not established, the full potential of BPM will never be realized.

IT's View of Itself

Despite the many synergies between process and information technology, they are very different subjects that require different perspectives and expertise. In many IT organizations, adopting a process approach has been limited to acquiring an IT tool and templates for documenting and retrieving processes. If this is all that gets achieved, the potential of BPM will not be realized. The very fact that in many cases "process" is a new mandate that IT is "selling" to the organization causes it to err on oversimplification, corner cutting, and integration with current practices instead of adequately explaining the potential benefit to the business.

How IT goes about its work of designing systems and applications is also hampered by its functionally focused view. In the same insurance company IT shop described earlier, once a project has completed the requirements phase, there is no more responsibility or accountability for that project within the group. It all shifts to the next silo in the line—the application development groups—so any insight into how the process should work stays locked in the silo and one can only hope that the requirements documents somehow reflect what needs to be done.

In organizations where resources are the fixation, getting resources (that is, the budget) becomes all important to business managers and IT alike. Most of the IT portfolio management practices we have seen have a common feature of project approval/go ahead based on ROI. This presents an immediate impediment to taking our approach to improvement projects.

ROI assumes you know both the benefit and the cost of a particular project. In order to know or estimate the costs, you must already know what the solution is. Thus, most IT projects are funded projects to implement a predetermined solution. At one company, even the brief initiation document that described a project at only the highest level of detail required the proposed IT system to be listed.

This contributes to the idea that analysis is not really needed—we already know the solution. It may sound obvious, but for a number of organizations, this realization about funding practices was the explanation of why they had had such a hard time taking a process approach to their work. Instead of starting from a solution-neutral position, they had been trying to reverse engineer the projects from the predetermined IT solutions to a full process design.

In another organization, we noticed that because projects were funded as IT projects, any other process issues that were found during analysis could be resolved only if they could fit under the same budget. This meant that many process problems were going to be ignored. And even when non–IT solutions were identified, the project team had difficulty in finding the resource to manage and implement the solution, because it did not have partnerships with training, HR, and others.

There is a better way for IT to do its work, but it will take many changes. We think it is an urgent issue for IT and we are not alone. . . .

IMPLICATIONS

If the IT department is to operate as we have described in this chapter (that is, as an effective partner to business, as a guide in the wise application of technology to business needs, as a leader in designing and managing the business as a Value Machine), there are implications in the following areas:

- How IT executes its strategic role
- How IT defines process/workflow
- How IT defines work
- How IT defines requirements for systems being developed
- What IT's role is in improvement projects
- How IT structures itself and interacts with other partners in making changes
- How IT projects are funded
- How IT is held accountable for performance

IT's Strategic Role

Because technology has become so important to the strategic aims of many companies, IT departments have become (or have the potential to be) critical players, even leaders, in establishing or redirecting the strategies of the businesses they serve. To carry out this role in a structured, thorough way, IT leadership should consider taking the lead in defining the Value Dimension of the business. This can be done by documenting the "is" Value Creation Architecture of a given business, and then leading the design of a "should" VCA that guides the strategic and tactical decisions of management, including decisions about technology development, deployment, and maintenance.

Depicting Process/Workflow

IT has always seen the value of capturing, defining, designing workflow as it relates to information systems. They rightly realize that they must understand how the work flows if they are to design/redesign the system so that it supports or enables the work. Accordingly, most IT groups have emphasized various forms of workflow mapping as a part of their work. Unfortunately, this is not the "flow of work" as we mean *work* in a value creation context.

IT workflow diagrams are usually at the lowest level of the Value Creation Hierarchy (Figure 11.3)—at Level 5 or below. The content is heavily procedural usually detailed information describing the interface between a user and the system, because ultimately that is the level of detail needed to build and maintain an IT system (code).

IT workflow maps often contain odd phenomena, put there because they make sense to IT but not to ordinary business users. For example, IT workflow maps often mislabel a repeatable routine as a process. In the course of working in any one of a number of processes, a performer may send an e-mail. IT would like to have one universal set of requirements for e-mail sending, so the tendency is to treat that activity as a process and try to arrive at one set of requirements.

Another example comes from Accounts Payable: while we may have one Accounts Payable system, do we really want the same process for paying critical vendors for scarce raw materials

Figure 11.3 Level at Which Workflow Mapping Is Performed

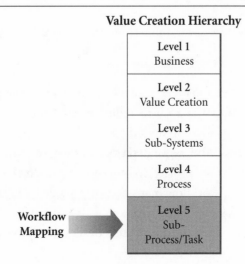

as we do for paying the vendor who provides light bulbs and copy paper? Looked at in a value creation context, these are not the same process, but they may have some things in common. But IT is likely to label these two different situations as the "Accounts Payable Process."

In an IT workflow map, the flow is not the flow of work but a view of what the technology is doing in the process. IT generally tries to depict all of the interfaces and instances that a user or group of users has with a system, so the resulting map may not really be a process sequence (in a value milestone context). IT is quite simply trying to answer the question, "What are all the things that the human wants the system to do or the system does during these interactions?" This approach to workflow design may indeed optimize the technology or job efficiency, but neither necessarily optimizes value. And often in an IT workflow map, the work being depicted is parts of several processes. But the maps don't make that clear because they focus only on system.

IT's Approach to Defining Work

Most IT organizations use SMEs (subject matter experts, usually users) to help when defining and redesigning processes, but this can lead to problems:

- The SMEs usually have a siloed functional view of the work. In fact IT often has a more cross-functional view because more and more systems cut across the work of several functions (for example, ERP systems).

- The SMEs will tell you only a user perspective at the job level. This is encouraged by the fact that IT wants this level of detail.

- The SMEs usually don't recognize that they may be working in several processes (it is just their job).

- The SMEs will state all of the requirements for themselves and their job and few, if any, of the requirements of those who work downstream in the process. They often have no idea what happens next in the process.

- Even if IT engages SMEs from several functions, the designs typically end up as the sum of all of the functional bits.

The fact is, SME teams often don't feel empowered to redesign the process. They view their role (and they are told as much) as to help redesign what the system will do for them in their job. The focus is on the system, so nobody is looking for opportunities to address non-system issues with the process. And as we described earlier, very often only systems work is within scope of the funding for the project, so other ideas couldn't be implemented anyway.

The result is that typical IT workflow maps do not provide enough context to understand the work, to make good *process* design decisions that then drive good systems decisions. It is an incomplete context upon which to base process design decisions, including the role of IT in the process.

It takes a value-centric view to understand how the system should be supporting the achievement of a value milestone or several value milestones. On that basis you can make better tradeoffs and decisions about the functionalities required, how much reuse and standardization versus supporting unique instances, and all other design decisions.

Yes, once you have the value context and have made those high-level decisions, you still need to drive the level of detail down to individual users, use cases, scenarios, but now you are doing it in the context of the business as a Value Machine.

In summary, many IT practitioners need to consider changing their approach to defining, documenting, and redesigning work—in short, documenting the value context first and then linking the necessary IT information flows, use cases, and other documentation to that value context.

The value context view needs to be a business view, so it is critical that the business leaders participate in the building of the Value Creation Architecture. IT can guide this work—but it cannot own this view of the business. Real *business* process maps should be the linking point for all IT work and documents.

IT's Approach to Requirements Definition

Requirements gathering should begin with an understanding of the value view of the work.

We have seen many approaches to requirements definition, but most large IT projects include some process definition and design in the requirements phase. We have already discussed the workflow mapping that is a part of this work. In addition we have observed the following approaches that tend to get in the way of getting to a good set of system requirements that are linked to process requirements.

- *A functional approach*. Separate SME groups (users from the business) and Domain groups (IT system groups), all working on one process, deciding to hold independent meetings to develop requirements for each domain/functional group and then leaving the domain groups to figure out the interface issues. Amazingly enough, this well-intended effort began with a high-level cross-functional process map, but then the team members took each box on the map and drilled down separately all the way to the lowest level of detail. Out of these excruciating (not to mention inconsistent) pieces, the domain groups were expected to reassemble the whole process. Instead, they defaulted to building a few interfaces here and there, ones already predetermined to be needed.

- *IT representing the business*. The practice of insulating the business from interactions with IT on projects (Don't bother the business people—they are too valuable and busy!), through the use of Business Analysts to represent the business's needs and requirements. From what we have observed, most of the Business Analysts have IT backgrounds, not business backgrounds. They are also usually not empowered to make any decisions beyond system decisions, so they have to ignore most of the Effective Process Framework.

- *Ineffective toolsets for working with the business.* Use of nonvisual tools (prose documents, gargantuan lists) to elicit and document requirements. Teams we have interviewed have admitted that there was such a sea of words that they sometimes didn't know what they were validating and signing off on; they just wanted to stop the madness.

- *Technical decisions in advance of process designs.* We have observed project teams that complete the technical deliverables first and then build the process around them. We even know of some organizations where this is a formal handoff from IT to the training development group. T&D then builds the training and process pieces because they need to train in a process context. These IT groups recognize that their work is impacting process and so this is their way of addressing process, but we would say the approach is backward.

We think that good system design needs to begin with process design—process in a value context. The cross-functional process map is the place to begin requirements definition. It is only at that level that

- Work can be judged to be value adding (Could steps/work be eliminated?) and potentially providing competitive advantage.
- The best performer to do the work (skills/costs/flexibility) can be determined.
- The tradeoffs between what the human should do and what the system should do can be effectively decided.

Those tradeoffs ultimately determine what technology's role should be in a process or task, what it does, how much should be automated, and so on. For the design of any given work task or process, the designer (or let's call him or her the Performance Architect) can follow this logic:

I can apply human skill, knowledge, or capability to the work to get it done.

Or

I can apply technology to get it done.

Or

I can apply a combination of the two.

How would I know the best way? I should consider the availability and cost of the resource for sure, but also the following:

- Is the work primarily algorithmic or heuristic? (Algorithmic lends itself more easily to technology.)

- Is the work subject to compliance requirements? (Which will be easier to engineer for compliance, ensure compliance, and prove compliance? How much risk is there?)

- Does competitive advantage dictate which way I should go? If speed is the competitive advantage, which is faster for this work—human or technology? If flexibility is the advantage, which can react faster—human or technology?

- How adaptive does this work need to be? We are doing it this way for our given products/services and situation today, but do we foresee the need to be able to quickly adapt this work to new circumstances in the near future? Which will be easier to reconfigure/adapt—a human work system or technology?

- Is there a management consideration? Will one option provide better insight into the process than the other, making it easier to manage? The system might provide data, but the work is also happening in a black box, with no human to see, or watch, or ask.

A need for rational design tradeoffs makes eminent sense if you spend any amount of time in the bowels of IT, watching the designers attempt to make thousands of little changes to hardcoded work systems to accommodate or adapt to a new requirement for the business. You look at all that work and think, "An old manual system would have cost ten times less to change and deploy and been ten times faster." Sometimes nobody appears to consider that when they tally up the savings (headcount) for an automated process.

Contrast that to organizations that have taken the Value Creation Architecture approach to their business issues: "I think that the process information can nicely fit into the Use Case models underway in the [...] group, which is already connected to system models and code. So, in essence, we should be able to trace your process work down to code. Very cool."

IT's Role in Improvement Projects

IT has many roles to play in an improvement project, and it requires different authorities and different skill sets. If we look at our RPM methodology and compare the role of the business and the role that IT should play in the project, we can see parallels and critical points of collaboration (Figure 11.4):

- During the Align Phase, it is critical that both IT and the business provide vision and constraints. IT must bring the technology strategy to bear and both paint the possibilities as well as state the boundaries of what technology can do for any given process. The IT strategist and Enterprise Architects need to collaborate in this role.

- Early in the Analysis Phase, different skill sets are needed from IT. The experts in the systems that currently support the process must help to create the as-is picture and voice what is and is not working well in the current process. Later, during the "should" strategy sessions and throughout the Design Phase, we need the visionary thinkers back on the team as well as those who have expertise in existing technologies that possibly could be leveraged.

Figure 11.4 RPM Methodology with Business and IT Roles

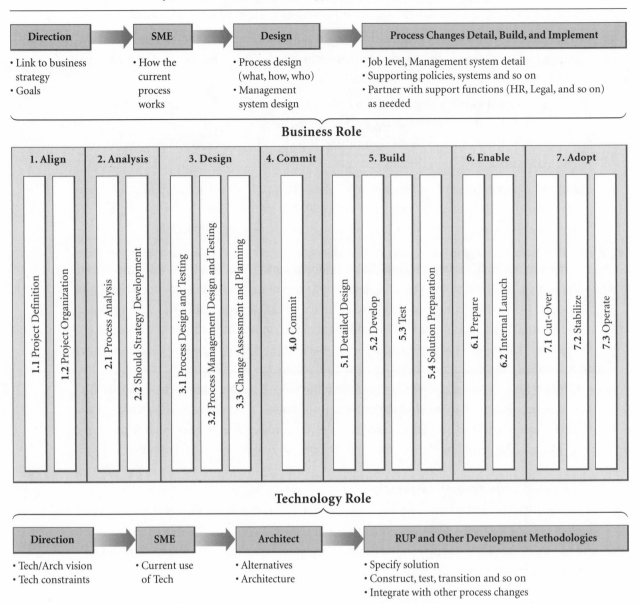

- During the Build, Enable, and Adopt phases, we bring to bear all the specialized IT resources required to construct, configure, test, and so on. This is where RUP and other IT-specific development methodologies can kick in.

The fact is that IT needs partners in the "change business." In organizations in which the primary portfolio of change is in IT, there is the opportunity for IT to lead the way in building the required alliances with the other internal business partners required to bring about effective change, including:

- Linking up with Six Sigma and other process excellence groups
- Leveraging the shared Value Creation Architecture view of the business—the basis for a common view and language
- Determining how the methodologies link together and how roles will play out during an improvement project
- Using a process approach to improvement before determining and contracting for specific solutions

IT's Approach to Funding Change

We have already described the predominant ROI funding model for IT portfolio management. We now describe the alternative.

We propose that the portfolio in the future needs to be approved on a different basis (not ROI). Improvement projects should be chosen on the basis of the value to the business of solving a business issue (for example, increased sales, decreased abandonments, decreased costs, and so on). Let's call this Business Case #1: It does not assume anything about the nature of the solution. Instead, the funding is for determining and designing the solution (Phases 1–4— Align through Adopt—in the Rummler Process Methodology).

Once the solution is known, the project is approved for the building and implementation of the solution (more likely the solution set). Only then can you have a full ROI-based business case. Let's call this Business Case 2. This approach allows the project to be solution neutral enough to determine the best solution given the needs and constraints.

IT's Accountability

In the IT organizations that have made this kind of change, accountabilities have also changed. Traditionally, a large part of IT accountability has to do with bringing in projects on time and on budget. We have seen the Project Management Office run-amok version of this in action on several projects, where the ultimate and only goal becomes to get the project done in time and on budget in spite of the solution quality. The result was argument about whether IT missed requirements or the business didn't state requirements, or some other endless finger pointing.

In this new process-centric approach, IT, along with the other partnering solution providers, is held accountable for process results.

We see this opportunity for IT as a challenge but worth the uphill climb. Much of our work in the past few years has been focused there, and we continue to seek opportunities to help organizations make this shift.

For example, a developer in an organization whose primary business is software development wrote to us:

> It is sort of cool isn't it. ☺ We've worked hard on making sure that we have complete traceability from Strategy -> Process Framework -> Process- >Requirements -> Use

Cases-> Information Models -> Service Layers -> Code. If you've worked here a while, you know that the last item is the one most folks care about, but w/o the rest it's a tough sell in the long run. It's the kind of story we should be able to tell all across the business! Your team's work has really helped bridge the gap from **Strategy** to **Code**. There's probably a book title in there somewhere. ☺ We're getting ready to start blue-printing this whole process so we can replicate it—we need to start showing this to more execs!

CHAPTER TWELVE

Summary

In this final chapter, we revisit our reasons for writing this book and our hope for its usefulness. We point out what we consider to be the "big ideas" contained in these pages.

We also point out what we believe are the important implications of the contents of this book for two parties. The first is the staff organizations that, together, have the potential to redirect the process movement in a more productive direction and their leadership. The other key party is, of course, the executives and managers of the organizations that can benefit from a better way to understand and utilize the power of process.

WHY THIS BOOK

This book was written in response to the many requests that Geary Rummler and his partners received for a follow-up to *Improving Performance*, and we also came to see it as a way of sharing our experiences and observations about the process movement since that book was published. This book was meant to catch up with you and to continue a conversation started in 1990, when the early promise of process design and improvement was just beginning to be glimpsed. Since that early conversation, much has happened to pull the concept of process in different directions—some good, some not. So one purpose of this book was to identify those influences, critique them, and try to put them into perspective—in particular, in the perspective of the ultimate purpose of organizations, which is to create and sustain value.

The other purpose was to point a way forward, for those who continue to believe, as we do, that the concept of process—design, improvement, and management—is still the greatest management idea to come along in a hundred years.

THE "BIG IDEAS"

This book has succeeded if it convinced you of the importance of the following ideas and concepts.

Value Creation

Process is the fundamental building block for defining and organizing the work required to create value. As such, it is the vehicle for articulating the Value Creation Dimension of an enterprise so it can be:

- *Properly designed* for effective, efficient performance and possible competitive advantage
- *Managed* for optimum performance
- *Supported* effectively (that is, by IT and other enabling groups)

There are two dimensions to every organization—the value dimension and the resource dimension—that need to be designed and managed in concert for optimum organizational results.

The Value Creation Hierarchy — pg 30 + Fig 2.4

The *Value Creation Hierarchy* is a framework for identifying and defining processes and their relationships. The hierarchy can be made visible with the tools contained in the *Value Creation Architecture*.

The Effective Process Framework   pg. 22

The Effective Process Framework (EPF) identifies the variables affecting the performance (that is, results produced) of any process, regardless of the level in the Value Creation Architecture. The EPF is a valuable tool for:

- Troubleshooting why a process is failing
- Designing a new process

RPM METHODOLOGY   pg 31

Based on these three "big ideas," the Rummler Process Methodology (RPM) is a methodology for systematically defining, designing, improving, or managing a:

- Sub-process
- Single process
  - Primary

◦ Contributing
- Multiple processes or sub-systems
- Entire business

Value Creation–Managed Organization

The move to a Process-Centered Organization is really a move to a *Value Creation–Managed Organization*. As such, there are two parts to this transformation:

1. The ***design*** of an effective Value Creation System (that is, by building a Value Creation Architecture)
2. The ***management*** of the VCS

This book is focused on the first of these; our companion book for managers is focused on the second.

The Performance Architect

The expertise we are calling the *Performance Architect* guides an enterprise as it articulates its Value Creation Dimension, improves process performance, and moves toward Value Creation Management. Information Technology can provide a most valuable contribution to the Performance Architect role because IT advises on the strategic potential of technology and develops and maintains technology that can be an essential element in both process performance and Value Creation Management.

IMPLICATIONS

We see the implications of this book and its contents as of greatest importance for two "groups." The first group includes those staff organizations that could potentially take on the role of Performance Architects and do the kind of process work we have been describing. The second group comprises those people for whom such work should be performed—that is, for the managers and leaders of organizations.

Potential Performance Architects

We have described Performance Architects as coming from various disciplines inside companies—from the classic functional staffs of IT, HR, Training, Quality, OD, Industrial Engineering, and from the newer, process-oriented groups calling themselves Process Excellence, Six Sigma, and the like. None of these groups by itself is sufficiently broad in its skills and experience to guide an enterprise in defining its Value Creation System as we have outlined it; such work requires collaborative effort across these disciplines and in close partnership with the business they help.

All of these disciplines can bring something to the party. Next we group these disciplines and summarize their special contributions in light of our arguments that in today's organizations, the performer is either a human being with a computer or a network of computers.

Information Technology We have said a great deal about the shortcomings of IT and its credibility issues with the business side, but, on the other hand, we have recognized how critical IT has become to process performance and overall organizational success. We realize there are IT organizations that are heading in a new direction. If it so wishes, IT could take the lead in collaborating with the other disciplines to educate and guide leaders in the design and management of their organizational Value Creation Systems. But this would require an end to fixating on technology and instead fully joining the business team.

Human Resources, Training, Organizational Development This collection of functional specialists tends to concentrate on the human performers and their managers. They offer advice, tools, methods, and systems to deal with what is often called the "soft side" of business. Fair enough, this side needs plenty of attention and always will, unless everyone is automated out of a job. But in order to be effective performance architects, these specialists need as much as IT does to become knowledgeable about the business and, probably even more challenging to some in these ranks, to become knowledgeable about technology.

There are some practitioners who insist that their focus is on "human performance technology," but if you accept the fact that most human performers in business can't do their jobs today without information technology, you can't be very helpful if you don't understand what affects human performance. Technology is one of the biggest of those effects—witness any employee doing virtually any job in any organization.

Quality, Industrial Engineering, Human Factors Engineering These were the original process experts. Many of the tools and concepts of the process movement of the 1980s and 1990s were not, of course, new; they were derived from industrial engineering. These folks were largely focused on manufacturing processes, but so many of their insights—about process flow, bottlenecks, value-added steps, and so on—have migrated to nonmanufacturing organizations that you don't hear the argument as much anymore, "Well, this stuff is great for manufacturing, but not for us."

Where these groups could make a contribution today, however, is in the area of technology—specifically regarding the so-called business–IT gap. They are experts in improving the interaction between "man and machine." Fifty years ago, the machine may have been a lathe or a drill press; today, it's a laptop. But the principles these specialists have used for decades to understand and redesign the workplace for optimum performance are a potential gold mine for IT developers. If only collaboration would happen.

Business Management

The second audience for this book is of course the executives and managers who lead organizations. The Performance Architects we hope are inspired to act because of this book can accomplish little unless the leaders of their organizations see the need for their help. And that will happen only if the leaders agree to the fundamentals we propose:

- That the purpose of a business is to create and deliver value
- That processes are the chief means to create and deliver that value
- That process performance has to be carefully designed and managed
- That the task of management is to design and manage both the value and the resource dimensions of their organization, thus ensuring consistent, predictable results

Our companion book directly addresses the role of senior leaders in value creation and management. We hope we have said enough here to convince those leaders of the importance of process and the possible opportunities it provides.

What can you do to practice what we outline in this book? Find a serious sponsor—someone who agrees that value is organizational mission and he or she could use your help. That's where we started.

IT'S NOT OVER . . .

For devotees of Geary Rummler—and there are many such "Rummlerites"—it may be natural to wonder whether the publication of this book also signals the end of his work. That will not be the case.

The partners at the Performance Design Lab, Geary's final company, sorely miss him, and they fully intend to carry on his legacy in a variety of ways:

One is the publication of this book.

Another is the publication of the companion book for executives and managers.

And the third is a continued use and development of his concepts, tools and methods.

Geary always believed that there was something more to be learned by trying new ideas or pushing existing ideas in new directions—and so we endeavor to continue that way.

BPF   Business Process Framework

CBI   Critical Business Issue

EPF   Effective Process Framework

HPS   Human Performance System

RPM   Rummler Process Methodology

TPS   Technology Performance System

VCA   Value Creation Architecture

VCH   Value Creation Hierarchy

VCS   Value Creation System

CHAPTER ONE: THE SILVER ANNIVERSARY OF PROCESS

1. Today, the association is known as the International Society of Performance Improvement (ISPI).

2. Some early readers of this book have expressed concern about citing Motorola, Inc., as a paragon of process excellence, given its business ups and downs since its days of triumph in the 1980s and early 1990s. We think, however, that the saga of Motorola validates one of the major tenets of this book and our work with organizations: all organizations must be adaptive to changes in their external environment—adapt or die.

   Certainly there is still much to learn and to emulate from Motorola as it transformed itself from a troubled company to one of the leading corporations to take on the Japanese economic juggernaut. That story is still true, and still worth studying. If we were to establish a rule of thumb not to pay any heed to companies that once were strong and then were troubled, we would have virtually no companies to study. And it's not just Motorola that has had its difficulties. As others have pointed out, many of the companies cited in such books as *In Search of Excellence* and in *Good to Great* have suffered setbacks since their glorification in those books. Then do we cite nobody?

   We have also been urged by some readers to render an opinion on the reasons Motorola has had problems, since they adopted what we, to exaggerate a little, seem to be describing as the eternal passkeys to success. Some readers even venture to ascribe Motorola's difficulties to those very practices (that is, Six Sigma). But from what we can surmise through reading and talking with other Motorola watchers, the company's difficulties have had nothing to do with Six Sigma. Their biggest mistake was in the mid-1990s, when they tarried in making a decision about whether to get into digital cell phones, while Nokia snuck behind them and took away a huge swath of market share. That was a leadership problem, in other words. Yes, a solidly designed management system will aid leaders in making decisions—but make them, they must. There was, in fact, a different generation of leaders at the helm in Motorola by that time, and we know from sad experience that an incoming leadership team can dismantle a management system a whole lot faster than they can build one.

3. Geary A. Rummler and Alan P. Brache, *Improving Performance: How to Manage the White Space on the Organization Chart* (San Francisco: Jossey-Bass, 1990). Revised and updated edition published by Jossey-Bass 1995.

4. Michael Hammer and James Champy, *Reengineering the Corporation: A Manifesto for Business Revolution* (New York: Harper Collins, 1993).
5. Rummler and Brache, *Improving Performance.*

CHAPTER THREE: THE VALUE CREATION HIERARCHY

1. Michael E. Porter, "What Is Strategy?" *Harvard Business Review* 74, no. 6 (November—December 1996).
2. There are several interesting points about contributing processes/processing sub-systems.

As indicated in Figure 3.6, there are potentially many contributing sub-systems and processes in a business. We show just a sample for the general area of Human Resources.

Other Human Asset and Resource Management sub-systems include:

- Human Capital Productive

- Human Capital Portfolio Grown

Other general areas of contributing sub-systems include:

- Physical Assets and Resources Management

- Stakeholder Management

There is frequently confusion among the titles/names of support functions and the processes that support functions participate in. A good example is the Human Resources (HR) function of a business. A key process in which the HR function plays an important role is the "recruiting process." (Note that in the example we use in Figure 3.6, the recruiting process is called the "Human Capital Obtained" process. We follow that naming convention wherever possible to emphasize the desired outcome of a process.) Most everyone in an organization refers to the recruiting process as an HR process—but is it?

Like every contributing process, the recruiting process is cross-functional. If we were to develop a cross-functional process map of the recruiting process for Belding, we would minimally have swimlanes for:

- HR management (who will be setting relevant policies and requirements regarding operation of the process)

- Recruiting function (who will be executing parts of the process)

- Operating units (who are the recipients of the recruits, will specify the number and qualifications of the recruits, and will screen and ultimately select the new hires)

- Colleges, employment agencies, or other suppliers of recruits

- Employee candidates

Certainly, HR plays several important roles in the recruiting process. But it is one of several important players in this fairly typical contributing process. For example, the design/redesign of a recruiting process is done jointly, involving the operating units/primary processes who require recruits and the HR/recruiting experts. The operating units (customers) specify the outputs required (number and qualifications) and some process requirements such as throughput time.

The HR/recruiting experts specify various process requirements necessary to meet college, company, and governmental standards that are mostly likely unknown to the operating units.

The process execution involves both HR and operating parties. The operating unit sets output requirements for a period of time (number and profile of recruits), interview/screens recruits, and makes the final hiring decision. HR/Recruiting identifies possible candidates, screens candidates, presents candidates to the operating unit for a decision, and introduces the selected individual into the hiring sub-process.

Process management is done jointly. Operations is concerned with the effectiveness of the process in producing the number of qualified new hires. HR/Recruiting is concerned with the process meeting all the policy and regulatory requirements. Process maintenance is the concern of the Recruiting organization.

So is recruiting really an HR process? Perhaps, like many contributing processes, it could be said to be a *joint* process, "hosted" by the HR organization. In the final analysis, both parties need to be accountable for the effectiveness of the process.

When redesigning or improving a contributing process such as "recruiting," *handle with care!* Regarding contributing processes, there is a tendency to say, "It is only a support process—how big a deal can it be?" From our experience, contributing processes can be a very *big deal*. They present these special challenges:

- Since they support multiple customers/users with different requirements, there are more stakeholders involved in identifying requirements, participating in the design of the process, and having final approval of the end product. Stakeholder management is a challenge.

- There are special process design challenges. The process must have flexibility capability built in, to accommodate different end-user requirements. And the process must be easily modified and updated, as stakeholder requirements (for example, government regulations, corporate policies) will likely be in a continual state of flux.

- As you can begin to see with our Human Capital example in Figure 3.6, most contributing processes are wrapped up fairly tightly with other contributing processes to constitute a Contributing Processing Sub-System. As we keep mentioning, "It's a system." You can't rip a process out of the larger processing sub-system and make changes and then simply reinsert it back into the sub-system. Careful attention must be paid to the interface with other processes, which becomes part of the stakeholder management task.

- A robust process management system must be designed to assure that the process continues to meet its relatively complex set of performance requirements.

Again we emphasize that when tinkering with a major contributing process, handle with care. If we were bidding on the redesign/improvement of a major contributing process versus a major primary process, we would most likely estimate 30% more time and 50% more cost for the contributing process project.

With some predictable frequency, in a standard "manage the resource dimension" mode, a business notices all those costs sitting in the various staff functions. And with visions of all those resource savings in their heads, executives launch a big program to downsize the budget (that is, headcount) of those support units. So we have an effort to take a sizable chunk out of the resource dimension absent any clue as to the impact it will have on the critical value-adding work being done through contributing processes to the Value Creation System. Historically, there are two dangerous paths businesses take to reduce these support costs.

One is to "downsize"—to simply whack 10%–15% out of every support organization's budget—and let the chips fall where they may. The longer-term impact of this approach on contributing processes that in turn provide critical input to primary value-adding work processes in the Value Creation System is frequently disastrous. An alternative approach is for the business to target apparently high-cost contributing processes for systematic analysis and redesign, involving all key parties and following a sound process redesign process such as the one we recommend in Chapter Six. In fact, in the interest of continually fine-tuning the vital Value Creation System, the business might schedule these contributing process redesign projects on a regular schedule rather than wait for some profit margin crisis.

The second is to "outsource"—usually select some sub-function and outboard it. In most cases, this constitutes making a resource dimension decision with little or no understanding of the impact on the value dimension. Such decisions have the affect of either tearing contributing sub-processes out of processes or processes out of processing sub-systems, again with disastrous results. (However, these bad results tend to show up sooner rather than later.) Pardon us for making one politically incorrect observation here: "Hey stupid, it's a system!"

CHAPTER FOUR: DEVELOPING THE VALUE CREATION ARCHITECTURE OF A BUSINESS

1. Some people we've encountered over the years have trouble with the notion of describing organizations as "machines." They argue that the machine metaphor seems to leave out the recognition of hard-working human beings with complex emotions and motives, reducing them to mere cogs in the big, all-consuming "machine." Way too mechanistic for their taste.

   We respond by saying that we fully recognize the importance of people inside businesses—Level 5 of the VCH is, after all, about the performer—and we certainly don't view people as machines. But it's the businesses they work inside that are machine-like—or should be. As complex and multidimensional as a given business might be, it should also be predictable, capable of being designed, operated, managed. The problem with many of today's organizations is that they are too convoluted and strangely designed to lend themselves to being understood as "well-oiled machines." But that's exactly the problem, and that's why a VCA can be the first step in making them more machine-like.

   Some of our clients and friends have suggested that we adopt the term *ecosystem* to describe the complex modern organization, and this term has become popular in the business press to describe what we call an organization's "super-system." We're fine with that term, because to us it expresses the same notions about organizations that we mean when we call it a Value Machine: it is a highly complex system of multiple, interdependent moving parts that have to be carefully designed and managed in order to achieve consistent high performance. So if "ecosystem" works for you, great.

2. Currently, a number of "architectures" have been developed as a means of capturing various aspects of organizations. To date, all these have emanated from the world of Information Technology—to explain the relationship of technology applications to each other, and supposedly, the business (for example, enterprise architecture, business architecture, and technology architecture). Our Value Creation Architecture starts from a different vantage point altogether, with a different objective. We are interested in capturing the value-adding work structure of an organization, as represented by the Value Creation Hierarchy. The result is a management-centric model of the work required for a business to deliver valued products and services. In Chapter Eleven, we describe the possible relationship of the VCA to the various IT-generated architectures.

CHAPTER SIX: A FRAMEWORK AND METHODOLOGY FOR VCS DESIGN

1. A. William Wiggenhorn endorsement of Rummler and Brache, *Improving Performance*, inserted into the first edition of the book (1990).
2. Rummler and Brache, *Improving Performance*, 1990, 1995.
3. The HPS has been used by performance analysts and others for some forty years to diagnose and even predict the behavior of human beings in given performance situations. The earliest version of this model was created in the 1960s by Geary Rummler and Dale Brethower. Today, there are any number of versions, but the original is still powerful and relevant to anyone interested in understanding or improving performance.

CHAPTER NINE: OTHER RPM APPLICATIONS

1. From Michael Hammer, "Reengineering: The Implementation Perspective" seminar, 1993.

Note: Page references with *fig* indicate an illustrated figure; page references with *t* indicate a table.

Performance Design Lab (PDL) is a research, consulting, coaching, and training organization. PDL is an acknowledged thought-leader and pacesetter in the process design, improvement, and management methodology space. Our methodologies and concepts have been adopted worldwide by Fortune 100 companies, other consulting companies, as curricula for business schools and by government regulatory agencies. Our books, *Improving Performance: How to Manage the White Space on the Organization Chart* (Rummler & Brache, 1990, 1995) and *Serious Performance Consulting According to Rummler* (2004), have become standard industry reference works. We have worked directly with a myriad of top-tier companies across a variety of industries helping implement large-scale transitions effectively while creating lasting value for our clients. Our fundamental belief is that performance can be designed. That performance improvement is not magic, but *science.*